CREATIVE DESTRUCTION

How to start an economic renaissance

Phil Mullan

P

First published in Great Britain in 2017 by

Policy Press
University of Bristol
1-9 Old Park Hill
Bristol BS2 8BB
UK
t: +44 (0)117 954 5940
e: pp-info@bristol.ac.uk
www.policypress.co.uk

North American office:
Policy Press
c/o The University of Chicago Press
1427 East 60th Street
Chicago, IL 60637, USA
t: +1 773 702 7700
f: +1 773-702-9756
e: sales@press.uchicago.edu
www.press.uchicago.edu

© Policy Press 2017

British Library Cataloguing in Publication Data
A catalogue record for this book is available from the British Library.

Library of Congress Cataloging-in-Publication Data
A catalog record for this book has been requested.

ISBN 978-1-4473-3611-2 paperback
ISBN 978-1-4473-3613-6 ePub
ISBN 978-1-4473-3614-3 Mobi
ISBN 978-1-4473-3612-9 epdf

The right of Phil Mullan to be identified as author of this work has been asserted by him in accordance with the 1988 Copyright, Designs and Patents Act.

Cover design by Soapbox Design
Printed and bound in Great Britain by TJ International, Padstow
Policy Press uses environmentally responsible print partners

Contents

List of figures and boxes

Figures

List of figures and boxes

Boxes

List of abbreviations

ARPANET	Advanced Research Projects Agency Network
BEA	the US's Bureau of Economic Analysis
BED	Business Employment Dynamics
BIS	Bank for International Settlements
BLS	the US's Bureau of Labor Statistics
CBI	Confederation of British Industry
CEO	chief executive officer
DARPA	Defense Advanced Research Projects Agency
ECB	European Central Bank
ERM	enterprise risk management
EU	European Union
FRED	Federal Reserve Economic Data
G7	Group of Seven (US, UK, Japan, Germany, France, Italy and Canada)
GDP	gross domestic product
GFCF	gross fixed capital formation
ICT	information and communications technologies
ILO	International Labour Organization
IMF	International Monetary Fund
JOLT	Job Openings and Labor Turnover
LSE	London School of Economics and Political Science
M&A	mergers and acquisitions
MFP	multi-factor productivity
NBER	the US's National Bureau of Economic Research
NESTA	the UK's National Endowment for Science, Technology and the Arts
NIPA	national income and product account
NRC	the US's National Research Council
OECD	Organisation for Economic Co-operation and Development

ONS	the UK's Office for National Statistics
OPEC	Organization of the Petroleum Exporting Countries
QE	quantitative easing
R&D	research and development
TFP	total factor productivity
UN	United Nations
VAT	Value Added Tax

Acknowledgements

The ideas in this book are inspired by my political engagement since the 1970s, and by my business experiences in the internet and telecommunications industries over the past two decades. These gave me convenient vantage points for viewing three big financial crises during those 20 years.

First, in 1996 and 1997 I was rolling out the Cyberia internet cafe franchise in Bangkok and in Manila, allowing me to appreciate the effects of the Asian financial crisis at first hand. A couple of years later I worked through the dot.com boom and bust, still with Cyberia, and also as a board member of the communication services company Easynet. Both businesses were operating at the frontier of the information and communications revolution. By the time of the financial crash of 2008 I was one of Easynet's managing directors, running its UK business during those turbulent times.

Those experiences provided privileged opportunities to ponder the interaction between the real and the financial parts of the economy. I am grateful to the people who brought me to work with these companies: Keith Teare, David Rowe and Eva Pascoe. They afforded me the livelihood to be able subsequently to take time off to research and write this book. As well as being original and successful businesspeople, they are shrewd thinkers about matters of the world: economic, technological and beyond. We have talked about these things together on lots of occasions, and in some charming places.

Those reflective discussions point to how this book is primarily the product of *collaboration*. Not just with these and other work colleagues. Nor only with the ideas of the writers and speakers that have stimulated me to think more deeply about the West's economic malaise. On top of these, direct collaboration with scores of people has been invaluable in getting to this stage.

Having heard or read earlier versions of the arguments, many have offered me constructive feedback.

All the best bits in this book have been gleaned from the wisdom of others: some consciously, many more no doubt subliminally. Of course this doesn't mean that any of my collaborators will agree with everything, or even most things, that I have written.

Out of too many to mention, copious thanks to a few:

- For reading earlier drafts and offering challenging thoughts and suggestions that helped me enormously to develop and refine the arguments: Frank Furedi, Philip Sadler, Daniel Ben-Ami, Rob Lyons, Angus Kennedy, and Mina Toksöz.
- James Woudhuysen: first, for his intellectual opinions and input, not least in matters of technology and innovation. But thanks also for spending too much of his time trying to improve my writing style. His only partial success is due to my ingrained bad habits, not any lack of effort from him.
- My friends Claire Fox, Mick Hume, Austin Williams, Bernhard Blauel, Brid Hehir, Wendy Earle and my sister Patricia, for their advice and encouragement to stick with it, not least through the arduous times in this lengthy project.
- My unofficial editors Gavin Poynter and Mike Fitzpatrick, who read drafts, challenged me, commented, and suggested improvements. Then, after all that wasn't enough, they got stuck into editing chapter drafts. Our afternoon get-togethers over tea and biscuits were for me always a source of learning, stimulation and mirth, mixed with some awe of two extremely smart people, and a frustration that I had gone through life so poorly read in comparison.

And, most heartfelt, for dealing with my doubts and difficulties during it all, for her assistance with the writing and production, and for everything else, thanks to my lovely and long-suffering wife and best mate Para.

INTRODUCTION

A decade after the Western financial crisis

> Growth has ground to a halt almost everywhere …
> a grim new reality: the world is stuck in the slow
> lane and nobody seems to know what to do about
> it. (*Foreign Affairs* editorial, March 2016)

It was no surprise that the Western financial crisis of the late 2000s, the greatest since the Wall Street Crash of 1929, was followed by a severe recession, particularly affecting the developed economies.[1] Yet ten years later, despite the stabilisation of the financial sector, the major focus of concern has become the persistent absence of any substantial revival of production.

The United Nations (UN) annual *World Economic Situation and Prospects* report in 2016 described how earlier hopes for a more dynamic recovery had once again been dashed. Stagnant investment has become well established, exerting downward pressure on productivity, employment and growth 'across a large set of economies'.[2] The sclerosis in productivity has become the big economic story of our times. Governments seem powerless to do anything to revive it.

Some interpret the decay in the pace of productivity growth as the arrival of an era of 'secular stagnation'.[3] More pragmatically, Olivier Blanchard, a former chief economist to the International Monetary Fund (IMF), warned that we should expect lower underlying productivity growth in the future as a 'fact of life'.[4] Meanwhile the consultants McKinsey were advising their clients to consider lowering their sights on investment returns over at least the next 20 years, painting a picture of continued sluggish growth.[5]

Advanced economies are caught in a cycle of depression. The apparently self-reinforcing character of low growth resulting from a dearth of investment amplifies the prevailing sense of despair. Inadequate investment depletes the economy of productive capacity, which in turn slows growth, income, and investment. The dismal science of economics is plumbing new depths.

Box 0.1

RECESSIONS, CRISES AND DEPRESSIONS

'Recession', 'economic crisis', 'depression' each mean different things. Recession is a temporary period when economic activity contracts, generally identified by two consecutive quarters of falling GDP. Economic crisis is a longer-term state characterised by low levels of investment and by decay in the economy's capacity to create new sectors and good jobs. The current economic crisis began with the recessions of 1973-75. Depression signifies a severe period of economic crisis that has become self-reinforcing: it is characterised by the atrophy of the machine of production. The current protracted depression is labelled here the 'Long Depression', distinguishing it from the 'Great Depression' of the 1930s.

Why no revival of growth?

Three popular narratives have emerged in response to the post-crash lethargy. 'Banker-bashers', with varying degrees of sophistication, blame a bloated financial sector for the continuing difficulties of the wider economy. The diversion of capital into speculative activities, the volatility of the money markets and the burden of debt are all cited as enduring constraints on productive investment.

'Techno-pessimists' argue that technology is exhausted and a continuation of the past couple of centuries of economic growth is unlikely. Many add that the demographic headwind of an ageing population is making things worse. By contrast, 'techno-optimists' believe that innovation has never been so powerful. Electronic commerce and the anticipated arrival of driverless cars and artificial intelligence prove it. Some enthusiasts believe that the growth indicator gross domestic product (GDP) underestimates the contribution of new technologies.

A common feature of these narratives is their fatalist resignation to how the Western economies are operating. Those who highlight the damage from the financial crash conclude it is unrealistic to expect other than a 'new mediocre' of puny growth for many years.[6] Those who focus on the role of technology also incline towards a determinist acceptance of the current economic situation. Either technological exhaustion is making low growth inevitable. Or technological progress means that people can ignore the appearance from the economic statistics of minimal growth: there is nothing really wrong, so no need to fix anything.

Complementary arguments about demographic change slowing growth are presented as natural and difficult to alter, even as 'unpreventable'.[7] A greater deference to nature coexists with the notion that torpid growth could persist for a long time. From all directions these perspectives seem reconciled to current economic trends.

The consensus message is that society should get used to a world of minimal expansion in GDP. This acquiescence to sluggish growth is in accord with the prevailing environmentalist view that faster growth risks more ecological harm. However, it also condemns Western societies to the continuation of productive decay with damaging human consequences. Without interventions that shake up the economy there can be no resumption of healthy investment and decent productivity growth. Prosperity will erode further. The extra resources needed to deal with existing and future social challenges, including environmental ones, will evaporate.

Let's look at these three perspectives more closely.

The burdens of financialisation

Many commentators warned Western leaders to expect a prolonged economic hangover as the price to be paid for the roaring financial party they had enjoyed in the preceding twenty years. Richard Koo, who had researched the 'lost decades' of the Japanese economy after 1990, suggested that the West could be entering a similarly prolonged 'balance sheet' recession.[8] In his view, the private sector would not soon get back to spending and borrowing. It would be focused instead on 'deleveraging', paying down its huge debts. Heavy borrowers, whether individuals or businesses, would be obliged to go through a cleansing period to reduce their crippling levels of debt.

In their definitive account of the financial crisis, Carmen Reinhart and Kenneth Rogoff pointed to the historical experience that deep financial crises tend to be followed by slow recoveries.[9] Given the scale of the 2008 meltdown, they argued, nobody should be surprised by a prolonged period of substandard growth. From this perspective, it was inevitable that the demand for new borrowing would be weak. Fragile financial institutions are reluctant to lend as they restructure and attempt to stabilise. Furthermore, high public debt acts as a constraint on growth[10] and government austerity measures tend to have a short-term deflationary effect.

Yet as events unfolded, financial explanations for economic torpor did not prove persuasive. Despite predictions, there was not much deleveraging,[11] and private sector borrowing recovered fairly rapidly. By the middle of the post-crash decade nonfinancial businesses were borrowing at a faster rate than ever before.[12] Individuals have also been borrowing strongly again.[13] In relation to lending, financial institutions did not take long to get back to reasonable health, facilitating the renewed expansion of business borrowing. The UN assessment was that the post-crash recovery of the financial sector had in fact been swift and had significantly outpaced the real sector recovery.[14] After the scars of the financial crisis healed, economic growth should have picked up under this narrative, but it remained slow.[15]

It appears that something other than the repercussions of the financial crash must explain languid economic activity. Even as businesses have been borrowing again, they have not been investing in more efficient plant and equipment to improve and expand their operations. Over the same period many businesses have succeeded in boosting their profits,[16] so a shortage of financial means cannot be the reason for low investment.

The exhaustion of growth

Commentators who attribute the stagnation of production to technological exhaustion tend to trace the productivity slowdown of the past decade to a longer-term decline in innovation. Tyler Cowen, for example, argued in 2011 that after the great technological advances of the 20th century, including electrification, the telephone, the internal combustion engine, we had 'eaten all the low-hanging fruit' and had reached a plateau.[17]

For Cowen, the 1969 moon landing was the symbolic dividing line between an era of rapid technological transformation and one of significantly slower progress. Robert Gordon broadly agrees: for him, the year 1970 marked 'the distinct breakpoint between faster and slower growth'.[18] Gordon argues that the impact of recent computer and communications-based technologies has been much less than that of the inventions of the second industrial revolution.

Though the scientific advances have been spectacular, their impact has been largely confined to entertainment, media, retailing and finance. Unlike the earlier innovations, they have not yet, despite high levels of anticipation, revolutionised manufacturing and production related to food, clothing, housing, transport, or health.

It is clear that digital technologies are currently being implemented in only a limited range of productive activities. It is also apparent that this is a significant factor in the continuing stagnation of productivity. But this is a failure of investment in innovation, not of technology itself.

Box 0.2

THE FOUR INDUSTRIAL REVOLUTIONS

The first industrial revolution was that of the steam engine, the spinning jenny and the railways from the 18th century. The second industrial revolution occurred during the second half of the 19th century, centred on the telegraph, the telephone, electricity and the internal combustion engine. The third one began in the mid-20th century with nuclear power, jet propulsion and computerisation, leading on to the internet and other digital technologies. The fourth industrial revolution is the one needed now to escape the Long Depression.

The evasions of the techno-enthusiasts

Enthusiasts for new technologies dispute the view that innovation has reached some sort of technical or social terminus. They point to the dot.com boom of the late 1990s when new enterprises seized the opportunities provided by the internet and personal computers. They cite the explosion of mobile phone technology as another sign that, far from being stuck in the past, we live in a global society in which 'the pace of change is accelerating'. They proclaim the promise of nanotechnology and genomics.

Yet, as we have seen, the techno-pessimists have a point when they note the narrowness of the digital revolution. Personal gadgets, games consoles and smartphones have transformed the way we consume and spend our leisure time. But since the rollout of the word processor and the data spreadsheet of the 1980s, information and communications technologies (ICT) have done relatively little to transform the production process, or establish new productive sectors.

Some techno-enthusiasts claim that the statistics that guide economic interpretation fail to capture many of the growth and prosperity effects of digital technologies. Free smartphone apps improve our lives in diverse ways, enabling us, for example, to find our way home by sat nav, or call a cab from Uber. Though, they say, this may make us happier and more productive, it doesn't get counted in the main statistic for economic output: GDP.[19]

From this perspective, a services-driven and information-intensive economy is not well measured by 'industrial era' statistics that are better at counting widgets than bits of digitised data.[20] Though GDP stagnates, quality of life is improving. Furthermore, they insist that improvements in the quality of ICT-related products are underestimated and their prices are not discounted appropriately. Inflation is therefore overstated and, as a result, real output figures are understated.[21] Real productivity is higher than reported.

But adjusting for quality has always been difficult. This potential error in GDP measurement did not start with computers: consider the improving performance of cars during the 20th century. It is unclear why the scale of this error should have increased in recent years, during the period of declining productivity that is being pondered. In fact improvements in data collection techniques are more likely to have reduced rather than magnified this inaccuracy.[22]

Techno-enthusiasts also argue that much of the consumer welfare benefit from digital services and products is missing from the GDP figures. The data omit, for example, the value of access to free information and entertainment through the internet. But this measurement deficiency is also not new. Official figures have always aimed to measure market activity, not consumer welfare. Such data never valued some of the most important benefits of earlier innovations, such as electric lights and fridges, telephones and televisions. While we reap many unquantified delights from our PCs and smartphones, their exclusion from GDP does not invalidate the data. This cannot explain weak productivity growth.

It is also a misapprehension to claim that, because ICT saves people time or money, this amounts to an improvement in 'productivity' that is missed by the reported statistics. Productivity is a measure of efficiency in production, not of what people do in their leisure time. It also doesn't matter to the measurement of productivity if something useful to production is free rather than costing money. If, for instance, easy internet searches increase a person's output over a given period, productivity grows. This will register in standard productivity measurements, whether or not there is a payment for the search engine.

A brief survey of these explanations for the failure of sustained economic recovery since 2008 confirms a pervasive sense that modern capitalist society has hit some substantial barriers in its attempts to restore growth. Whether these are identified as the parasitic character of the financial system or the limits of technology, there is a widespread acceptance that they are formidable, if not insuperable, obstacles to progress. Even the techno-enthusiasts seem resigned to low GDP growth, though for the different reason of mismeasurement. Contrary to these narratives, the main economic difficulties are not financial, determined, or illusory. They are to do with production. They are susceptible to human intervention. And they are real.

It also emerges from a consideration of these different perspectives on the absence of recovery that the problems of the mature Western economies did not begin in 2008. Tendencies towards stagnation and decay in the economy's capacity to create new sectors and decent jobs have been apparent for several decades – indeed since the onset of the Long Depression in the early 1970s.

The Long Depression

For more than two decades following the Second World War, Western economies enjoyed the most sustained period of expansion in history. After nearly thirty years of war, political turmoil and economic devastation, the US, and, under its hegemony, Europe and Japan came to enjoy steady growth, full employment and rising living standards.

The recession of 1973–75, however, signalled the onset of a period of economic stagnation that has continued to this day: the Long Depression. For the past four decades the pace of productivity growth has dwindled and these economies have been unable to achieve a decent sustained rate of growth. Figure 0.1 shows that the tempo of economic growth in the Group of Seven (G7) leading Western economies[23] fell sharply between the 1960s and the 1970s, and has since tailed off steadily, decade by decade. (Although GDP has many limitations – see Box 0.3: Measuring economic performance, at the end of this chapter – it is the best comprehensive indicator of wealth creation.) Productive decay in the US is evidenced also in the marked slowdown in the pace of net job growth in successive recoveries (see Figure 0.2).

The indicator GDP per person, which takes account of the effects of the changing population size, provides the best measure of the capacity of societies to afford the things that make for good and improving lives. Figure 0.3 shows how the growth in this indicator has declined since the 1960s, most dramatically in Japan, but across all the advanced economies.

As a result of chronic economic stagnation – starting long before the 2008 crisis – standards of housing and transport, education and health have continued to lag behind popular expectations. Social problems, from mass unemployment among young people to those arising from the needs of an ageing population, appear to multiply beyond the capacity of public intervention.

Figure 0.1 Real economic growth by decade across the Group of Seven

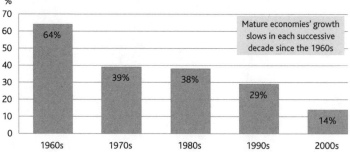

Source: Organisation for Economic Co-operation and Development, Gross Domestic Product by Expenditure in Constant Prices for the Group of Seven, Main Economic Indicators. http://dx.doi.org/10.1787/data-00052-en. Retrieved from FRED (Federal Reserve Economic Data), Federal Reserve Bank of St. Louis. Copyright OECD. Reprinted with permission. https://research.stlouisfed.org/fred2/series/NAEXKP01G7A661S/

Figure 0.2 US net non-farm payroll gains seven years on from previous peaks

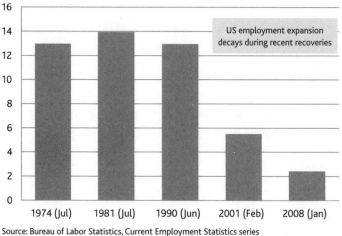

Source: Bureau of Labor Statistics, Current Employment Statistics series CES0000000001. http://data.bls.gov/timeseries/CES0000000001

The fact that many people have continued to experience rising living standards over recent decades reflects how economic decay is neither absolute nor uninterrupted. During the four decades since the crisis began, the rate of new business investment and the pace of productivity growth have deteriorated. Yet output has grown, corporate profits have expanded and living standards, for

Figure 0.3 Real GDP per person average annual percentage growth

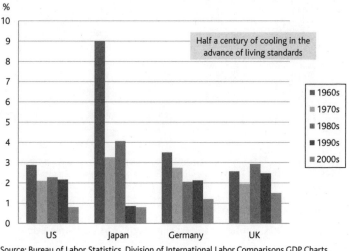

Source: Bureau of Labor Statistics, Division of International Labor Comparisons GDP Charts.
http://www.bls.gov/fls/home.htm#tables

most, have improved. Economic development always takes place unevenly, never more so than in times of depression. Decay is a tendency, not an iron law. The pattern is not one of unmitigated decline. Rather, an underlying dynamic of decay interacts with offsetting bulwarks of resilience, occasionally even producing bursts of vigour. This is owed primarily to the effectiveness of capitalism's coping mechanisms.

Some national economies have derived temporary respite from new developments. The extraction of North Sea oil and gas provided a boost for Britain and some other European countries in the 1980s. The commercialisation of the internet offered opportunities in both hardware and software in the 1990s. The shale energy boom has been a bonus for North America in more recent years and other countries, including the UK, are seeking to exploit this resource. As we shall see later, these windfalls have also provided the opportunity to avoid tackling fundamental problems of investment and productivity.

Three factors have made more substantial contributions to the resilience of the system; they are explored further in Chapter One. One is the impact of periodic recessions, playing their historic dual role. On the one hand, they express tendencies towards crisis. On the other they offer a mechanism of renewal through the destruction of less competitive firms and the consequent boost in productivity. Another is the contribution of international capital flows. These took the form of 'petrodollars' following the oil price crises of the 1970s. More recently, ailing Western economies have received massive inward flows from China and other emerging economies. A third, and most important, factor is the emergence of financialisation, the ascendancy of financial rather than productive activities, in close association with the state. The fusion brought about a powerful coping mechanism: *state financialisation* (described further in Chapter One). The combined effect of these counteracting forces has been to disguise the scale of the underlying problems of production.

The Long Depression has been, for the most part, a *contained depression*. As a result the urgency of the problems of poor productivity has been obscured, facilitating acquiescence to a status quo complacently labelled as 'the new normal'.[24]

The state and the zombie economy

There is much disagreement among economists over the factors causing the decline in productivity since the 1970s. There is, however, a consensus that in the 1980s, the decade of Reaganism in the US and Thatcherism in the UK, a resurgence of market forces was associated with the retreat of the state from economic life. For many, the upsurge in the financial sector associated with measures of deregulation paved the way towards the catastrophe of 2007-08. As Martin Wolf put it: 'the financially-driven capitalism that emerged after the market-orientated counter-revolution has proved too much of a good thing'.[25] From this perspective, unrestrained market forces, expressed in diverse forms of speculation, lavish executive bonuses and increasing social inequalities, led inexorably to the crash.

In Chapter Eight, we question this consensus, which is often proclaimed mistakenly as the triumph of 'neoliberalism'. Rather, markets are even less free than they used to be. The state did not retreat from economic life in the 1980s. Under the banner of 'deregulation', the form of state intervention changed significantly. While retreating from the traditions of economic policy aiming to encourage growth, the state offered subsidies to sustain industry and encouragements to the financial sector. Nor was there much evidence of an unleashed entrepreneurial spirit among capitalists. They preferred to avoid the risk of investment in new technologies or new areas of production, in pursuit of quick returns through financialised activities.

Policymakers have generally stumbled into solutions for immediate problems when they could no longer evade them. For instance, somewhat inadvertently, they fostered the extension of financialisation to provide a potent coping mechanism for capitalism in the 1990s and early 2000s.[26] Its subsequent efflorescence culminated in the financial crash.

Government policy in response to the crash followed the same pragmatic and myopic approach of successive governments since the 1980s. As Wolf put it, the objective was to do 'the minimum needed to "put the show back on the road"'.[27] Government policies have attempted to restore economic stability at the expense of establishing a solid dynamic for growth. Yet such state-led measures are ultimately counterproductive. Trying to stabilise the economy in its current state has the perverse effect of preserving its moribund features and stunting its development. While state intervention has moderated the worst features of decay, the economy has become increasingly sclerotic.

Short-term expedients have brought temporary respite while allowing deeper problems to fester. These policies have ultimately made the slump worse. By sustaining a stagnant productive base, the state has forestalled the process that Joseph Schumpeter named 'creative destruction'. Instead of encouraging the replacement of ailing companies by more dynamic enterprises, the government has opted to maintain a 'zombie' economy. Various forms of state support prop up firms that are incapable of boosting productivity through investing in new technologies. A dead economy is thus given the semblance of life and the appearance of resilience disguises a continuing process of decay.

It will not be easy to escape the grip of the Long Depression. Though a comprehensive restructuring of production is needed to restore capitalism's value-creating capacity, the default option is always to avoid disruption. But 'creative destruction' on a significant scale is essential to restore growth. Older, less productive capital assets will have to be written off and replaced by a wave of transformative outlays on the latest technologies in newly emerging sectors of production.

Since the financial crisis the underlying problems of sluggish investment and growth have become increasingly apparent. Yet there remain too many economists, politicians and members of the public alike, who are inclined to downplay or avoid the warning signals. Unanticipated events do sometimes jolt the elites into recognising better the weak state of the economy. The 2016 British referendum vote to leave the European Union (EU) and Donald Trump's US presidential election victory were each driven much more by people rejecting technocratic policies and cultural values, than they were by economic factors. Nevertheless the shock effect of both results influenced perceptions about the economy. They shook up the elite's complacency over the extent and impact on people of the post-2009 recovery.

However, even when economic decay gets more attention, instead of pursuing growth-obsessed policies there is a widespread inclination to endorse strategies of muddling through. There is a persistent evasion of confronting the challenges of stagnation with the appropriate determination to make a real difference. Many who have recognised something of the scale of the problem tend to take a fatalistic view of the persistence of no or low growth.

This means that the biggest challenge to restoring growth is not economic, but political. It lies in the failure to recognise the constraints holding back the development of production and that these are potentially under human control. Contrary to the words of Lawrence of Arabia in David Lean's eponymous film, our fate is not 'written'. The future is not set. The process of decline is not inevitable. The first step towards reviving economic dynamism is to understand the character and drivers of the Long Depression.

Box 0.3
MEASURING ECONOMIC PERFORMANCE

Official economic statistics are not absolute truths. They are always based on estimates and samples. The national economic output figure, which we know as gross domestic product, measures the wealth being created in an economy. It seeks to quantify the *new values* being generated in a period of time *within* a territory (that's what the 'domestic' refers to). GDP adds up estimates of the values as measured in the final market prices of goods and services newly produced by all sectors of the economy – agriculture, manufacturing, mining, energy production, construction and, the biggest of all, services.

GDP changes are a reflection of changes in population – specifically the hours spent productively engaged in work – and of productivity – the average output for each hour, measured at market prices. Because real prices fall with technological advance and improved productivity, GDP as a real *price* measure will generally underestimate increases in *material* wealth in the sense of the quantity of things that are represented by a particular value. Nevertheless a shift up or down in the GDP statistics provides a good indicator of the direction of an economy's production: expanding or contracting.

The trend of the GDP growth rate across the G7 has halved from more than 4% at the end of the 1960s to 2% in the mid-2010s.[28] Less than a quarter of this slowdown is due to a halving of population growth since the late 1980s when it was about 0.6% a year. The main contributor has been the decline in labour productivity growth.

However, as a representative measure of an economy's health and level of prosperity GDP has plenty of shortcomings. It fails to measure all there is to life. Many social improvements, from running water and sanitation to falling infant mortality, do not get counted directly. GDP doesn't measure qualitative change like better health, living longer, or enjoying more leisure time.

Diane Coyle, who wrote an entire book on the GDP statistic, called it 'a made-up entity'.[29] GDP depends on assumptions about what's included and what is not. Changing the assumptions changes the output data, sometimes considerably. Recently, for example, EU statistical guidelines changed to include in national output some black market activities, such as dealing in illegal drugs and prostitution. More prosaically, the US expanded its definition of investment, thereby adding 3.6% to the size of its GDP in 2012 – rather more than a full year of growth.[30]

One of GDP's biggest economic defects is the inclusion of activities which, even if useful, embody no new economic value. For example, many, though by no means all, financial services are necessary for the market economy to function. They allow goods and services to be exchanged for consumption either by individuals or by other businesses. They help to allocate capital to fund additional production. Production, the arena where value *is* added, could not happen in a market economy without the help of these services. But these financial intermediation services exchange, or move about, *existing* value; they do not create *new* value. However, financial services appear within GDP figures.

Unsurprisingly, coming up with credible figures for their contribution to GDP is fraught with problems. As Stephen Burgess, a manager at the Bank of England, stated, 'there are many conceptual difficulties associated with measuring output in finance'. Users should not have 'unreasonably high expectations' of some of the proxy measures that are used to estimate output in the financial sector.[31] In other words, don't expect the financial sector component of GDP to mean much. Moreover, with the huge expansion of debt and the financialised economy in recent years, the inclusion of financial services in GDP has led to major distortions in the economic growth reported.

Despite all GDP's deficiencies, paraphrasing Winston Churchill it is the worst measure of wealth production, except for all the others being put forward these days. As David Pilling concluded a review of its criticisms, GDP may fail entirely to capture the complex tradeoffs between present and future, work and leisure, 'good' growth and 'bad' growth. But its great virtue remains that it is a 'single, concrete number'.[32]

Part I
The state we're in

Productivity isn't everything, but in the long run it is almost everything. (Paul Krugman, *The Age of Diminishing Expectations*, 1994)

ONE

Decay and resilience

Signs of stasis and decay are apparent across Western countries. Growth is anaemic everywhere, as illustrated by the three charts in the Introduction. Since the financial crash performances have deteriorated further. Ed Conway, an economics editor, calculated that seven and a half years after the crash, global industrial output was comparatively lower than it was seven and a half years after the great crash of 1929.[1] Productivity – what each worker can produce in an hour – has not recovered anywhere. In America average annual productivity growth of below 1% between 2009 and 2016 is less than half the level of the half-decade before 2008.

In post-crash Britain, productivity flatlined for many years. Britain's return to pre-recession levels of output per person took much longer than the 1930s. Japan had its own financial crash in 1990–91 and has since endured more than two 'lost' decades, averaging annual output growth for each person of less than 1%.[2] In Spain since the start of the 2010s more than one in five workers have been unable to find a job; for young Spaniards it has been one out of two. And in the advanced economies where unemployment has fallen to relatively low levels, many of the new jobs are of poor quality and generate inadequate incomes.

Yet, because of the enduring resilience of the capitalist system, it has been possible for much of the past four decades, especially before the crash, to regard such manifestations of decline as unfortunate episodes, exceptional occurrences, blips in the long-term trend of increasing prosperity. Fears arising from the inexorable demise of traditional manufacturing industries in the West have been allayed by the apparent vitality of the global capitalist system with the rise of China and other emerging economies, and by the expansion of services and the promise of new digital technologies at home. Even with the post-2010 gloom about protracted torpid economic growth, few people anticipate a calamitous collapse in living standards, just more of the same, with the resumption sometime of rising prosperity.

In the industrialised world, output has risen and consumer goods – phones, cars, washing machines – have become more versatile. Man's new gadgets, such as the iPhone, impress. Especially because of such advances in ICT, we seem to have been moving quickly. Yet appearances can be deceptive. A hamster on a wheel, after all, can work hard, run fast, and even enjoy the process: but it is not going anywhere.

The broad-based, unrestrained dynamism that characterised the 25 years of boom after 1945 is no more. Transient features of economic vigour mask an underlying process of decline and loss of dynamism. Though a range of mechanisms has allowed the economic system to survive – and even, for periods, to expand – the trend since the end of the post-war boom in the early 1970s has been one of decay in the Western economies' capacity to create new sectors and provide decent jobs.

However, perceptions of general, if perhaps uneven, improvements in living standards over several decades have nurtured a tendency to ignore deep-rooted problems of sluggish investment and growth. As mentioned in the Introduction, this impression arises because the underlying trends towards stagnation are masked by a number of factors that contribute to the resilience of the system. They have enabled it to retain the appearance of advance despite the persistence of decay. Three factors stand out: the impact of recessions, international capital flows, and financialisation. Let's take these in turn.

Recessions

Through their cleansing effect, recessions create the conditions for a renewal of production, creating space for more productive firms to set up or expand.[3] The weaker and least productive businesses either go bust, or get taken over by stronger businesses at bargain basement prices. The survivors are those with cash generating operations and the most profitable of them adopt newer technologies to surge ahead. Meanwhile, the new businesses that have more space to expand also invest in the latest technologies. By the 'batting average' effect alone, productivity across the economy usually picks up and recovery takes off.[4]

The rise in unemployment during recessions when companies close down or lay off employees also supports the remaining businesses to recover, since it becomes easier to keep wage costs down. This helps the cash flows both of the surviving companies and especially the new businesses that go on to drive the recovery.

Recessions and many of the other long-established market features that help offset decay, such as foreign trade and cutting production costs, were evident in the first decade of the Long Depression. The recessions of the mid-1970s and early 1980s helped clear out some of the weakest parts of the economy, and each ushered in temporary periods of economic recovery and expansion.

International capital flows

In the 1970s, high oil prices, resulting from geopolitical instability in the Middle East and the declining value of the dollar, encouraged flows of international capital into the crisis-stricken economies of the West. 'Petro-dollars' – surpluses built up by the oil-exporting nations – were used to buy up Western financial assets or were lent to developing countries via the major commercial banks, some of which helped to fund the purchase of Western exports. Through both avenues, this provided a helpful transfer of value from developing countries to the West, thereby bolstering resilience and alleviating the effects of the West's economic slowdown.

The rapid expansion of the Asian economies since the 1990s has provided a parallel source of capital for the West. Considerable value was being produced too quickly to be entirely absorbed at home, making it available for lending elsewhere. Spearheaded by China, the import of capital from the emerging parts of the world has been a boon to the old West in allowing it to maintain an aura of prosperity.

Financialisation

International flows of capital helped to finance the most important supportive mechanism of the flagging economies of the West: financialisation – the expansion of financial activities to compensate for the weaknesses of productive enterprises. At a time when productive operations are struggling to create new values, the extension of credit allows businesses and individuals to continue to produce, consume and operate despite the relative inadequacy of newly produced values. Subsequently banks and governments rely increasingly on debt to finance their activities too.

To maintain the semblance of vitality, Western capitalism has become increasingly dependent on expanding debt levels and on the expansion of fictitious capital. The latter is made up of financial assets that are only symbols of value, not real values. For example, company shares that are traded like goods and services do not in the same way embody value. They are tokens that represent part ownership of a company and the potential of a distribution of future profits in the form of dividends. The paper or electronic certificate itself is not a genuine value that can create more value. Rising share prices are often presented as evidence of a healthy economy, but the amount of money a share changes hands for says nothing definitive about the value of the company's assets or about its productive capacity. On the contrary, it is when real capital stagnates that the amount of fictitious capital tends to expand.

The expansion of the financial sector is the most recognisable aspect of financialisation. However, a more telling part for how the workings of the economy change is the adoption of financial activities by the nonfinancial corporate sector, by the wider industrial economy. The core feature of financialisation is the fusion of industry with financial activity. Troubled nonfinancial firms turn to financial activity to raise cash and shore up profitability.

These financial activities start with raising debt to fund business operations working at sub-par profitability. They extend into financial engineering, where buying and selling shares or acquiring companies take precedence over productive investment and organic growth in the underlying businesses. Financial services companies are often helpful in conducting these activities. The drive though comes from the nonfinancial businesses that are obliged to pursue financial activities when their original productive ones are less profitable and remunerative.

The rise of financialisation illustrates a key feature of the Long Depression that has evolved over recent decades. Market-driven mechanisms counteracting production's decay have been supplemented by powerful *muddle-through* policies enacted by the major Western states. Since the 1970s Western state institutions have, often haphazardly, stumbled upon ways either to extend some of the existing counteracting methods, or have come up with new measures to cope with the slowdown.

While the tendency towards financialisation arises from the existing market relationship between finance and production, state intervention has allowed it to flourish. The potential for financialisation to thrive was triggered by a decision of the US state in the early 1970s to bring the Bretton Woods post-war currency agreement to an end. By breaking the link between the dollar and gold, and the pegs between other currencies and the dollar, the financial system was set free.

This state-determined return of explicit fiat money – money not backed by gold – moved the West onto pure paper currencies. As a result banks had more leeway to create money and the credit system was less constrained. State institutions have since promoted and entrenched the financialised transformation of all the Western economies, not least through the actions of the central banks.[5] They have been such a driving force in the evolution of this phenomenon that it is appropriate to characterise this process as 'state financialisation'.

Governments across the Western world have provided the infrastructure for financialisation, facilitating both the growth of debt and that of the financial system. In Britain, the City of London, the product of Britain's 19th century industrial and commercial world leadership, was given state backing in the 20th century to help offset the decline of productive industries. In the 1960s, for example, the British state was happy for London to operate as the major offshore trading centre for the emerging eurodollar market. (This is a market in dollars held outside the US and therefore beyond the control of the US Federal Reserve.) State support has assumed ever greater importance since the 1980s, when the British government directly promoted financialisation through Margaret Thatcher's 'Big Bang' financial sector reforms of 1986.

Before examining the failures of conventional economic models to grasp the key significance of weak investment and stagnating productivity to the Long Depression, it is worth pausing to consider some of the deficiencies of the radical critique of financialisation because of how it can mislead. Critics often attribute current economic woes to the ascendancy of 'neoliberalism'. As noted in the Introduction, this is a doctrine that proposes a diminished role for the state and greater scope for unrestricted market forces. They argue that financialisation is a result of the *retreat* of the state from the economy. Quite the reverse: while it is possible to cite many instances of financial liberalisation and deregulation, these represent greater, not less, state engagement in economic life.

For example, in the US in 1999 the Clinton administration repealed the 1930s Glass–Steagall Act, which had separated investment and commercial banks. This action gave financial operations greater flexibility, and the government further decided not to subject over-the-counter derivatives to regulation. These financial instruments featured prominently in the leadup to the 2008 crash. Yet, at the same time, new forms of regulation were being introduced. For example, since 1988 capital adequacy ratios were set for banks through the series of Basel Accords under the auspices of the 'central bankers' bank', the Bank for International Settlements (BIS). Although ultimately ineffective in preventing instability in the financial system, these measures are indicative of the continued official oversight and control of the financial system.

Instances of financial liberalisation should therefore not be interpreted as reflecting the absence of regulation. As Costas Lapavitsas, a radical critic of financialisation, observed, finance has continued to be heavily regulated both domestically and internationally.[6] The form of this regulation has simply changed, responding to the needs of the wider economy.

State financialisation has been remarkably successful in compensating for decay and preventing it from appearing as an uninterrupted phenomenon. Yet, like the other coping mechanisms, financialisation cannot resolve the moribund state of production. Nor can these coping measures indefinitely maintain a semblance of prosperity. The 2008 Western financial crisis illustrated the limits of coping with productive decay through the devices of financialisation and debt.

The proximate factor precipitating the crash was a bubble of debt. Too much money from debt went into boosting spending levels and the appearance of prosperity in the present. Far too little went into investing to create durable prosperity for the future. The growing dependence on debt for funding consumption was not because people became irresponsible about their finances. Rather, people turned to borrowing because their incomes were not growing enough to fund their intended spending. Similarly, businesses initially turned more to borrowing to finance their necessary expenditures. This points to the kernel of the problem: the economy wasn't producing enough new value. Instead of creating value, it became dependent on debt.

False dawns and flawed forecasts

Following the 2008 banking crisis, Her Majesty the Queen famously upbraided a gathering of eminent economists at the London School of Economics (LSE) for their failure to anticipate the crash. Her criticism of the inadequacy of the economists' models echoed that of the immediate post-war US president Harry Truman, who expressed a wish for 'a one-handed economist' – to spare him from the equivocation of expert advisers who always counselled 'on the one hand, this; on the other, that'. Over the 60 years between the comments of Truman and the Queen, economic modelling has acquired greater mathematical sophistication, but not much greater accuracy in predicting events. Always relying on data from the past and on definite assumptions, models have proven of limited value in foretelling a changing future.

Twentieth century economists generally moved away from the quest of the great classical economists (Smith, Ricardo,

Mill) to understand the fundamental dynamics of capitalism in favour of analysing the movements of markets, prices, levels of demand and constraints on supply. Focusing on superficial signs of resilience, economists have failed to grasp the underlying tendency towards decay. A failure to disentangle surface appearances from underlying dynamics – or to work out the mediating links between these different levels – clouds both analysis and prognostication.

On a number of occasions over the past 40 years, mainstream economists have proclaimed the end of the Long Depression and heralded a new era of sustained expansion. One such false dawn coincided with the era of Thatcherism and Reaganomics, named after the two Western leaders who presided over a rejuvenated Anglo-American alliance in the 1980s. Another was dubbed the 'New Economy', acclaimed as the consequence of the commercial exploitation of the internet and the new information technology of the late 1990s. A third moment of capitalist optimism was triggered in the mid-2000s by the prospect that the extraction of shale gas could deliver the US cheap energy and end its dependence on Middle Eastern oil. Before we assess these, it is worth recalling from Figure 0.1 that despite these factors G7 growth has slowed in *each successive decade* since the 1960s.

The Thatcher/Reagan effect

By the mid-1980s, it appeared that a decade of sluggish economic growth and rising prices – 'stagflation' – was at an end. In Britain Margaret Thatcher (prime minister from 1979 to 1990) and in the US Ronald Reagan (president from 1981 to 1989), both deeply committed to conservative economic and social policies, presided over a period of expansion following sharp recessions. The upturn followed the collapse of much traditional manufacturing industry and bitter trade union disputes. On both sides of the Atlantic, economists and politicians proclaimed a new era of dynamism and prosperity based on private enterprise liberated from state tyranny and trade union power.

Celebrations of the end of the Long Depression proved premature. By 1987 stock markets crashed, including the largest ever one-day fall in American stock markets. So traumatic was this collapse that some commentators even anticipated a return to 1930s-type economic conditions.[7] The crash in financial markets was briskly followed in 1990-91 by a return to international recession, a recession from which the world's then second largest economy, Japan, has yet to recover. Rather than confirming the strength of the system, the transient 1980s recovery merely marked the transition to a new phase of the Long Depression. It was one characterised by the reduced pricing power of Western corporates, expressed in lower rates of inflation, combined with moderate levels of economic growth.

The dot.com boom

In their enthusiastic response to the takeoff of internet-related enterprises in the late 1990s, economists provided an even starker instance of their inclination to get carried away by the promise of a new technology to deliver Western economies from the grip of the Long Depression. Though the internet and digital technologies were more developments of post-war military and industrial research than the fruits of contemporary scientific innovation, they were greeted as the harbingers of a New Economy. New industries boomed and a networked society flourished. The beneficial economic effects of the new technologies were particularly evident in the US, but were also pronounced in Britain, Finland, Sweden and South Korea, and rippled out across the rest of the world.

Though for a brief period there were signs that productivity was rising again after two decades of torpor, by the turn of the millennium the New Economy was already in trouble. In 2000, the dot.com bubble burst. The crash was followed by another (relatively mild) recession affecting most Western nations. More significantly, within a couple of years growth in productivity in the US had stalled: the forces of decay soon reasserted themselves. Once again, signs of resilience in the form of new technology had been misinterpreted as grounds for optimism about the prospects of emergence from the Long Depression.

The shale energy boom

In the early 2000s 'fracking' – the extraction of gas and oil from shale reserves through horizontal drilling and hydraulic fracturing – transformed the North American energy landscape. In addition to liberating the US from dependence on overseas sources of oil, the prospect of lower energy prices was widely hailed as a potential boost to the competitiveness of industry. In 2011 the Boston Consulting Group popularised the idea of an American 'manufacturing renaissance' in an influential report, *Made in America, Again: Why Manufacturing Will Return to the US*. For its authors, shale energy offered US manufacturers new opportunities to compete on the world stage, at a time when rising Chinese wage costs were also beginning to undermine China's competitiveness.[8] At the 2013 Davos World Economic Forum, US energy secretary Robert Hormats argued that the rapid availability of cheap, plentiful gas had the potential to transform the American economy.[9] Eighteen months later the IMF claimed that the 'shale revolution' would boost US industrial production compared to higher gas price regions like Europe.[10]

Though it is too early to assess the long-term impact of shale energy, in 2015 in terms of volume the US was still more dependent on energy imports than it had been in the mid-1980s, or before the mid-1970s. While America's trade deficit in energy has improved in value terms, it is still higher than it was in the 1980s and 1990s (see Figure 1.1). The impact of the energy-fuelled 'industrial renaissance' on the rest of the merchandise trade deficit is so far even less tangible: the figures show a continuing deterioration. (The temporary improvement in 2008-09 was the familiar effect of recession: imports fall away as a result of declining household consumption and less domestic production requiring imported inputs.) The overall trend suggests that, contrary to expectations of an embryonic industrial resurgence, the US is becoming more, rather than less, reliant on overseas production.

This rising trade deficit accompanying a return to sluggish growth reveals how productive decline remains the more potent force on the US's external account. Again, resilience is being confused with durable economic revival. A positive addition to the economy is mistaken as being truly transformational.

Figure 1.1 US merchandise trade balance

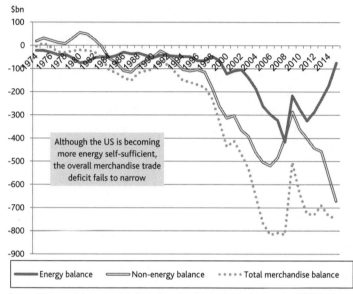

Source: US Energy Information Administration, Monthly Energy Review, October 2015, table 1.5. http://www.eia.gov/totalenergy/data/monthly/archive/00351609.pdf

The 'resource curse'

A proper concern about the US shale energy boom would not be the conventional one, that it might peter out too quickly, but that it could last long enough to put off the economic restructuring that is already much overdue. The beneficial effects of fracking could become the 2010s equivalent of the ICT revolution – a force that obscures decay while being unable to reverse its rule. The shale energy boom could become America's version of the 'resource curse'.

It has long been recognised that, for a developing economy, having energy or other natural resources *can* – though it doesn't have to – become a distraction from economic development and progress. Capital – domestic and foreign – often focuses on the resources sector alone, at the expense of broader economic development. Because of the nation's resource wealth, other sectors seem to have less incentive to pursue productivity improvements. This can produce the paradox that countries and regions with an abundance of natural resources often experience slower economic growth and worse development outcomes than countries with fewer resources.

This has become known as the resource curse, the paradox of plenty, or the Dutch disease; the latter term coined in 1977 by *The Economist* to describe the decline of the manufacturing sector in the Netherlands after the discovery of a large natural gas field in the late 1950s. If the US genuinely experiences a sustained energy boom, that resource curse could become a bigger problem than if it were merely a passing phase. The false belief that the US economy was 'on the mend' could further distract attention from addressing its economic problems.

Another Western country provides recent evidence of this possibility. Britain's North Sea oil boom in the 1970s and 1980s disguised how far the underlying British economy had sunk. Michael Edwardes, then the chief executive and chairman of Britain's ailing motor giant, British Leyland, warned the 1980 conference of the Confederation of British Industry (CBI) of the dangers from Britain's own resource boom. He argued that if the Cabinet did not have the 'wit and imagination' to reconcile industrial needs with the benefits of North Sea oil, they would 'do better to leave the bloody stuff in the ground'. He was ignored: North Sea oil came and went, and Britain's inexorable economic decline continued.

TWO

Productivity in decline

The capacity to produce more in a shorter period of time is the most fundamental indicator of social progress. Rising productivity has underpinned the spectacular development of human civilisation over the past 200 years. Fluctuations in the growth of productivity distinguish alternating phases of capitalist expansion and capitalist crisis.

The slowing pace of productivity growth in all the major industrialised economics at the close of the 1960s was the clearest indication that the post-war boom was coming to an end. The subsequent failure of productivity to recover its earlier dynamism signified that this turning point also marked the start of another depression. The fortunes of productivity define the contours of the Long Depression better than any other measure. Figure 2.1 illustrates both the overarching tendency towards stagnation and the effect of counteracting resilient tendencies.

The fates of different advanced economies in the Second World War dictated different patterns of post-war development. The destruction of capital assets in Germany and Japan as a result of military defeat facilitated a more thoroughgoing economic restructuring and higher levels of productivity than in the UK or US, where restructuring was more the consequence of the industrial demands of war than physical devastation. It is striking that relative productivity levels in the 1960s were inversely proportional to the extent of homeland bombing two decades earlier. When the post-war boom faltered, the slowdown in productivity was more readily apparent in Germany and Japan where it had reached higher levels.

Figure 2.1 Productivity average annual percentage growth

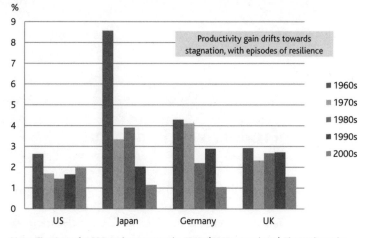

Notes: Figures are for GDP per hour, except the 1960s (GDP per employee). The UK figure for the 1970s covers only 1971-79 (instead of the standard 1970-79).
Source: Bureau of Labor Statistics, Division of International Labor Comparisons GDP Charts. http://www.bls.gov/fls/home.htm#tables

In this chapter, we first consider why productivity is central to economic development, to living standards and to the welfare of society. Second, we review the evidence of deteriorating productivity underlying the Long Depression, its differing manifestations in different advanced economies and the impact on living standards. We then examine what drives productivity with reference to some of the influential economic theories on the question. We finally assess two major controversies about productivity over the past 20 years: these illustrate some dominant misapprehensions about productivity growth that need to be clarified.

Why productivity matters

Productivity tells us two main things about what an economy can provide. Its absolute level tells us how wealthy we are today. Its pace of change tells us how much wealthier we could be tomorrow.

Increasing productivity means an increasing amount of goods or services produced in a given time. A doubling of productivity should mean a doubling of wealth as expressed in double the *volume* of units produced. However, since it is not feasible to compare and aggregate in technical terms the volumes of all sorts of different useful things being produced, the amount of *value* of the goods or services produced in the same time has instead become the standard measure.[1]

The power of productivity is enhanced because its growth is cumulative: productivity growth begets more productivity growth. It generates the extra resources that can be devoted to the next round of productivity-enhancing investments. Also more productively created, lower-cost goods or services feed back into production by stimulating productivity improvements to bring costs down in other areas. For example, increasing productivity to produce a cheaper machine tool is likely to encourage the spread of this equipment to other areas of production, thus raising productivity more widely.

Higher productivity techniques in one area will usually be applied to boost productivity in others – a process known as productivity diffusion.[2] Thus the moving overhead lines pioneered in the Chicago meatpacking industry in the late 19th century were subsequently copied as assembly-line technologies in the automobile industry and then in other modes of transport (ships and, later, aircraft). Similar techniques were deployed in the production of household appliances and, in the post-war years, electronic goods. Unfortunately this virtuous cycle turns into the opposite when productivity slows: weak productivity also becomes self-reinforcing. Productivity sclerosis also diffuses.

How does growth in productivity improve living standards? This is often explained by the fact that more productive companies can pay higher wages. But this is only part of the story. Certainly companies in a specific sector gain competitive advantage by innovating first and raising the productivity level for some product or service. These more technologically advanced firms will benefit from selling more at lower prices and higher profit margins. Many will share some of this expanding profit with their workers through wage increases. As other businesses follow these pioneers in the use of new technologies, wages for their workers will also eventually rise.

The broader relationship is that in an economy in which productivity is growing across many sectors, everyone can enjoy higher living standards. Introducing better ways of producing goods and services makes them cheaper for all. Since each particular product or service takes less labour time, an item previously priced at £10 might now have a £9 price tag. A unit of something becomes cheaper so everyone is able to buy more of it with their dollar, pound, yen or euro.[3] Productivity growth thus has a 'double' impact on living standards and prosperity. Incomes will rise for people working in particular sectors where productivity is growing, while everybody benefits from these cheaper goods and services.

In contrast, weak growth in productivity results in little or no improvement in the purchasing power of money, while real incomes also remain stuck or grow only slowly. Temporary factors can mitigate this link between productivity and living standards and allow people to sustain the latter. Personal debt can expand to finance consumption, stock markets can boom to make us wealthier on paper, and house prices can rise, also making us feel wealthier and more open to borrowing from the future. Over longer periods, however, when these artificial props for prosperity give way, people find they are no better off than they were some years earlier. Their disillusionment is compounded when they can only get low productivity employment that offers poor pay and high insecurity.

Productivity growth also underlies social development. The steady growth in productivity in Britain since the late 18th century provided the basis for advances in health and welfare. The *particular* way a society has developed has been the product of human decisions over how to use increasing wealth: for example, creating a pension system, or a safety net for the unemployed, or a public health service, or universal childcare. Without the material basis provided by rising productivity, human possibilities and ambitions would have been correspondingly constrained.

Productivity growth is the fundamental driver of economic and social development, raising living standards and humanity's control both of nature – to use natural resources efficiently – and also of time – reducing the labour time necessary to produce things. Not only is this essential to prosperity, it gives society the opportunity to expand leisure time. It gives us more time, in the words of Victor Frankl, for contemplation so as to obtain 'fulfillment in experiencing beauty, art or nature'.[4]

The deterioration in productivity

The pace of productivity growth has been on a downward trend since the 1970s, becoming more pronounced from the early 1990s in most industrialised countries, and in the US from the early 2000s. This trend has become more widely recognised by economists in the aftermath of the 2008 financial crash.[5] The recognition is due less to deterioration in the fundamentals of productivity than to the erosion of previous offsetting and obscuring influences, not least those arising from the debt bubble.[6] Non-enduring mechanisms that successfully supported output had also sustained reported productivity.

An IMF study published in 2015 recognised that the post-crash productivity slowdown was the continuation of one long-term trend across the advanced industrial economies: underlying output and productivity growth had been in secular decline for the previous four decades.[7] The Fund report also went on to describe how the secular productivity trend had been masked by the ups and downs associated with the financial cycle, together with other temporary uplifts. The expansion of low-cost debt has provided an important transitory boost to output and productivity: debt-supported businesses crank up production to meet artificial debt-supported demand.

Complementing this mechanism, businesses have shored up productivity more directly by persistent efforts to cut jobs as a principal way to reduce operating costs. While output has been maintained by borrowing, managers have found ways to eliminate layers of staff without investing in physical assets. These efforts to cut labour costs have been implemented under a variety of fashionable management and organisational models including business process re-engineering, lean techniques, Six Sigma, and the flattening of hierarchies.

The combined effect has been to squeeze more out of the remaining workers, flattering productivity figures. While an effective temporary substitute for investment-driven productivity, the resulting intensification of work eventually hits physical limits. Without investment in better technology people can only be driven so hard over the course of the working day.

In different countries we can identify differing ways in which transient uplifts have interrupted the secular process of productivity decline.

Britain

The shakeout of some of the least productive industries in the 1973-75 and 1980-81 recessions – especially steelmaking, shipbuilding and cars – followed by the expansion of financial services provided the most important contributions to British resilience. The temporary effects of North Sea oil production in the 1980s and 1990s also helped, as did the even more short-lived boost from sterling's devaluation and interest rate cuts arising from Britain's forced exit from the European Exchange Rate Mechanism in 1992.

Germany

Industrial reorganisations following national reunification in 1990 were mainly responsible for the 1990s uplift. German productivity growth subsequently slowed sharply and since the turn of the century it has been the weakest of the four economies featured here. This is not the familiar economic narrative about Germany, because while productivity growth slumped, it had other reserves of resilience as a substitute for domestic investment. In particular, Germany has been able to sustain its economy by taking advantage of its leading position in the eurozone group established in 1999: exporting capital and goods to the other, especially the southern, eurozone countries, and benefiting from a low exchange rate for exporting globally.

The US

The ICT boom of the late 1990s and early 2000s produced an upward blip in US productivity. In retrospect many economists now see this as less transformational than it was then perceived to be.

In all cases, though, none of these upward movements proved enduring and they were unable to restore anything like the dynamism of the booming 1950s and 1960s. The US Conference Board has produced an aggregate chart (Figure 2.2) for the advanced mature economies that smooths out some of these country volatilities and clearly shows the trend of slowdown in labour productivity growth since the end of the post-war boom.

Figure 2.2 Trend growth of labour productivity in the mature economies

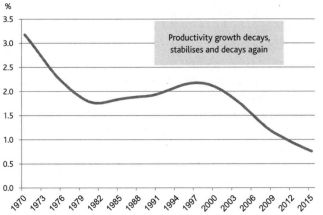

Notes: GDP per person employed. This trend line is based on HP-filtering.
Source: The Conference Board Total Economy Database™ (Adjusted version), November 2016.
http://www.conference-board.org/data/economydatabase/

There are two broad phases to the decline. Overall, mature economy productivity growth fell in the 1970s from about 3.25% to about 2.0% a year. The combined effect of the first wave of counteracting forces then stabilised growth rates during the 1980s, even producing a small uplift. However, as the most effective of these measures exhausted themselves decline took over again from the late 1990s. Growth rates fell to about 1.25% in the mid-2000s and, subsequent to the financial crash, fell again to below 1%.

The impact on living standards

To put productivity statistics into a human perspective, growth rates of the earlier 3.25% mean that living standards double about every 20 years (assuming reasonably stable employment rates and hours worked). With a growth rate of only 1%, this would instead take about 70 years. By contrast, over the 100 years before 1970 – including the devastating inter-war depression – productivity on average grew at around 2% a year, so that living standards doubled every 35 years. This represents approximately a doubling in each generation, providing strong grounds for the assumption of post-war parents that their children would be better off than themselves.

Slowing productivity has also sapped income growth. The recent tendency to stagnation in wages across many Western nations has been evident in their average levels, notwithstanding some recent post-crash recovery (see Figure 2.3). (Average 'mean' wage levels are also influenced by changes in earnings dispersion.) While average wages have been decidedly flat in Japan ever since its financial bubble burst at the start of the 1990s, growth rates have also been slowing in the other advanced economies, and have lagged behind their rates of economic growth. In Germany, average and median (midpoint) wages rose until the mid-1990s,

Figure 2.3 Average real wages

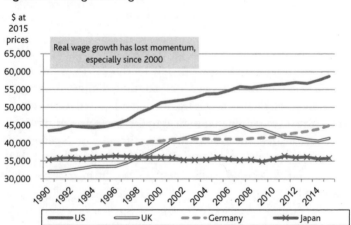

Source: Average annual wages (2015 constant prices at 2015 US dollar Purchasing Power Parities). Copyright OECD. http://stats.oecd.org/Index.aspx?DataSetCode=AV_AN_WAGE

when they flattened out. They then fell by nearly a tenth in real terms between 2003 and 2008.[8]

In the US and Britain it took until the financial crash for income stagnation to become fully evident,[9] though signs were already there earlier. For Americans in full-time employment median earnings have been flat since the turn of the new century, and have fallen for men.[10] Even more striking, for non-managerial workers hourly pay was lower in real terms in the mid-2010s than it had been in 1973 at the start of the Long Depression (see Figure 2.4). In fact, 1973 represented a high for US private sector hourly earnings that has never been attained since.

Figure 2.4 US average hourly wages

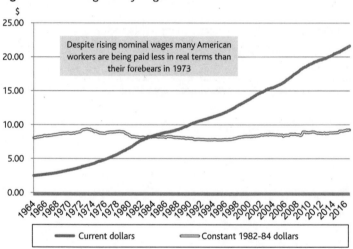

Source: Bureau of Labor Statistics, Current Employment Statistics series CES0500000008 and CES0500000032. http://www.bls.gov/ces/home.htm#data

Since the 1950s more women working has boosted median household income in the US because of more double-income households. This measure has also been on a falling trend since the turn of the millennium: in 2015 it was below its level in 1999, more than a decade and a half earlier (Figure 2.5). In the UK, median wages continued to grow in the 1980s and 1990s, but growth began to tail off from 2003 before falling in real terms since 2008 (Figure 2.6).

Figure 2.5 US real median household income

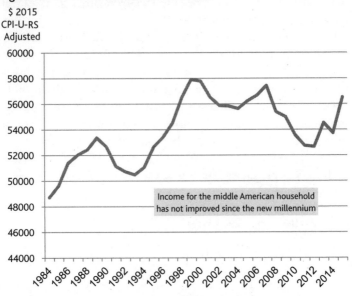

$ 2015
CPI-U-RS
Adjusted

> Income for the middle American household has not improved since the new millennium

Source: Bureau of the Census, Real Median Household Income in the United States [MEHOINUSA672N], FRED. https://research.stlouisfed.org/fred2/series/MEHOINUSA672N/

Figure 2.6 UK real median full-time gross weekly earnings

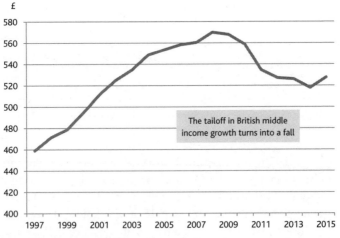

£

> The tailoff in British middle income growth turns into a fall

Note: Constant 2015 prices.
Source: Office of National Statistics, Annual Survey of Hours and Earnings. http://www.ons.gov.uk/employmentandlabourmarket/peopleinwork/earningsandworkinghours/bulletins/annualsurveyofhoursandearnings/previousReleases

Given the relative success of the factors compensating for decay expressed in rising GDP figures, these adverse trends in wage growth may suggest a decoupling between economic growth and pay levels. This underlies the huge focus on inequality: in particular the belief articulated in Thomas Piketty's best-selling book *Capital in the Twenty-First Century* that the rich have been advancing themselves at the expense of the rest of society. There is, however, a simpler, more fundamental explanation for poor income growth. Most wages are still connected to growth; they have simply been tracking the inadequacy of the productivity trend. Slowing, flatter productivity has been the biggest contributor to slow, flattened income growth.

Productivity: investment and innovation

The reason for the secular decay in productivity growth is straightforward. Productivity's growth comes from new and better ways of doing things: from the application of new inventions through investment in new technologies and new processes. The persistently inadequate levels of spending since the 1970s on science, research and business investment have reduced the amount of new higher-technology capital for each worker.

A combination of basic research, that comes up with and develops the new ideas, and of transformative capital spending is required to drive productivity forward. Business investments that introduce innovations serve either to revolutionise existing production processes to greater levels of productivity, or introduce new higher productivity sectors. These innovations are the source of all genuine growth in labour productivity.[11]

Innovation gives a temporary advantage to its first users. They will be able to reap superprofits from both product and process innovations. Product innovation will allow them to sell the new goods or services at a premium because of their originality and initial absence of competition. Process innovation that boosts productivity will allow them to sell at prices low enough to undercut the other producers using older technologies but high enough to earn a premium.

Soon competitors will seek to follow this path and replicate the innovation. The improvement in product or process will become generalised. The originator's superprofit will deplete as prices standardise. Social productivity rises, either directly from the improved technological means of production or indirectly where the improved service or product re-enters the production process as a better input. The consequence is that a breakthrough innovation ends up enhancing productivity far beyond its immediate direct impact.

Take the use of 3D manufacturing techniques. The first users of these technologies make huge superprofits. But as others adopt the same techniques, the original superior approach becomes the norm and the premium profit disappears. Society then benefits from the generalised adoption of the improved technologies in raising productivity and lowering prices.

Complementing the technological upgrading of existing businesses, sustained productivity growth therefore requires having a sufficient degree of *turnover* of businesses. Healthy business dynamism, in the sense of businesses closing and opening, is necessary to facilitate a continuing shift of resources from low productivity to higher productivity areas. Unless resources of people and capital can move out of less productive areas to allow more productive ones to establish and expand then economy-wide productivity languishes.

Researchers at the Organisation for Economic Co-operation and Development (OECD) concluded that the main source of the recent productivity slowdown is not a slowing of innovation by the most globally advanced firms, but rather a slowing of the pace at which innovations *spread throughout the economy*: a breakdown of the diffusion machine. Indeed, the OECD found that while the productivity growth of the globally most productive firms remained pretty robust in the 21st century, the gap between those high-productivity firms and the rest had risen.[12]

This study confirms that the major economic problem of the Long Depression is not an absolute disappearance of investment and innovation but the wider economic atrophy that hinders their spread. When too many resources are stuck in low productivity areas and in zombie businesses – businesses that are too weak to invest in their underlying operations but have enough income from somewhere to survive – then the potential for the wider positive impact of particular innovative business investments will be frustrated.

Growth models

The simple explanation for weak productivity as being rooted in inadequate transformative investment is blurred by the main post-war economic theories about growth. These theories have relied on mathematical models that break down growth into discrete parts, including labour time, labour quality, capital investment, and technological progress or innovation. The terms sometimes change but the methodology is similar. This approach has watered down the analytical appreciation of what are the *effective* drivers of productivity, as opposed to its arithmetical constituents.

The result is that the vital role of a particular type of investment, transformative investment (investment that embodies innovation), is lost sight of. The *fusion* that is decisive for productivity to thrive, between a particular type of capital investment and the innovation it brings into the production process, is decomposed.

Nobel laureate Robert Solow developed what became the standard post-war 'neoclassical' growth accounting model in the mid-1950s.[13] It had the intent, moulded by the Cold War, of highlighting the limits of extensive economic development, of simply throwing resources at a particular economic sector, as the Soviet Union was doing with respect to key industrial sectors. Solow assumed decreasing returns to investment so that, in the absence of technological progress, growth over time would be choked off.

His model, and its derivatives, had the big intrinsic limitation that they could not explain the technological progress constituent – also known as total factor productivity (TFP) or multi-factor productivity (MFP). In the model this factor was left over as a 'residual' after all the other numbers had been entered for labour and capital. Solow interpreted this leftover technological progress as external, or 'exogenous', implying that it originated outside the production process. This interpretation denied the essential understanding of innovation as being more than ideas or inventions; innovation is only realised through the process of production within the aspect of capital investment.

It is not surprising that such a static and technical approach was unable to explain productivity growth.[14] Solow found that economic output was growing much faster than could be explained by the growth of inputs from labour and capital. In his original exercise the residual accounted for a whopping *seven-eighths* of the increase in US productivity between 1909 and 1949. This rather large residual was so significant that his fellow growth theorist Moses Abramovitz famously described it as 'the measure of our ignorance'.[15]

We can lose this ignorance by recognising that the rate of productivity growth primarily reflects the amount *and* the technological level of capital investment available to workers. The two are intrinsically connected, not distinct elements as in the models. The pace of the accumulation of new capital for each worker is therefore crucial for productivity growth.

Empirically, this close relationship between investment and productivity growth is strong. In his academic life before joining the Board of the US Federal Reserve, Ben Bernanke produced an analysis (with Refet Gurkaynak) which found strong statistical evidence that a country's rate of investment in physical capital is strongly correlated with its long-run growth rate of output per worker.[16] They therefore rejected Solow's interpretation.[17]

Unfortunately other influential critics of the Solow model have not helped clarify the necessary relationship between capital investment and productivity. The 'post-neoclassical endogenous growth theory'[18] school of thinking, led by the economists Paul Romer and Robert Lucas, was a response to the deficiencies of the Solow model. Their approach rejected the idea of technological progress as an exogenous or windfall factor. Instead they argued that growth was to a large extent 'endogenous', arising from factors *internal* to business. Their thesis highlighted the role of knowledge in bringing about technological change.[19]

Such knowledge-based models of growth put innovation in the prime position. They acknowledged that innovation is too important to simply fall out of the model as a leftover. Unfortunately this advance came at the analytical cost of downplaying the role of physical investment. Innovation remained divorced from capital investment. Instead this theory's advocates gave a superior position to spending on human capital – primarily education and training – and on research and development (R&D) above the role of capital investment. The endogenous school's counterposition of these 'intangible investments' to tangible physical investment muddied how productivity grows in a different way.

This approach's elevation of spending on intangibles rests on the presumption that knowledge is now playing a more central role in modern economies. But there is nothing qualitatively new about knowledge recently that justifies the notion of a distinctive 'knowledge economy'. It is better to see that knowledge and production are intertwined, and this applies throughout the history of technology.

There is not even anything new about *recognising* knowledge's productive contribution. In 1890 Alfred Marshall, author of the classic textbook of capitalist economics, *Principles of Economics*, described knowledge as 'the most powerful engine of production'. Though rather less in step with modern environmental sensitivities he emphasised how knowledge 'enables us to subdue Nature and force her to satisfy our wants'.[20]

Knowledge has always underpinned the realm of production; it informs the way production works as well as how it develops. This applies both to the *tacit* knowledge – the sort that's difficult to write down or to verbalise, but which ironically is the most talked about today – as well as to the *explicit* knowledge that people can be more easily trained in. Talk of today's as a knowledge economy gives the false and deceptive impression that knowledge didn't rate as much in the industrial economy of earlier times.

The prominence given to knowledge today is better explained by the way the mature economies now appear. With the decline of traditional heavy industries, production seems to have become less visible. This invisibility arises partly because more manufacturing takes place offshore with much located far away in the emerging economies. In addition, the provision of services that have expanded in the West does not share some of the material features of manufacturing goods.

The promotion of 'knowledge capital' also chimes with contemporary themes and cultural ideas. It fits well with environmentalism and the heightened distaste with ecological damage attributed to production. Knowledge and intangibles are mostly immaterial and are less obviously contributing to pollution, global warming and climate change. The intangible economy's association with a greener world makes a virtue of the decline of material production as if this is a good thing for society.

The main problem with this approach is that knowledge is being privileged over necessary aspects of the production process that are deemed to now be less important. This focus contributes to the evasion of the tangible material prerequisites for reviving the West's productive capabilities. When knowledge is deemed to be the pivotal economic driver then the restructuring of material productive assets has less priority.

The key role of capital investment as the embodiment of innovation and technological advance is underestimated and belittled. Robert Atkinson, president of the Information Technology and Innovation Foundation think tank, is correct to criticise the 'intangible-capital fundamentalists' as people who unreasonably dismiss the contribution to growth of investment in tangible high-tech equipment.[21]

Contrary to the methodology of both exogenous and endogenous theories, the dynamics of growth cannot be properly grasped when it is viewed as discrete components. Economic growth is not an arithmetical sum of various inputs, but is the measure of a process by which society develops its productive capabilities. The driver of technological progress cannot be understood without seeing its tangible physical, as well as its intangible, constituents as part of the whole.

Elevating intangible spending over tangible investment actually damages how society can benefit from its reservoirs of knowledge. Knowledge and intangible spending – especially that on R&D – need to be intertwined with tangible investment to be effective. Neither can flourish in isolation. Immaterial and material economic developments are not alternatives; they advance together. Innovation suffers in a culture where the immaterial is fetishised at the expense of the material.

We can transcend the debate over these alternative models by acknowledging that the source of productivity growth is *both* internal and external. The physical investment that produces gains in productivity has to incorporate some new way of doing things, some sort of tangible technological advance. Otherwise it will only be repeating previous ways of producing things and productivity remains stuck.[22] The innovation embodied in 'internal' transformational investment will often derive from 'external' research and experimentation.

Productivity controversies

Over the past 20 years two major controversies have raged around the issue of productivity – one in the US and one in Britain. The first centred on the impact on productivity of the revolution in information technology in the US in the late 1990s. This debate revived an earlier discussion of the apparent failure of the introduction of computers in the 1970s and 1980s to boost productivity. The second area of controversy concerned the persistent failure of productivity to recover in Britain in the aftermath of the 2008 financial crash.

A new ICT economy?

In the late 1990s, after more than 30 years of slackening growth, the US experienced a surge in productivity,[23] widely attributed to the impact of the new information technologies. After average productivity growth of about 1.5% over 1970–94, it shot up to nearly 2.3% during 1994–2004 (though still below the 2.7% of the post-war boom), before fading again to 1% between 2004 and 2015.[24] The spurt clearly marked a significant departure from the long-term pattern of decline.[25] The familiar claim was that the advent of ICT heralded the end of an unusual period of economic lethargy and the birth of a 'New Economy'.

Everyone agrees that the US's productivity figures improved in the late 1990s, but key elements of this surge have remained controversial. The most basic is the question: what caused it? In particular, what was the role of the new information technologies? A second area of controversy arose from the

evident divergence between US productivity figures and those
of Europe – where productivity continued to lag even though
the deployment of mobile technologies was, arguably, more
advanced than in North America. Another set of issues emerges
from the apparently narrow scope of technological innovation
in the US economy. The areas that recorded highest growths
in productivity – the retail and wholesale trade, and finance
– were tangential to the productive economy. And, finally, if
technological innovation cannot explain the 1990s productivity
leap, how can it be understood? Let's take these questions in turn.

Did ICT definitively cause the US productivity surge?

To many in the US, the dot.com boom seemed to provide
a delayed response to the earlier jibe that the development
of computers had evidently failed to trigger a revival of the
economy. Back in 1987, Robert Solow had observed acerbically
that 'we see the computer age everywhere except in the
productivity statistics'.[26] This became known as the 'Solow
paradox'. Now we could suddenly see computers everywhere
– in our workplaces, in our homes, and increasingly accessible
on the move, first from internet cafes and then via mobile
handsets – and in the productivity statistics. At last information
technology had registered in terms of productivity growth; it
had merely taken longer than anticipated.

This productivity recovery spawned an updating of economic
models, which 'showed' that it had been caused by ICT.
Economists such as Dale Jorgenson, Kevin Stiroh, Stephen Oliner
and Daniel Sichel represented the mainstream perspective with
their models attributing a large proportion of the uptick roughly
equally to the *production* of and to the *use* of ICT equipment and
software.[27] The former effect is readily understandable: the heavy
demand for new ICT products that accompanied the dot.com
bubble boosted productivity in the production of these products
during the late 1990s. Any area facing robustly rising demand
will usually see extra output being squeezed out in advance of
the extra recruitment of staff. Meanwhile the latter effect from
the rise in the use of ICT by others seemed to substantiate a

positive relationship between the internet's takeoff and a return of economic dynamism.

The confidence of so many economists about the emergence of a more dynamic computer-led economy derived in part from further methodological limitations of the familiar growth models. The models have a self-fulfilling character: the outputs reflect how the input data is broken down. When models were revised to incorporate the particular role of investments in ICT, these became a dominant factor in explaining rises in productivity, even though ICT was never more than a third of total investment.[28]

ICT was separated out as one type of capital investment, while all other non-ICT investment was lumped together as a single line 'other' with supposedly minimal impact. But this apparently small non-ICT component – representing the other two-thirds of total investment – contained many big positive and negative influences, which in absolute terms were each on a par with the effects of ICT. Because these influential non-ICT investments were not individually broken down, they were mostly ignored in the analysis and commentary.

As Martin Baily put it: 'growth accounting decompositions, however valuable, do not prove that the hedonically inflated IT capital is really being used productively. They simply assume that is the case.' Baily instead suggested that reverse causality had also been at work: economic expansion in the 1990s in part caused the surge in ICT spending rather than vice versa.[29] While ICT spending did take off in the late 1990s, the models could not establish this as the cause of a wider productivity revival.[30] While the timing appeared congruent for resolving the Solow paradox, these econometric studies primarily reflected the myopic New Economy thinking of the time. Unsurprisingly, their conclusions then affirmed it.

Why no productivity surge in Europe?

One challenge for people attributing US productivity growth to new technology was the disjuncture between the US and European productivity figures even though ICT was spreading rapidly on both sides of the Atlantic. Noting that European productivity growth was decelerating, rather than advancing, Robert Gordon reasonably deduced that the explanation for the US productivity hike must go 'far beyond' the use of ICT.[31] How could ICT be the main source of the US growth revival, when European businesses used the same PCs and the same software, and, even more awkwardly, Europe was ahead of the US in the use of mobile telephony?[32] The presumed benefits from Silicon Valley innovations could not be contained by national borders. Though American firms did not hesitate to sell their digital products and services to other parts of the world, the productivity growth recorded in the US remained elusive overseas.

The Europe–US contrast, Gordon concluded, flew in the face of the 'widespread evidence' offered that investment in ICT was the source of the US achievement. He argued sensibly that the failure of Europeans to achieve the same accelerated growth in productivity after 1995 should have shifted the focus of causal explanations away from universal technological advances such as the internet, to country-specific factors that encouraged or discouraged productivity.[33]

The relative importance of consumption in the US compared to Europe helps to explain the productivity divergence. Household spending supported by debt was more marked in the US (and the UK) than in continental Europe during the 1980s and 1990s,[34] and the retail sector accounted for more than half the productivity differential.[35] Larry Elliott and Dan Atkinson concurred that this was the main difference in productivity levels between the US and Europe. They came to the blunt conclusion that the US 'productivity miracle is something of a myth'.[36]

Retailing and finance

One persistent finding from several studies threw light on what was really causing those impressive productivity figures. Besides ICT manufacturing, two other sectors exhibited high productivity growth and stood out from the wider economy: the wholesale and retail trade, and finance, especially trading in financial securities.[37] Computer hardware and software was being most extensively used in these two sectors, but these studies confirmed the limited reach of the New Economy.

Productivity failed to revive in broad areas of US industry. This included agriculture, construction and utilities, and large parts of the manufacturing industry: food, drink and tobacco, textiles, mineral oil refining, coke and nuclear fuel, chemicals, plastics and motor vehicles. The list of exclusions extended to substantial service industries: health, education, hotels and catering, the sale, maintenance and repair of motor vehicles, inland water and air transport, and 'miscellaneous' business activities.[38] A substantial portion of the economy missed out on the much hyped 'renaissance'.

The focus on ICT is more indicative of the otherwise limited character of technological change during the Long Depression, rather than revealing its transformative character. The flowering of internet services was the exceptional experience of innovation and technology that proved the rule of decay across the economy.

The prominence of retail and finance reflects the significant sources of economic resilience in the 1990s; it does not indicate that the economy was regaining its dynamism. Few commentators seemed to notice that the two areas where productivity had grown fastest were those most removed from productive activity. Speeding up financial transactions or expanding opportunities for consumption does not create a more productive economy. At best they assist the financing of productive activities, and the exchange of things created in production. Neither of these functions, however necessary they are, directly creates the new value that defines what is productive in a market system.

Retail and finance grew to compensate for the decay of genuinely productive enterprise. The strength of financial trading reflected the shift in the economy from reliance on producing real goods and services to financial activities. In parallel, rising household debt levels helped drive the consumption that sustained GDP and the personal sense of continued prosperity, showing up in the expansion of shopping.

Attributing the growth of either trade or finance to ICT puts the cart before the horse. Supported by the Federal Reserve central bank, increasing financialisation in the 1990s, not particular technologies, underpinned the short-lived US productivity revival. Seeing it the other way around revealed the technology-tinted glasses with which many people have been viewing the world. Finance and retail jumped out from economic models focused on ICT because any expanding sectors will tend to make use of current technologies, which in the 1990s happened to be information and computer based.

Causation ran the opposite way to the conventional presumption: from growth to technology, rather than from technology to growth. ICT did act as an enabler of financialisation, but it was neither its cause nor the driving force behind higher output and growing productivity. In the early 20th century the electrification of the automobile industry facilitated factory production, but it was not the reason the market for cars took off, nor why national economies expanded.

Some technologies are more readily adaptable to some uses than others. For example, financial activities are especially susceptible to being digitised; hence the emergence of the 'fintech' sector that promotes the use of ICT in the provision of financial services. Venture capitalist Bill Janeway claims that in no sector of the world economy did advances in computing have a more 'revolutionary' effect than in finance, because of its technical suitability for developing and trading complex financial instruments. Wall Street, Janeway asserts, was the key market for innovative ICT.[39] The expansion of the financialised economy had causes independent of new technologies, and in fact helped these technologies' rapid development.

Explaining the growth in productivity

The temporary reversal in the late 1990s and early 2000s of the Long Depression's productivity slowdown in the US was the result of a range of counterforces that centred on but went beyond the particular benefits of financialisation. The US's relatively vigorous productivity record was broader testimony to its capacity to draw on wider sources of resilience. For example, as the world's hegemonic power, the US was able to use its global leadership position to take special advantage of the opportunities offered by the ending of the Cold War. These included the benefits accruing from the rise of Asia, including low-priced consumer goods, as well as large and cheap capital inflows – especially from China.

The US was also able to use the status of the dollar as world money to get away with currency depreciations that supported production for export. The US dollar fell by more than 15% on a broad trade-weighted basis between 2002 and 2004,[40] encouraging more exports and fewer imports. Production and productivity rates were boosted to higher levels than would otherwise have been the case.

Cost-cutting activities also helped US firms to increase reported productivity. Finding pockets of spare labour capacity to get rid of, while often simultaneously intensifying work for those who remain, is a sure way to raise productivity, at least in the short term. These can increase the *level* of productivity but don't permanently raise its *rate* of growth.

Such methods were widely used in the wake of the brief 2001 recession. For Tyler Cowen, the subsequent rises in productivity were more attributable to cost-cutting than to innovation with 'stunning new technologies': the approach of 'discovering who isn't producing very much and firing them' had generated the biggest productivity gains of the early 2000s.[41] Gordon too recognised that, when ICT investment had collapsed after 2000, sharp cuts in labour costs produced transient improvements in productivity.[42]

Nobel laureate Edmund Phelps further suggested that firms had adopted a more short-term outlook, shedding employees who had been involved in research and corporate planning, but who were not essential to current production. He also pointed to the role of labour hoarding: firms had been overly optimistic when the economy initially slowed, hanging on to workers in the expectation that business would soon improve. As expectations became more realistic, they shed this hoarded labour and productivity rose again.[43] Thus, non-ICT factors have been more important than technology in US productivity changes over the past 20 years, just as these are more relevant to trends in other developed economies.

Revisiting the Solow paradox

This is not to deny that post-war developments in ICT represented a significant advance. But the transformative productivity effects of these technologies mostly predated the bursting of the dot.com bubble, and have otherwise still been far too limited in their application. The computer revolution really began around 1960 and reached its climax in the dot.com era of the late 1990s.[44] Contrary to Solow's dismissal of the economic contribution of computer technology, the biggest productivity impact of ICT *preceded* the commercial explosion of the internet.

The initial applications of computers in the 1970s and 1980s were transformative, raising productivity in many administrative tasks and functions. Examples include bank ATM machines, electronic billing and electronic publishing, all of which eliminated the need for much monotonous administrative and secretarial labour. However, the resulting gains in productivity were not substantial enough to avoid being swallowed up by the downward forces of decay.

By the mid-1980s, computers had become widespread in offices; by the 1990s they were ubiquitous. From this perspective, the dot.com boom was more a marker of the end of a period of technological transformation in production, rather than the onset of a new era. The economic historian Alexander Field explained that what was striking about Depression-era technological progressivity was its broad base, both within and beyond manufacturing. In contrast, during the New Economy period of US productivity growth the advances within manufacturing were narrowly concentrated in durables; and within durables, it was in computers, software and telecommunications.[45]

ICT retains the potential to enhance cooperation within and between industrial sectors. As Joel Mokyr emphasises, science does not just drive technology; technology can drive science. Digital technologies can, for example, provide better tools for scientific discovery.[46] Yet society has proved too slow in extending the boundaries of science since the 1970s compared to the century before. It has been too limited so far in realising the substantial potential of ICT in advancing areas such as medicine, genomics and robotics.

The UK productivity puzzle

Whereas the problem in the US was to explain the burst of productivity growth in the late 1990s, the challenge facing economists in Britain was how to explain the failure of productivity to grow in its customary manner following the 2008 banking crash and the subsequent recession. By 2014, productivity remained about a fifth lower than the level it would have reached if the growth trend up to 2007 had continued,[47] prompting the Office for National Statistics (ONS) to comment that 'such a prolonged period of essentially flat productivity is unprecedented in the post-war era'.[48]

Conventional solutions to Britain's 'productivity puzzle' failed to stand up to scrutiny. One explanation was that during the downturn companies had hoarded labour to a greater extent than in the past, thus dampening growth. But empirical research showed that during the 2008-11 downturn, there had been an increase in the rate of job losses compared with the previous four-year period. The subsequent expansion in recruitment – even though much new labour was casualised – also cast doubt on the significance of labour hoarding.[49] Nor could low productivity figures be dismissed as a mere statistical artefact.[50]

The real explanation of Britain's exceptionally poor performance lay in the withering in the contribution of earlier factors counteracting the dominant tendency towards stagnation. Whereas, as we have seen, in the US a range of coping mechanisms (including the role of new technologies) contributed to a short upturn in productivity, in Britain the declining effectiveness of counter-crisis measures – particularly those involving the financial sector following the crash of 2008 – exposed the underlying weakness of the economy, expressed in chronically stagnating productivity levels.

While Britain was not unique in the industrial world with regard to its low productivity, it had an unenviable record, not just in lagging business investment, but also in neglecting R&D, together resulting in slothful technological advance and innovation. British spending on R&D fell from 2.2% of GDP in 1981 to 1.7% in 2014, a figure not only well below that of the US, Japan and Germany but also below China and South

Korea.[51] By 2014 output per hour in Britain was 20% lower than that of the rest of the G7, and more than 30% below that of France, Germany and the US.[52]

The real underlying question was how leading up to the 2008 crash UK productivity growth had seemed relatively strong when so little was committed to R&D and to innovative capital investment. The answers to this question are to be found in the way that productivity figures were boosted by counteracting factors, notably by the direct contribution of the financial sector and the wider role of financialisation in sustaining inflated demand for business operations through corporate and personal debt.

Productivity benefited both because the financial sector's phoney contribution to GDP did not require lots more workers, and also because repeated cost-cutting exercises restricted employee numbers across the rest of the economy. When the financial collapse deprived British business of the benefits from expanding financial services and booming debt, productivity fell back in line with economic reality. The stagnant productivity figures following the crash reveal the true state of the economy beneath the froth of financialisation.

To clarify the persistent stagnation in levels of productivity in the UK after 2008 we need to look more closely at both the direct role of the financial sector and that of the wider process of financialisation in the years leading up to the crash. We can then review the state of denial of some of these harsh realities among mainstream economists.

How the financial sector helped to mask low productivity

During the 2000s up to the peak of the financial crisis in 2008, financial services (also known as 'financial intermediation', which includes insurance companies as well as banks) grew by 53%, far outpacing the 19% growth in the whole economy. Without this sector, accounting for almost one-tenth of the economy, the average annual economic growth rate in Britain would have looked less impressive at 1.8%, instead of being artificially boosted by more than a fifth to register 2.2%.[53] A study produced at the LSE in 2011 analysed the sources of the 2.8%

annual growth in productivity in the 'market sector' (excluding public sector areas like health, education and government administration) that occurred between 1997 and 2007. It also found that 0.4% of the growth increase was directly attributable to the financial sector.[54]

An ONS report highlighted the fact that the biggest sectoral drop in UK productivity between the pre- and post-crisis periods was in the finance and insurance sector. Productivity growth of 4% a year in this sector in the pre-recession period compared with annual declines of almost 3% in the subsequent three years, a drop in annual productivity growth of almost 7 percentage points.[55] This reveals the statistical illusions that arise in an economy with a major financial sector. These distortions are exacerbated by the above average productivity attributed to workers in the sector, despite the fact that none of their labour creates value.[56]

A Bank of England report further emphasised the disproportionate impact of the financial services sector on the British economy leading up to 2007. An assessment of the relative contributions of different sectors to the reported fall in productivity between 2007 and 2013 found that the two biggest contributors, each representing about one-fifth of what was then a 16% productivity shortfall, were 'mining & quarrying' – reflecting mainly oil and gas extraction in the North Sea – and financial services.[57]

The reference to North Sea oil confirms the historic role of this windfall for the British economy: production peaked in the late 1990s and by 2010 it accounted for only 2.3% of gross value added. Productivity in the energy sector fell even faster than production, because as the depleted reserves became more difficult to extract, relatively more workers were needed to extract less energy.

Another group of researchers came to similar conclusions, ascribing one-third of the decline in productivity after the banking crash to the same two sectors.[58] They also concluded that one-third of all British total factor productivity in the years leading up to the crash came from the financial sector. One of this team later claimed that a quarter of that 16% productivity shortfall could be attributed to financial services alone.[59]

The role of financialisation

In addition to the *direct* contribution of the financial sector to raising GDP and productivity artificially, the explosive growth in debt and other features of financialisation have also played a major, probably a bigger, role. Credit-fuelled spending has boosted output and productivity in business services, in consumer services, and in firms dependent on government contracts, all of which saw their customers – business and personal – purchase more with the help of debt expansion than they could have based solely on the new value they had created. This extra output at a time of tight business controls on labour costs helped to inflate productivity statistics. Michael Saunders, from Citigroup and subsequently a member of the Bank of England's Monetary Policy Committee, identified that a 'sizeable part' of the pre-crash positive record of UK productivity growth was misleading, either a statistical artefact or a temporary surge.[60]

In Britain, total debt between 1990 and 2008 grew at an annual rate of around 4% a year, almost double the growth rate of GDP. British household debt alone grew by 40% of national output between 1990 and 2008.[61] If, say, only a quarter of that went into buying things that sustained British output and productivity (with the rest going into bricks and mortar or spent on imports), the equivalent of about 0.5% of national output a year, that would have made a significant contribution to sustaining the output and productivity growth recorded.

According to Bill Martin, the asset price bubbles and the fiscal largesse they licensed may have 'substantially flattered' Britain's growth performance between 1995 and 2007 by about this amount: 0.5% a year. Without the misvaluation of stock and housing markets, some, perhaps much, of the decline in unemployment might not have occurred and growth would have stayed 'significantly below' the pace of annual expansion that gave credence to the idea of Britain's 'New Golden Age'.[62]

Martin suggested that by 2007 the level of activity and therefore productivity had been artificially inflated by about 6.5%. This is close to the size of the fall in GDP in the initial recession from early 2008 to mid-2009. The post-financial crisis recession can be seen as removing the artificial growth that financialisation had helped produce, restoring the economy's size closer to its true level.

It is important to recognise that productivity borrowed is not the same as productivity earned. Productivity gains that are the result of sustained productive spending on R&D, technology and business investment in innovation are very different from productivity which is the statistical by-product of a society living off debt – effectively borrowing wealth from the future – while keeping employee numbers under tight control.

Economists in denial

By downplaying these significant effects of financialisation – while recognising only the direct effects of the financial sector – Dan Corry, Anna Valero and John Van Reenen dismiss the impact of finance on productivity. Their analysis and thinking informed Britain's 'Growth Commission', also based at the LSE, which explicitly challenged the notion that Britain's economic growth has been heavily influenced by a 'finance-driven statistical mirage'.[63]

In fact, their LSE study lists some relevant effects of financialisation before the crash. Of the previously mentioned 2.8% average annual productivity growth in the previous decade, it identified that the biggest chunk came from the category 'business services and the renting of machinery and equipment' at 0.8%, followed by 'distribution' at 0.7%.[64] These findings, far from belittling the role of finance, reveal some its broader ramifications.

'Business services' include areas such as consultancy, accounting and legal work, which have assisted the expansion of financial activities by other businesses, often in partnership with the financial institutions. For example, the explosion since the 1980s of the mergers and acquisitions (M&A) financially engineered route to business growth has pulled in consultants, lawyers and accountants, as well as bankers and brokers. The growth of these areas is evidence of the impact of financialisation, not of its limited influence.

'Distribution', which covers retail and wholesale trade, transport and storage, is another beneficiary of a more financialised economy. Its disproportionate expansion has been fuelled by the growth of debt. Consumer credit, growing at annual rates of around 15% between 1995 and 2005, provided a substantial boost to retail sales.[65] Just as in the US where distribution was a big contributor to the productivity surge of the late 1990s, so in Britain these areas expanded about the same period as part of the shift to a debt-supported, consumption-driven economy.

In conclusion

In the two decades from the 1987 stock market crash productivity in Britain grew at around 2.0% a year.[66] The direct and indirect contributions of financialisation can be conservatively estimated at 0.4% and 0.5% respectively, a total of 0.9%. Subtracting this contribution yields an estimate of annual productivity growth of closer to 1.1%.

This contradicts any notion of a period of British economic and productivity dynamism in the leadup to the financial crash.[67] It also compares unfavourably with the 2.5% productivity growth recorded over the earlier part of the Long Depression (1975–87), and, of course, remains well below the 3% average over the post-war boom.

Following the 2008 crash, as the mechanisms of debt and financialisation lost much of their capacity to boost productivity, the fundamental weakness of the economy was simply exposed in the UK productivity statistics. As the financialised economy is restored, aided by the state, Britain's productivity statistics may pick up but the underlying real productivity torpor will remain.

THREE

Innovation puzzles

The past four decades have seen great change and no change.

On 4 April 1973 Martin Cooper, general manager of the communications systems division of the technology giant Motorola, was standing outside the New York Hilton in midtown Manhattan. He was feeling apprehensive. Holding something like a white brick whose electronic insides he had invented, he tapped into it and made the world's first public call over a mobile phone. Some say he initially dialled a wrong number.

It took another 10 years before Motorola began selling the DynaTAC mobile phone that Cooper prototyped. The commercial model weighed getting on for a kilo and, even excluding its 20cm antenna, was nearly 20cm long. It cost US$4000 – about US$21,000 in today's money. Also back in 1973, private sector workers in the US earned about US$22 an hour in today's money.[1]

More than 40 years later, some things had changed – but some had not. In September 2014, Apple launched the iPhone 6. It was less than 14cm long, very slim, weighed a sixth of the 1983 DynaTAC device, and, manufactured in China and priced at US$649, cost a thirtieth of that first mobile phone. It could do almost anything you could reasonably ask it to do – even make phone calls to correct numbers – and worked 120 million times faster than the onboard computer that guided Apollo 11 to the moon and back.[2]

And what was the average hourly wage among American production workers in September 2014? At US$20.68, it was actually slightly *lower* than it had been when Cooper made that famous first mobile call. Lots of American workers may have smartphones but, as mentioned in Chapter Two, they were getting paid less each hour in real terms than their equivalents were earning *more than four decades earlier.*[3]

Silicon Valley endlessly trumpets its achievements in innovation. Yet ingenuity in the world of consumer products has not been matched by ingenuity in ways to raise wages. The production of wealth in the US, the West's strongest economy, has not improved enough to bring about an increase in wages over more than 40 years. The peculiar coexistence of areas of striking innovation alongside areas of stagnation suggests the relationship between innovation and productivity is not straightforward.

In the previous chapter we examined the West's decline in productivity growth, explaining its roots in the dearth of the transformative investments that embody innovation. Yet many people, not only those imbibing the Silicon Valley air, believe, as was discussed in the Introduction, that we have the good fortune to be living in one the most technologically dynamic periods in human history: a feast of innovation, in which 'the pace of innovation has never been higher'.[4]

Futurist Ray Kurzweil believes that we live in unusually rapidly changing times. According to his 'law of accelerating returns', the rate of change in a wide variety of systems, including technologies, tends to increase 'exponentially'.[5] This thesis draws upon another 'exponential' observation, described as a law, formulated by Intel founder Gordon Moore, that the number of transistors that can fit on an integrated circuit doubles approximately every two years. In their 2011 book *Race Against the Machine*, Erik Brynjolfsson and Andrew McAfee also claimed that 'innovation has never been faster': they argued that the digital revolution is accelerating innovation, driving productivity, and irreversibly transforming employment and the economy.[6]

Yet there are many others, including technologists and scientists, who take a less sanguine view of the pace of innovation in the advanced industrial economies. Peter Thiel, a San Francisco-based venture capitalist and a founder of PayPal, and Garry Kasparov have described a slowing of innovation, attributing 'the whole post-1970 era of bubbles, busts and wage stagnation' to 'the depressed rate of technological progress since the 1970s'.

While recognising genuine progress, they claim the contemporary fixation with ICT has 'induced a misleading sensation of technological acceleration', masking the relative stagnation in many other sectors: energy, transport, space, materials, agriculture and medicine. They contrast the post-1970s slowdown to the gains of the post-war boom when 'we bounded forward in the 1950s and 1960s thanks to a generation of scientists who did not just believe in a better future but invented it'.[7] Moreover, even ICT is no longer making the strides of earlier years. Thiel has complained that Silicon Valley entrepreneurs now seem inclined towards 'incrementalist' improvements rather than working over longer periods at solving the social challenges that require radical new science and technology.[8]

Physicist Andre Geim, co-inventor of the nanotechnology compound graphene, is also concerned by the relative decline in technological advance and believes that we are in the midst of a 'technology crisis'. Disruptive new technologies now appear less frequently than steady economic growth requires. In the past two decades, 'apart from social media, it has been less about disruption, more about honing the same gadgets'.[9]

There is therefore great ambiguity over what is happening in the world of innovation. In this chapter we explore the complexities of innovation and some of the controversies associated with this subject, aiming to separate myth from reality. The aim is to establish why innovation is so important to the economy – and why its decline has damaging implications for society. A fundamental difficulty in confronting the paucity of productive innovation in advanced economies is the absence of consensus on the very existence of the problem.

Measuring the contribution of innovation is also difficult; we consider various attempts to quantify this process – using proxies such as citations, spending on R&D, and patents. The unsatisfactory character of all these metrics has led to assessing the contribution of innovation in terms of its qualitative impact. This is the crucial factor, ultimately expressed in higher productivity. This chapter concludes with a brief survey of the importance of research in relation to production and the role of the state in fostering – and neglecting – this foundation for effective innovation.

The meaning of innovation

> Great powers cannot become, let alone stay, great just because they are good at trade, or have copious reserves of rice, wheat, coal, oil or money. They need to be able to foster and exploit continuous technological innovation. (George Magnus, 2011, p 41)

Perhaps in an unconscious acknowledgement of the paucity of genuine innovation in the course of the Long Depression, the very concept has acquired a quasi-sacred status. Economists and politicians constantly proclaim their commitment to innovation. They almost believe that the incantation of the word will conjure up its transformative effect upon production. They commonly see innovation where no real technological transformation has occurred and apply the concept to phenomena far removed from the sphere of production.

According to the Google 'Ngram Viewer' the word 'innovation' registers in twice as many books published in the last few years compared to the start of the Long Depression. It has become part of popular culture through reality television programmes like *Shark Tank* in the US and *Dragon's Den* in Britain, in which aspiring entrepreneurs pitch their 'innovations' to potential investors.

The pervasiveness of the concept reflects a tendency to use it indiscriminately, in relation to business models, forms of organisation, marketing, and types of financial instruments and financial platforms. The British government applauds these 'wider', non-technological forms of innovation, explaining that this concept should not be restricted to the development or use of technology or other forms of product and process change.

For Britain's now renamed Department for Business, Innovation and Skills it was sufficient to purchase new computer software or hardware to qualify as an 'active' innovation company.[10] Thus merely upgrading software or replacing PCs now ranks officially as innovation. The British think tank NESTA also promotes 'social innovation', defined as the development of new ideas to tackle social problems, or to meet social needs through improvements in public services.[11] Some even claim that being 'customer-led' is itself a form of innovation.[12] Such promiscuous uses of the term innovation help to obscure the real problem of stasis in modern industrial economies.

Given all the hype and confusion surrounding innovation, we need some definitions. Here we use the term innovation as directly linked to the production process and its outputs. Invention is different and comes earlier: making a new discovery, developing a new technology creates the *possibility* of innovation. Capital investment follows and *implements* this novelty in production. As Jim Collins succinctly put it, creativity plus implementation equals innovation.[13]

There are two types of productive innovation: innovation in the process of production, resulting in more efficient ways of producing things, and innovation in the products themselves, producing new commodities, satisfying a wider range of human needs. Both aspects are important for boosting prosperity, but the former is the fundamental driver of economic and social advance. Process innovation mediates between invention and productivity. Let's look at the distinction more closely.

Process innovation requires the application of new technologies to the ways in which commodities are produced, raising productivity, facilitating lower prices and higher living standards. For Joseph Schumpeter, innovation meant a historic and irreversible change in the way things were produced, a qualitative change that could not be reduced to a gradual series of steps. He gave the example of transport: adding together mail coaches will never produce railways in the way that the implementation of steam power achieved.

This is in contrast to new 'innovative' business models that may come up with cheaper ways of delivering existing services – retailing, renting property, taxis – but don't improve productivity's growth rate. 'Sharing economy' models are largely dependent on sweating existing assets. Similarly reorganising processes to make people work harder or smarter can boost productivity statistics for a time but, as noted earlier, are limited by workers' physical and mental capacities. The historic potential of *process* innovation arises from the fact that it knows no such limits.

Process innovations, by raising productivity and increasing wage levels, also facilitate personal consumption: luxuries in one generation become standard in the next. Product innovation – producing new things – can also bring qualitative improvements to our lives. New commodities, such as electric lighting, cars and planes, radio and television, antibiotics, all improve the quality of life and leisure.

Process and product innovations can interact. New products – such as those 3D printers – may be taken up by industry and drive process innovation. Products that have both personal and productive applications have the most wide-ranging impact for society. Taking a broad social perspective, the most important innovations are those that directly (process) or indirectly (products used within production) improve the efficiency of making goods or delivering services and are productive of additional value.

There is a danger, therefore, when an economy becomes narrowly focused on product innovation at the expense of process innovation: this has been a feature of Western economies during the Long Depression. Technological innovation has centred on communication and entertainment devices that are smaller, smarter and more capable. Though these have enriched lifestyles, they have had relatively little effect on process and productivity.

Today's plethora of consumer gadgets and 'toys' provide enjoyment, but they usually don't help in economising on resources used in the production of the essential needs of society. Promising new technologies like virtual reality are today more likely to be directed to the sphere of leisure than to industry. Technology applications in finance can be disruptive and help to raise funds or reduce expenses but, in themselves, they are not directly productive of value or beneficial to productivity.

Robert Gordon makes a useful distinction between the rapid *pace* of innovation and the restricted *impact* on productivity.[14] There is no determinate relationship between them when innovation is mostly restricted to life-changing consumer products rather than productivity-enhancing techniques of production.[15] The narrowness of innovation over the course of the Long Depression expresses how innovation has been constrained by production's stasis. It is much more through these qualitative shortcomings that contemporary innovation expresses the decay in the productive economy. However innovation's contribution is measured, it is not playing much of a role in enhancing production capabilities.

Measuring innovation

> Not everything that can be counted counts, and not everything that counts can be counted. (William Cameron, also attributed to Albert Einstein)

Confusions over what is going on with innovation are not helped by the absence of any commonly accepted unit of measurement. To fill this gap, various proxy measures have been put forward, though all have significant limitations. These metrics relate more to the 'raw material' of innovation – the ideas and the inventions – than they do to the consequent innovation. Hence they cannot do justice to the deployment of innovations. Furthermore, these proxies may be influenced by factors that have little to do with either invention or innovation. As a consequence even the directional trends can be deceptive, suggesting even the reverse of what is actually happening.

Citations

One common proxy is the number of mentions or citations in peer-reviewed journals received by a particular breakthrough. The recent growth in citations leads to the claim that innovation is proceeding at a healthy pace.[16] However, the number of scientific discoveries and inventions does not tell us anything about their commercial exploitation as innovations. We can have more science but less innovation.[17] Second, the number of scientific citations is not a reliable indicator of the significance of the work: quantity does not necessarily reflect quality. Adding to the volume of citations, advances in digital publishing have made publication easier, and academics and university departments are under greater pressure to publish to meet assessment standards.

Figure 3.1 Gross R&D spending as share of GDP

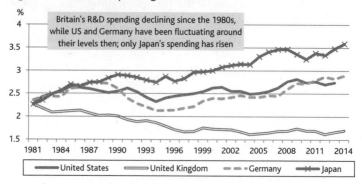

Britain's R&D spending declining since the 1980s, while US and Germany have been fluctuating around their levels then; only Japan's spending has risen

Source: OECD.Stat, Science, Technology and Patents: Main Science and Technology Indicators database. http://stats.oecd.org

Figure 3.2 Business R&D spending as share of GDP

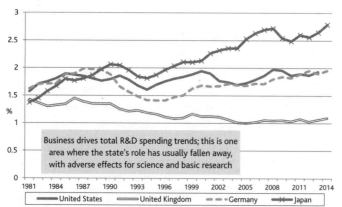

Business drives total R&D spending trends; this is one area where the state's role has usually fallen away, with adverse effects for science and basic research

Source: OECD.Stat, Science, Technology and Patents: Main Science and Technology Indicators database. http://stats.oecd.org

Research and development

The origin of innovation generally depends upon systematic science-based research. The importance of R&D increases as firms move closer to the frontier of the particular technology applications in their sector.[18] Such firms cannot advance by adapting existing technologies from competing firms, but only by pursuing solutions in the laboratory to the problems they experience in production. Spending on R&D has become probably the most commonly used proxy for innovation.

Charts for total public and private spending (Figure 3.1) and for business spending (Figure 3.2) on R&D relative to the size of the economy show a range of trends: rising in Japan, flatter in the US, fluctuating in Germany, and falling in Britain. Britain stands out as one of the lowest spenders in the advanced economies.

However, measuring R&D by spending, whether in money terms or as a share of GDP, does not tell us anything about innovation outcomes: 'crucially, it is the implementation of innovation, not merely the investment in it that matters for productivity'.[19] There is no determinate relationship between input (spending on R&D) and output (innovation). Research may end in a blind alley; experimentation may result in failure. R&D spending therefore does not account for the effectiveness of research. And while many innovations emerge from R&D, some may simply develop from existing productive activities, or from outside of formal R&D functions.[20]

Furthermore, the total amount spent on R&D does not take account of particular quantitative or qualitative trends within either research or development.[21] The 'R', research, part of R&D has been falling in both the private and public sectors, with relatively more being spent on development.[22] This shift might produce innovations in the short run, but over time will bring less of it.[23] If the priority objective is short-term commercial spinoffs, research with greater long-term potential may be curtailed.

Also changes in research methods could affect overall spending without any impact in terms of innovation. More big companies – pharmaceuticals illustrate this – are contracting out R&D to smaller companies or working in tandem with the public sector. These complementary outsourcing and acquisition models mean that large companies that formerly ran some of the most successful laboratories have cut them back or closed them down.[24]

From this perspective, the fashionable notion of 'open innovation' may be a way in which big companies avoid pursuing their own R&D challenges. Henry Chesbrough argued that large firms should not try to reinvent the wheel, but instead rely on others to innovate on their behalf, sometimes known as 'spin-ins'.[25] This approach partly reflects heightened levels of corporate risk aversion – what you don't spend on your own R&D you don't risk losing.[26] And partly also the goal of short term profit maximisation – acquisition costs are taken to the balance sheet, whereas equivalent in-house research expenses impact on profits. The effect of these changes in methods on overall R&D spending and on *its* productivity – in the sense of the degree of innovation arising from a particular level of spending – remains unclear. They are unlikely to be positive.

A further snag in interpreting spending levels is that its movements may simply reflect the changing focus of areas of innovation, or the changing national industrial structure, with different areas or industries having different R&D requirements. The overall consequence is that R&D spending can only be a tenuous gauge of innovation trends.

Patents

Judging from the number of international patent applications it could appear that we are living in highly innovative times (Figure 3.3). Patent statistics, however, are even less reliable indicators of innovation trends than citations or R&D spending. Here again, there is no basis for the number of patents having a determinate relationship to the pace of innovation. Pre-innovation patents are no guarantee of commercial possibilities, and patenting activity, like research, may be wasted effort if the new thing turns out not to be viable for the market.

A major difference between R&D and patents is that while the science and technology that emerge from R&D are necessary for most advances in production, the patenting process embodies an intrinsic constraint on economic development. Taking out a patent on a particular discovery or invention imposes restrictions on others using it and hence tends to inhibit the wider process of innovation. Unused patents in one field can prevent or hold back research and development work in unrelated areas.

Figure 3.3 Patent applications under the Patent Cooperation Treaty

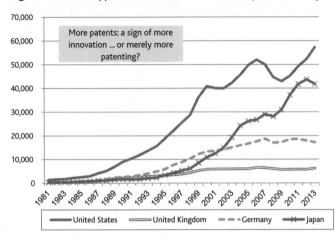

More patents: a sign of more innovation ... or merely more patenting?

Source: OECD.Stat, Science, Technology and Patents: Main Science and Technology Indicators database. http://stats.oecd.org

The recent explosion in patenting activity, not least into earlier stages of the development of knowledge, has reinforced the anti-innovation tendency. Patents can now be extended to 'upstream' research tools, and even to 'discoveries' of existing objects of study, such as genes.[27] This expansion has had a disproportionately harmful impact on research since these 'early-stage' patents have so many more potential uses and applications.[28] In the past, the award of a patent usually came *after* something useful had been achieved, rather than well before that stage.

Increasing numbers of patents also partly reflect changes to patent laws, and changes in the ways in which institutions and businesses can make money from patents. Unlike in that earlier 'age of invention' in the 19th and early 20th centuries, the frequency of patents has now become more a reflection of their litigation value to corporations, rather than an indication of perceived innovative and commercial utility.[29] The experience in the software industry especially illustrates that the increase in patent litigation is counterproductive in terms of innovation.[30]

There is also evidence that the trend towards lower business research spending is expressed in a rise in patent numbers, and a shift to cross-licensing in open systems, with the purpose of buying in technology (and the related patents) produced elsewhere.[31] More patents can reflect less R&D, never mind less innovation.

Our brief survey of proxies used to measure innovation confirms their limited value. Anecdotal patterns don't take us much further. The speed at which innovations are adopted is an oft-cited indicator of the acceleration of innovation.[32] Thus it is claimed that it took 46 years for a quarter of the US population to adopt electricity from the date of its first commercial availability, 35 years for the telephone, with television taking 26 years, the mobile phone 13 years and the web only 7 years.

This is indeed a striking sequence, but it is not necessarily a valid indicator of a more innovation-driven economy. The more extensive communication about new technologies as we get closer to the present accelerates awareness, while rising buying capacity – partly debt-funded recently – have enabled more people to purchase these technologies once they are available on the market. Another approach identifies when innovations first happened, comparing the 40 boom years before 1973, when the Long Depression began, and the 40 succeeding years.

1933-73

Synthetic rubber
Commercial plastic polymers
Synthetic fabrics
Nuclear power
Antibiotics[33]
Polio vaccine
Chemotherapy
The structure of DNA
Contraceptive pill
Heart transplantation
CT and MRI scanning
Black-and-white television services
Colour televisions
Household air conditioning
Microwave ovens
Radar
Computerisation: mainframe
and mini computers
ARPANET communications network
Word processors and
memory typewriters
Handheld electronic calculators
Personal computers
Robotics
The turbofan engine and jet aircraft
Supersonic passenger airliner
Wide-body (jumbo) jet aircraft
Rocketry and satellites
Manned space travel, including
landing on the moon
Credit cards
Barcodes
Mobile phones

1973-2013

DNA sequencing
Graphene
3D printing, also known as
additive manufacturing
Commercial internet
Websites
Online retailing
Smartphones
Social media
Bitcoin and the blockchain

And also since 1973 … oh yes, man has not returned to the moon during the past four decades, with the last visit being in 1972, while plans to visit the next closest celestial body Mars remain embryonic. Supersonic commercial air travel also ended – in 2003 – and there hasn't been much other progress in commercial air travel either. We fly more slowly now: the dominant workhorse of the 1960s, the Boeing 707, had a faster cruising speed than the current generation of airliners produced by Boeing and Airbus. The Boeing 707 flight time from Los Angeles to New York was 4.8 hours in 1958 compared to the 5.6 hours jet aircraft take today, and that excludes the extra time you now have to spend inside airports.[34] And more than 45 years after a Boeing 747 first carried passengers in 1970, we still fly in them.

This historical comparison seems compelling as a sign of the decline in the pace of innovation. However, it is a subjective exercise so cannot be conclusive; innovation enthusiasts could add further items to the post-1973 list. Also many claim that another wave of technologies is about to burst through, from smart robots to driverless cars.[35] So we need another approach to assessing innovation.

Innovation and productivity

Because innovation is a process rather than a discrete entity, we can only judge its relative strength or weakness by examining its economic effects, which are qualitative as well as quantitative. How great is the transformation wrought by the introduction of any particular technology to the productive process? This judgement is further complicated by the fact that the immediate or the originally intended applications of a new process may not turn out to be the most transformative ones. For example, the most significant impact of electricity was not, as first anticipated, its replacement of domestic gas lighting, but its consequences for the organisation of factory production.

In acknowledgement of this qualitative dimension of innovation, commentators introduce qualifying terms such as 'evolutionary' and 'revolutionary', 'continuous' and 'discontinuous', 'incremental' and 'radical'. These dualities lack precision and shift the difficulty onto how to distinguish between them. Such distinctions can also be misleading because all innovative change is built upon previous advances. Today no innovation is 'new' in the sense of being completely original. As Einstein observed, 'creativity is knowing how to hide one's sources'. The fact that innovations usually exhibit both the various dualities simultaneously raises further questions, such as what scale of 'incremental' change turns it into a truly 'radical' one?

Clayton Christensen attempted to resolve these difficulties by examining the impact of innovation rather than its inner characteristics, popularising the qualitative distinction between 'sustaining' and 'disruptive' innovations.[36] The former bring about improvements in a product or service that sustain the existing producers or providers. The latter disrupt an existing market and create a new one, displacing old producers by new ones. Thus mobile telephones spelt doom to some fixed line operators and digital photography sent camera film sales plummeting, pushing Kodak into bankruptcy.

Even this distinction is not without ambiguities as few innovations are intrinsically disruptive or sustaining. Henry Ford's application of assembly-line technology to produce the Model T Ford disrupted the market for horse-drawn vehicles and created a mass car market. From another perspective, this innovation sustained an emerging automobile market.

Christensen's approach can be extended from the assessment of the impact of innovation on a particular productive process to that of the impact of innovation in terms of productivity across the national economy. If productivity is growing systematically and durably in a particular country at a particular time, then that society can be judged to be innovating successfully. But when productivity growth is sluggish, innovation will be narrow, or episodic, or limited in some other way.

Innovation and production

The strongest evidence for a slowdown in innovation in the most developed capitalist economies is provided by the figures of productivity decay discussed in Chapter Two.[37] Though there have been spectacular technological advances in ICT over the past 40 years, this does not justify the hype about innovation in general. The potential for the wider social significance of ICT has been undermined by the slowness of complementary technological advances in other industrial sectors.

The scope for innovation is closely tied to the vitality of production in two ways. A dynamic economy sees adequate resources committed to the research that generates the discoveries and inventions that are the sources of innovation. It also sees sufficient resources given to capital investment in the new technologies that bring innovation to life.

In contrast in a stagnant economy, both the sources of innovation and the capital investment that realises it are constrained, so that productive innovation also grinds to a halt. By 2013 the trend growth for total factor productivity growth in the mature economies reached zero, leading the senior economist at the US Conference Board to conclude that innovation was stagnating.[38]

As a result the whole economic machine has suffered because economic growth is only secure through a combined process of continuous technological innovation, industrial upgrading and economic transformation.[39] 'Innovation' in the abstract cannot conjure up prosperity in the absence of an adequate dynamic of production.

Productive activity also provides the stimulus for invention. Much process innovation is driven by challenges arising in production: how to make a better widget or provide a better service? How to make it more cheaply? As Esther Dyson put it: 'I don't try to encourage creativity for creativity's sake.' 'Instead', she explained, 'I try to encourage creative solutions to real problems. Innovation is good only if it's useful.'[40]

The notion that the new ideas that form the raw material of innovation can develop in isolation from production is also false. This leads to the complacent view that the mature economies can stop worrying about the decay of manufacturing and other industries, yet still prosper through their scientific and cultural hegemony. In reality, Western decay is reflected in a decline in creativity as well as in innovation and productivity. Asked his view of the notion of the US as an 'economy of ideas', futurist Mark Anderson observed, 'I'm not buying any of it. I think that's bullsh--. The people who'll be the greatest innovators will live in an office above the shop floor. We're not going to have all those storytellers.'[41]

To develop creative solutions to problems of production, researchers and developments need proximity to the productive process. Hence Jeffrey Immelt, General Electric's CEO, concluded that separating design and development geographically from manufacturing does not make economic sense.[42] It is also not surprising that creativity and innovation have flourished in the East in tandem with its rising scale of industrial production. China now leads the world in areas such as prefabricated construction techniques (Vanke), telecommunication technologies (Huawei), as well as in nanotechnology applications and new energy sources.[43] The success of the Chinese economy has also enabled it to attract R&D from the US.[44] China is on track to become a science and innovation superpower by 2020.[45]

The state's role in R&D – and its neglect

Though the main barrier to innovation in the West is the dearth of productive capital investment, the decay of Western production is also expressed in a lack of commitment to the basic research needed to generate a new wave of technological advances. Because firms preoccupied by making profits are reluctant to engage in R&D projects of uncertain long-term benefit, governments have generally played a major role in this vital area, through a range of activities.

These include publicly funded laboratories and research at universities and nonprofit institutions. States also provide tax incentives to business and sometimes directly fund business research. When linked to long-term research projects, these sources of state financing go some way to compensate for the short-term perspectives of private enterprise.

Statistics on public R&D spending (Figure 3.4) exhibit some familiar limitations. For example, where some governments have been spending relatively more on development than on research, the combined figures may understate reductions in basic research. Nevertheless, flat or falling spending levels in recent years, especially in the US and Britain, do not bode well for generating scientific advances essential to reviving the mature economies.

Figure 3.4 Government-funded R&D as share of GDP

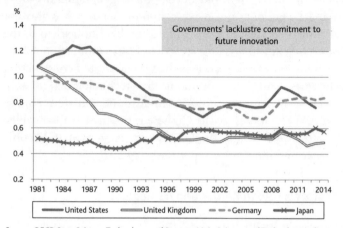

Source: OECD.Stat, Science, Technology and Patents: Main Science and Technology Indicators database. http://stats.oecd.org

The retreat of the state from scientific research is long-standing. Over the past 40 years government spending cuts have hit research in basic science hard, with consequences now reaching critical proportions. New discoveries still happen, writes Geim, but the rate at which they occur has slowed steadily.

The result is a reliance on derivative technologies that are incapable of sustaining dynamic industrial growth.[46] In 2007, America's National Research Council (NRC) reviewed developments in the physics of 'condensed matters and materials', a key area of state-supported research in the 20th century that prompted such innovations as the transistor, the integrated circuit and the laser. It noted that state funding for research in this field had not increased over the past decade, warning of the inevitable consequences for innovation in the future.[47]

One consequence of the relative decline of public funding is that it is now well exceeded by private R&D spending – though, as noted earlier this chapter, this does not mean that business has now taken up the job of basic research. This part of business R&D has been in relative decline since the 1990s.[48] The NRC found that most business R&D spending is in incremental improvements to existing products, while longer-range research has declined, now accounting for less than 10% of corporate

R&D. The decline in state funding plays a decisive role in weakening the impetus of scientific research across the board.

For Geim, the neglect of basic scientific research is critical. Though 'for a lay person, blue-sky research can appear a waste of money as it does not immediately provide the modern equivalents of bread and circuses', taking a longer view, there is no such thing as 'useless fundamental knowledge'. The silicon revolution would have been impossible without quantum physics. Einstein's theory of relativity might seem irrelevant to everyday life but satellite navigation systems would not work without it.

Geim warned that 'the chain from basic discoveries to consumer products is long, obscure and slow – but destroy the basics and the whole chain will collapse.'[49] When the state reneges on its previous active economic role investing in or sponsoring fundamental research the whole economy suffers, with grave consequences for growth, income and employment.[50]

FOUR

Why investment matters

The prolonged weakness of capital investment is the main explanation for the perpetuation of the Long Depression. Without the transforming investments that embody technological advances, innovation will remain deficient, sustained productivity growth will not occur and stagnation will continue. The research and science that come up with new ideas are insufficient to bring about progress on their own. They only acquire social value through the investment that realises them in innovating ways that add to human pleasure or prosperity.

A review of British productivity over the past four decades confirms the essential relationship between falling investment and declining productivity (see Figure 4.1). While the trend rate of expansion of the capital stock for each hour worked – the capital deepening that comes from capital investment – fell from 2% a year in the early 1970s to near zero, the trend in annual productivity growth declined from about 3% to 1%. According to the study, 'essentially all' of the reduction in the growth of labour productivity over this time can be accounted for by this decline in the rate of capital deepening.[1]

The consequences of inadequate investment for individual businesses are familiar: they will fall behind others in operational capabilities and in competitiveness. Profits will shrink together with the capacity to generate the cash required even to survive, never mind expand. The social consequences of an economy-wide failure to invest have also been widely recognised. A century ago Frank Knight observed that all forms of socioeconomic progress represent 'different modes of increasing the productive

Figure 4.1 UK productivity and capital stock trends per hour worked

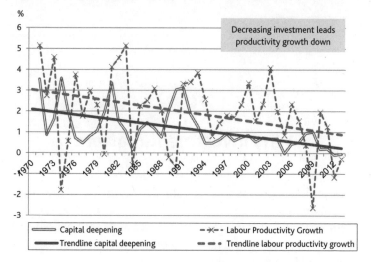

Source: Office for National Statistics, data used by Connors and Franklin, 2015, figure 3, p 7

power of society through the sacrifice or "investment" of present consumption'.[2]

Advancing economies require investments specifically in innovations that raise productivity, rather than investments that merely sustain production at the existing level of technology. They need the transforming innovation investments that result in 'intensive' growth, rather than the 'extensive' growth that results from simply replicating current production processes. The current weakness of Western economies is reflected in the dominance of 'extensive' investment: between 1960 and 2007, the 'great preponderance' of US economic growth was attributable to replication investment using established technologies.[3] The same study confirms the decrease in the relative importance of innovation-driven growth during the Long Depression compared with the preceding years of the post-war boom: a fall of one-fifth between the two periods underlies the deceleration in productivity growth since the 1960s.

The slowdown in investment that embodies innovation also impinges on job creation. Innovation stimulates new areas of production that can provide more jobs than the ones replaced by technology. Surveying trends in the US economy in the 19th and 20th centuries, Edmund Phelps has shown that investment in innovation was the decisive factor in fostering high rates of employment as well as growth in productivity. By contrast, declining innovation since 1973 is associated with rising unemployment and deteriorating wage levels.[4]

In this chapter, we begin by examining the Long Depression's failure of investment from two different perspectives, using two different indicators – gross capital investment and net business investment. 'Gross' is the measure of total investment. 'Net' subtracts the part of investment that goes to replacing the capital stock that has been used up during production.

The dismal record of investment is not only central to *explaining* productive decline. A revival of innovating investment is also critical to *overcoming* it. This chapter moves on to examine the increasingly popular counterview that capital investment is now less important for future prosperity.

Gross investment

Official statistics do not disentangle investment that results in innovation from that which merely replicates existing production. But as the direction of change is usually the same, we can begin with records of gross capital investment. Thus, the decline in public and private gross investment – gross fixed capital formation (GFCF) – dominated the West's economic history over the past four decades. A declining level of gross investment relative to output indicates a diminishing commitment of newly produced resources towards future growth, whether of the intensive or extensive varieties (see Figure 4.2).

At the start of the Long Depression, Japan and Germany were among the largest investors within the developed world. In the 1960s and early 1970s they continued to benefit from their modern post-war business infrastructure, which generated the profits that provided the means and the incentive to invest. As the international slump took hold in the 1970s, these two countries experienced the largest drops in investment, before beginning a more moderate decline from the early 1990s.

Befitting its status as the most mature of the four economies, Britain has been the tail-ender throughout the Long Depression.

Figure 4.2 Gross fixed capital formation as share of GDP

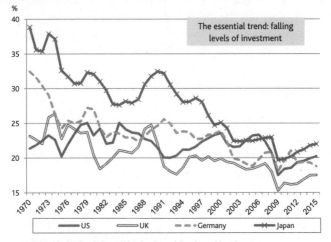

Source: World Bank databank. http://databank.worldbank.org/data/reports.
aspx?source=2&series=NE.GDI.TOTL.ZS&country=

Ever since the 1970s, Britain has been underinvesting in technology, capital equipment and infrastructure. A brief reprieve in the late 1980s, enhanced by a rise in investment in financial services[5] after the Big Bang and a surge in North Sea energy investment,[6] lasted only into the early 1990s.

While the US pattern falls between these two extremes, the course followed by the G7 economies collectively (Figure 4.3) is one of descent from boom to slump, followed by relative stabilisation in the 1980s, and a further sharp decline since the start of the millennium. Across the big seven industrial economies, absolute gross investment at the end of the first decade of the new millennium was below where it had started it – a decline aggravated by the effects of the financial crash. This miserable record provides tangible testimony of Western societies' loss of belief in the future.

While trends in GFCF are useful indicators of economic decay, *gross* investment statistics are of less value in assessing the *precise* dynamics of productivity. As a gross measure, it does not take into account wear and tear, or 'obsolescence': that part of the existing value of capital equipment and plant transmitted into the things they are helping produce. This replacement, or

Figure 4.3 Real gross investment growth across the Group of Seven

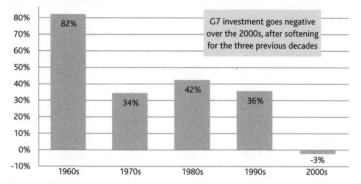

Source: Organisation for Economic Co-operation and Development, Gross Domestic Product by Expenditure in Constant Prices for the Group of Seven, Main Economic Indicators. http://dx.doi.org/10.1787/data-00052-en. Retrieved from FRED, Federal Reserve Bank of St. Louis. Copyright OECD. Reprinted with permission. https://research.stlouisfed.org/fred2/series/NAEXKP04G7A661S/

maintenance, part of gross investment does not generally add to productive capacity.

The amount is difficult to measure exactly and is approximated by making a charge for depreciation, which varies depending on the type of capital asset and how long it is expected to last. A computer, for example, will be assumed to depreciate more quickly than the factory premises in which it is assembled. Net investment figures take this depreciation into account and are a better indicator of changes to the value of capital stock over time, and hence to the pace of capital accumulation.

Another limitation of GFCF as a guide to business capacity arises from the fact that it includes capital investment in residential housing and public sector infrastructure, very little of which enhances business productivity. Though it is true that homes, schools and hospitals, roads and railways, are necessary to an advanced economy, they do not generally contribute to productive potential outside their immediate business sectors.

For example, it is possible that a major house-building programme could – in addition to improving the quality of life for many people – encourage the use of more advanced construction techniques and thereby boost productivity in the construction industry. It is also possible that improved transport links will – in addition to reducing the stress of commuting and easing congestion – also raise productivity within transport industries. However, these incremental infrastructure developments do not generally deliver productivity growth in other businesses. High quality public investment may confer many social benefits, but higher economy-wide productivity and faster economic growth are not generally among them.

Not having public infrastructure is another matter; its absence impairs overall productivity by disrupting what an industrial economy needs to function. As government spending is largely dependent on taxation, the slowdown in the creation of new values in production has also resulted in a decline in public sector capital investment. The most conspicuous results are potholed roads, disintegrating bridges and crumbling hospitals and schools.[7] The decline in public spending on infrastructure started in most countries in the 1970s, soon after the onset of the Long Depression, and it has failed to recover substantially at any time since – apart from in parts of Germany following its reunification.

However, that German blip didn't last long. Uniquely among the large developed countries, its net public investment has been negative for most years since 2002.[8] The German state has been running down its public capital stock in schools, transport and other infrastructure for more than a decade, with the worst affected parts in the west of the country which missed out on the reunification investment programme.

Everywhere the protracted character of the Long Depression means that sustained shortfalls in repairing, renewing and replacing road, rail and air facilities are now taking their toll on the wider functioning of the economy. The BIS in Basel argues that ageing infrastructure has become a potential drag on growth in the US, the UK and other advanced economies.[9]

The decay in net business investment

Statistics of net business investment offer a closer proxy for the innovation investment essential for raising productivity and creating good jobs. The national figures – not available in a consistent manner across all economies – reveal the declining trend over the years of the Long Depression.

The US

Net business investment relative to the size of the economy in the US has fallen from nearly 6% at the end of the post-war boom to about 2.5% today (Figure 4.4). This withering away of business investment over the past 40 years provides a stark illustration of the declining dynamism of the American productive machine. The fall to close to zero during the recession following the 2008 financial crash is especially striking.

Figure 4.4 US net business investment as share of net domestic product

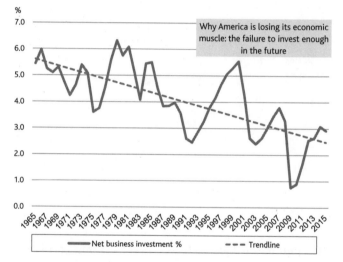

Source: Bureau of Economic Analysis, National Income and Product Account (NIPA) tables 1.17.5 and 5.2.5. http://www.bea.gov/iTable/index_nipa.cfm

As a result, business capital stock levels barely rose: quarterly statistics show they actually fell during 2009. For the first time since the Second World War, net investment in the US turned negative.[10] Though this was dismissed by some as an aberration caused by anxieties unleashed by the crash, such complacency is not justified by long-term trends. Since the late 1970s each post-recession peak reached by net business investment had been lower than its predecessor. A minor departure from this pattern occurred in 2000 when investment just regained the mid-1980s peak before crashing again. This transient achievement marked the high tide of the ICT boom.

Falling investment shows up in the slowdown in capital accumulation. This is illustrated by the reduced tempo, decade by decade, in the expansion of business capital stock (Figure 4.5), undermining the capacity of the US to provide for its own people or retain its global hegemony. The recent sharper deceleration can be expected to result in a further contraction in the underlying pace of US productivity growth.

Figure 4.5 US growth in net business capital stock

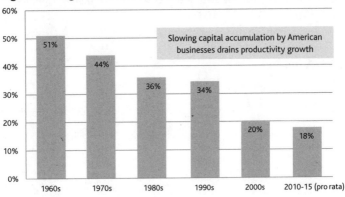

Source: Bureau of Economic Analysis, Fixed Assets Accounts table 4.2, growth in net stock of private non-residential fixed assets. http://www.bea.gov/iTable/index_FA.cfm

Another indication of productive decay is the rising age of capital assets. Falling investment means that assets are kept in operation for longer than is optimal, instead of being replaced. The average age of US capital stock has been increasing, most markedly from about 2000, since when it has risen from 14 to 16 years, a 15% increase.[11] This is notwithstanding the jump in investment in shorter-lived ICT equipment[12] and in new oil and gas wells since the shale boom started in the mid-2000s. Shale investments more than doubled as a share of all business investment in structures, from an average of 9% between 1990 and 2004 to 25% in the ensuing period (until the 2014–15 oil price falls caused a sharp deceleration). Without these countervailing rejuvenating effects on business equipment and structures, the age of US business capital stock would most likely have grown even faster.

Britain

Net business investment in Britain also shows a declining trend (see Figure 4.6). As in the case of gross investment, a temporary upturn in the late 1980s was a result of financial services and North Sea oil.

Figure 4.6 UK net private / non-financial business investment as shares of GDP

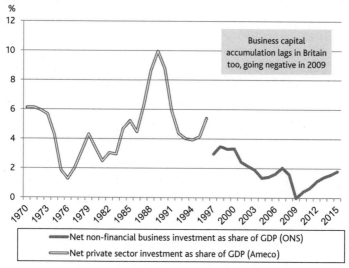

Note: The ONS publishes consistent data on business investment only since 1997.
Sources: Office for National Statistics, time series YBHA, FDBM and DBGF; European Commission AMECO Database. http://www.ons.gov.uk/economy/grossdomesticproductgdp/ http://ec.europa.eu/economy_finance/ameco/user/serie/SelectSerie.cfm

Though official figures for net business capital stock are available only for the past 15 years, breaking this period into three phases gives a good indication of the direction of change. Between 1998 and 2007 business capital accumulation grew at an annual average of 2.3%. During the 2008–09 recession the growth rate fell to 0.6%. And, in the subsequent sluggish recovery up to 2016, it crept up to 0.9%.[13] As in the US, a fall in net capital stock in 2009 marked a post-war nadir. Net capital stock *per employee* actually declined in both 2013 and 2014.[14]

Germany and Japan

Consistent with their more dynamic post-war legacies, in both Germany and Japan net business investment and capital accumulation still slowed but at a more modest rate than in the US and Britain. National reunification in Germany in 1990 caused a surge of investment, providing a temporary boost to net investment levels, which then fell away sharply in the eurozone years, troughing in 2009 at a level close to zero (see Figure 4.7).

Figure 4.7 Germany net private sector investment as share of GDP

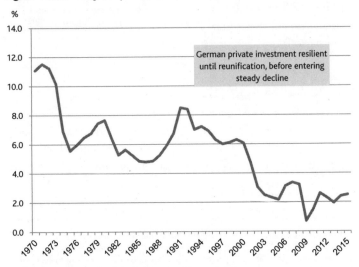

German private investment resilient until reunification, before entering steady decline

Note: West Germany for 1970 to 1990; Germany from 1991.
Source: European Commission AMECO Database, tables 3.4 and 6.1. http://ec.europa.eu/economy_finance/ameco/user/serie/SelectSerie.cfm

The capital investment slowdown in Japan began later than in other advanced economies but the subsequent rate of decline has been consistent with the pattern elsewhere (see Figure 4.8). After the 2008 financial crash, net investment went into the red and net capital stocks contracted every year from 2008 to 2012. Thus, while Japan fared best in the first two decades of the Long Depression, in the latter 20 years it has been hit the hardest.

Figure 4.8 Japan net total economy investment as share of GDP

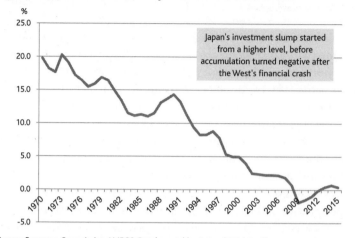

Japan's investment slump started from a higher level, before accumulation turned negative after the West's financial crash

Source: European Commission AMECO Database, tables 3.4 and 6.1. http://ec.europa.eu/economy_finance/ameco/user/serie/SelectSerie.cfm

In summary, the record of faltering business investment levels around the developed world is unambiguous. Investment's slowdown has been even more pronounced than that in GDP growth, subsequently pulling output growth down. The dearth of transforming investments has driven all the other features of decay: low productivity growth; the decline in good jobs; the growing dependence on external capital flows and debt.

Why investment still matters

Growing numbers of economists and politicians recognise that lower business investment has become the new norm, but they claim this no longer signifies the problems it once did. Diminished capital investment simply reflects the way Western capitalism has changed. Let us review some of these attempts to justify falling levels of investment during the course of the Long Depression.

A low growth era?

The idea that the West has entered an age of low economic growth – possibly secular, protracted stagnation – is gaining adherents with each year that the post-2008 recovery fails to arrive. As discussed in the Introduction, this is attributed variously to one or more of the fallout of the financial crisis, a permanent decline in the rate of productivity growth, or the effects of slower growing and ageing populations. As a consequence, this argument goes, with economic growth staying low, investment is bound to follow suit.

This reverses the standard 'investment drives economic growth' perspective and posits instead that the main factor determining investment levels is the pace of growth, or expectations of future growth.[15] Subdued growth implies there is no investment shortfall to be made up. Low investment is regarded as a symptom of economic sloth, not its cause. As a consequence, trying to boost the investment rate is the wrong goal for economic policy, most likely leading to increased waste and higher bad loans.[16]

This is less an explanation for low investment than an accommodation to economic torpor. It assumes the atrophy of production is a given, and thus precludes pursuing a plan to turn this around. Rather than consider what could be done to enhance the technological progress that underpins growth, this perspective is self-fulfilling. A fatalist acceptance of inadequate innovating investment gives up on the vital means for delivering faster economic growth.

The end of post-war exceptionalism?

Another expression of lowered expectations is the reinterpretation of the post-war boom as being abnormal, rather than the typical condition of capitalism. Economic growth of the 4–5% a year experienced in the 1950s and 1960s has come to be regarded as exceptional, and unlikely to be repeated. Thus, a lower tempo of investment since the 1970s is seen as a resumption of normal services, not a source for concern. A variant on this argument is that capital investment was bound to fall when post-war reconstruction had ended, reversing its jump as Japan and Europe rebuilt their economies after the wartime destruction.

However, a broader historical perspective undermines the 'what has gone up, must come down' justification for low productive investment now. First, post-war capital investment levels were not so unusual as to warrant lower subsequent investment levels as merely a return to normality. In the US, for example, the investment to GDP ratio was *lower* during the post-war boom than it had been before the First World War.[17] Second, in the war-ravaged countries investment was rising in the late 1930s to levels higher than today, long before the boost from post-war rebuilding.

These countries had already started to restructure their economies to pull them out of the slump before bombs and shells destroyed large parts of industry. Society did not need war-inflicted destruction to bring about much higher investment levels than we experience today. Moreover, the exceptionalism explanation doesn't account for the continued decline in investment levels since the 1970s, rather than them stabilising at lower 'normal' levels after the reconstruction-enhanced boom-time sugar-high ended.

The cheapening of capital goods?

Another claim is that the tendency for capital goods to become cheaper explains recent low investment figures. Reduced investment spending won't necessarily harm economic growth because it represents a greater volume of investment. Within this cheaper capital school of argument, the price of ICT investment goods is often highlighted: because of Moore's Law the quality-adjusted prices of computer hardware are falling particularly rapidly, accounting for less business spending on investment.[18]

The arithmetic underlying this view is sound: an increase in the volume of capital stock for each worker can be represented by a smaller rise in their *value* since they will be produced more cheaply over time, even with modest levels of productivity growth. The capital goods available to workers would expand less in value than in technical terms.

However this argument doesn't work when we look at inflation-adjusted investment levels *relative* to the size of the economy, rather than absolute expenditures. Productivity growth reduces the prices of all goods and services across the economy, not just capital goods. Thus the *ratio* of investment-to-GDP would not be much impacted, yet we've seen these rates steadily falling. Cheaper capital goods cannot explain away declining investment-to-GDP levels.

Deindustrialisation and the shift to services?

The most common of the relaxed explanations for low investment draws upon the sectoral shift from manufacturing to services and the presumption that services are less capital intensive than manufacturing. Everyone agrees that the manufacturing share of economic output has fallen substantially across the mature economies during the past four decades.[19] The conventional image of manufacturing is of factories and large machines requiring heavy physical investment, in contrast with the low-capital, high-labour intensity of many services. It seems self-evident that an economy that now earns its way more from providing services than from making things will need less physical investment.

This assumption about the low capital intensity of services is misplaced. Service sector capital intensity has increased sharply over the past two decades, and many of the expanding service industries such as telecommunications, education, utilities, health and transport are just as capital intensive as manufacturing, or even more so.[20] Also some services, such as retail and restaurants, that do not need much heavy machinery and other equipment still require substantial investment in property, fixtures and fittings.

The more relevant economic proportionality for assessing investment needs is not between manufacturing and services, but between low value adding and high value adding sectors. Generally it is the low value activities, whether making goods or providing services, that are of low capital intensity. This applies to simple manufacturing assembly operations, as it does to serving food and drink, cleaning, personal care, or shelf stacking.

High value industries, in contrast, whether manufacturing, extractive or services, are more likely to require capital investment to increase their capacity to produce at high levels of productivity. This applies as much to a modern transport system or a communications network as it does to advanced manufacturing. Even agricultural activities like dairy production – traditionally regarded as low-tech and labour intensive – are becoming much more automated and capital intensive: robots now milk cows.[21] A return to durable economic growth will require continuing levels of investment in higher value sectors – services or goods based – to expand, maintain and upgrade capital assets.

A more recent version of the structural argument focuses on the production shift to information-based goods and services, which has appeared to accelerate since the financial crash as smartphone ownership and apps usage have spread. The underlying digital technologies are said to be much less capital absorbing – necessitating little new investment – relative to the transformative technologies of the past.[22]

However, there has been little further structural transformation in the developed economies since the financial crisis to support this argument. The share of service sectors, including ICT sectors, has remained reasonably constant following the crash, undermining this as an explanation for the particular dearth of investment since then.[23] Sectoral shifts do not justify the falling investment record in the industrial economies.

The new knowledge-based intangible economy?

A popular variant on the service economy argument is that investment has not really fallen much, if at all, but instead takes a *different form* in modern knowledge-based economies. Tangible investment in physical things has been replaced by intangible investment in areas like research, human capital and marketing. This implies there is more of a measurement issue than an investment problem. Combine what remains of the previously dominant tangible investments with new intangible ones and, it's claimed, economies are still investing adequately. We should accord less significance to the low levels of old-fashioned measures of fixed investment.

This belittling of tangible physical investment is not new. It was implicit in the modern growth theories that were examined in Chapter Two. These models include capital investment merely as an input number, building in the exclusion of the dynamic possibilities of physical capital investment to account for technological progress. In a survey of economic growth theories, Maurice Fitzgerald Scott recounts that one of the main practical inferences that have been drawn is that while technological progress is a very important cause of productivity growth in the long run, capital expenditure is a relatively minor factor. As a consequence, the models suggest that share of investment to GDP is 'very unimportant' in the long run.[24]

The endogenous growth theorists took this de-prioritisation of physical investment further by suggesting that intangible forms of investment, such as spending on R&D and training, are more important for productivity than tangible investments in property, plant and equipment. Unsurprisingly, the models that factor in a range of 'knowledge capital' items as part of investment find that these intangibles are important drivers of growth.[25] Productivity models that are adjusted to incorporate intangibles as effective inputs find that intangibles have a significant effect on the productivity output. The models' results reflect the models' assumptions.

In the US and Britain around 30% of labour productivity growth is attributed to intangible investment by these adapted models, which is on a par with the contribution from tangible investment. Some even show a stronger positive association between technological progress and the contribution of intangible capital deepening than for tangible capital.[26]

Changing business spending patterns seem to justify giving this greater attention to intangibles. Across the OECD expenditure on them has been stronger than tangible investment since the 1990s. Between 1995 and 2007, on the eve of the financial crash, tangible investment as a percentage of GDP had generally been flat or falling, in line with our earlier analysis. Meanwhile intangible spending had risen, in some countries considerably. In the US it rose by almost a third.

This reflects how the US, like Britain,[27] is among the largest spenders on intangibles and 'invests' more in intangibles than it does in tangibles. On average, between 1995 and 2009 the US spent 9% of GDP on tangible investment and nearly 11% on intangibles. Carol Corrado, Jonathan Haskel, Cecilia Jona-Lasinio and Massimiliano Iommi concluded that for both the US and Europe this shift is a 'striking trend'. They argued that across developed economies gross investment rates become 5–10 percentage points higher when intangibles expenditure is reclassified as investment. [28]

Talking up the productive role of intangibles relies on an extended definition of investment to include a lot of business spending that historically has been accounted for as operating expenses – and much of it still is under company accounting conventions.[29] Economics studies, though, have broadened greatly what is included as 'investment'. This distorts the real picture of investment trends and distracts society from where it should be focusing for enhancing our productive capabilities, taking attention away from core spending in transformative technologies.

This discussion often uses the three broad categories of intangible assets that were first documented in 2005 by Corrado with Charles Hulten and Daniel Sichel: 'computerized information', usually measured by software – there is little disagreement about this representing a core modern investment; 'innovative property', starting with R&D, which is more contentious; and 'economic competencies', such as marketing, training and organisational processes, which stretch the measurement of investment into much more disputable areas.[30] These latter 'economic competencies' are usually estimated to make up about the same contribution to intangible spending as the other two categories combined.

Over the past couple of decades official statisticians have become more open to incorporating areas of intangible spending as part of gross fixed capital formation in the national accounts. The 1993 version of the *System of National Accounts*, agreed at the UN, sensibly recommended the inclusion of computer software as investment, as well as the more dubious incorporation of the costs of producing 'artistic originals'. Following this guidance, since the mid-2000s most national statistics now report computer software within their investment figures.

The UN suggestion to include 'artistic originals' – media productions such as films, television and radio programmes, music and books – in the investment statistics took longer to be implemented. The delay reflects that it has taken longer to dispel the commonsense view that spending on the production of these sorts of things is an operating expense rather than an investment in fixed assets.

Determining, for instance, which television programmes met the standard statistical criterion for being investment of having an impact lasting longer than 12 months appeared rather arbitrary. In the US, the answer provided by the Bureau of Economic Analysis (BEA) was to distinguish 'Long-lived television programs [including] situation comedies and drama programs' from 'Other types of television programs, including news programs, sporting events, game shows, soap operas, and reality programming, [that] have much shorter service lives and will not be capitalized.'[31] By this categorisation *Downtown Abbey* is an investment, but *The Voice* isn't.

More recently,[32] R&D has also been officially redefined as a capital investment, rather than as an intermediate expenditure.[33] This is a misleading change because, as discussed in the previous chapter, R&D is generally a pre-production activity, not final production expenditure.[34] While it is appropriate to spell out the important relationships between R&D, invention, innovation and investment, this does not establish that R&D plays the same role for production as does capital investment. Research works through experimentation, trial and error, sometimes with a dose of serendipity. It is not directly productive of goods or services. Lumping in this vital expenditure with investment clouds how a production process has to change *physically* to incorporate innovation through transformative investments. Investment is the necessary vehicle for any innovation; more R&D spending is not a substitute.

A study carried out for the British government's Intellectual Property Office exemplifies the intangibles thesis.[35] The UN-reclassified investment items – software, R&D and artistic originals – were calculated at less than half of the £127 billion of Britain's intangible investment in 2011. The other part – about 60% – is made up spending that is not, as yet, deemed investment by the UN.

This other part included, for instance, design work, making up about one-tenth of all intangible investment. This represents part of the labour time of architects, non-software engineers and graphic, product and clothing designers. So the designer of how a new smartphone looks, and even of the look of its advertisements and packaging, is included as investment on a par with the engineering activity that creates its innards. Also included here are relatively small amounts for developing 'new financial products' – new types of debt instruments – and for 'non-scientific' research conducted by social science and humanities academics. The investment value of academic research into areas that include the 'polka', 'kissing customs' and 'ritual masks' are left to our imagination.[36]

The remaining 50 percentage points of intangible investment are from the 'economic competencies' category, which are even more dubious in being treated on a par with physical investment. Some of these used to be called branding (advertising and market research costs: £14 billion), and training (£25 billion). This category also includes a substantial £25.5 billion – a fifth of total intangible investment – for 'organisational structure and processes', including spending on management consultants and a proportion of the salaries of employed managers.[37] (One could add that there is a danger of double counting here, since management consultants are said to charge for listening to what managers say and then repeat it back to them as their own suggestions, but that would be unfair on some consultants.)

The analysis feeds the conclusion that while capital investment has been in decline, not to worry. The intangible investment that is more relevant to a knowledge economy has taken over the lead role, and sustained overall investment levels much better (see Figure 4.9). At the start of the 1990s intangible spending was only about two-thirds of that on tangible investment, moving through the dot.com-inspired flourishing of the information era to be one-fifth ahead before the financial crash.

Figure 4.9 UK intangible spending relative to tangible investment

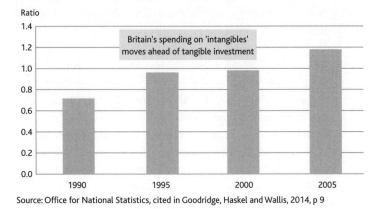

Source: Office for National Statistics, cited in Goodridge, Haskel and Wallis, 2014, p 9

As a result, although tangible investment fell away by almost a third as a share of GDP between 1990 and 2005, the growth in intangible spending meant that their combined share of GDP fell by a less dramatic tenth (see Figure 4.10).

This intangible model of investment is unhelpful in getting to grips with the sources of the Long Depression. Redefining everyday spending as investment covers up the decay in physical investment. Partly this is fed by a measurement illusion: as widely as intangible investment has been defined, even this spending grew little when presented as a proportion of GDP, rather than in nominal terms. A substantial nominal rise from £47.9 billion in 1990 to £118.1 billion in 2005 equates to a less impressive increase from about 8% to 9% of GDP.

Figure 4.10 UK tangible investment and intangible spend as shares of GDP

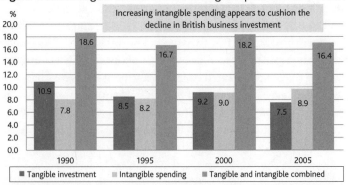

Source: Office for National Statistics, cited in Goodridge, Haskel and Wallis, 2014, p 9

More importantly, even this growth is predominantly accounted for by the expansion of spending that is the furthest from the production process. More than two-thirds came from intangibles *other than* software and R&D.[38] Software spending can be directly associated with productive activity, and R&D has the indirect relationship just explained. However, spending on areas such as branding, management consultancy and employee training test even their staunchest advocates in preparing credible return-on-investment justifications.

Spending more on 'economic competencies' does not substitute for capital investment by finding new ways to make businesses more productive. Rather, it is better viewed as a symptom of productive decay. Take the rise of spending on consultants. During the 1980s and 1990s management consulting expanded by offering services to businesses especially in the areas of strategy, information technology, organisation and M&A. This met a new demand for their services. In depressed economic conditions management was increasingly uncertain about how to ensure success, even to survive, in tougher economic conditions. Managers turned to outsiders for help, reflecting their own insecurities and an abdication of direct responsibility for charting a way through their difficulties.

While expertise in cost-cutting and business reorganisation was a source of lucrative revenues for these consultancies, their clients' underlying productive performance saw little uplift. Cutting expenses boosts short-term profitability and may lead to a one-off jump in productivity as workers are laid off. But businesses and national economies can't cut themselves to a higher rate of productivity growth.

Branding has also expanded alongside productive difficulties and the relative dearth of innovation. The transition into the Long Depression gave added impetus to the role of consumer marketing, advertising and branding. When products and services are less able to stand out through price competitiveness enabled by superior production technologies, or by offering distinctive product features, businesses look elsewhere in their desperation to promote sales and defend revenues. Spending on marketing and branding acquired greater importance in the eyes of businesses fearful of losing sales and concerned to protect their market share.

Yet the impact of brand spending is mostly ephemeral. The strength of a brand is ultimately the result of a successful product or service in the eyes of its users. A poor product or service cannot be successful for long however much is spent in advertising its brand features. Advertising can reinforce what people think about a company's products and services, but on its own it rarely changes people's long-term buying habits.

Moreover, it is hard to fathom how this 'economic competency' follows through into increases in GDP, never mind productivity. Even a successful change in one company's market share is usually at the expense of domestic competitors, leaving national economic output unaffected.

The marketing industry, however, has never been shy to claim responsibility for business sales and attribute value to its own contribution to business achievements. Rising stock market capitalisations seem to provide evidence for their assertions. In a financialised economy, equity values often rise faster than output, and faster than the company's net asset value on its balance sheet.

Marketing advocates have seized on this gap to claim that the excess of the stock market over a company's book valuation is attributable to the value of intangible assets and, in particular, the value of the brand.[39] Correlation, though, should not be confused with causation. When financial investors, supported by a financialised economy, buy shares and push up equity valuations this is usually driven by expectations about share prices and dividends, not brand analysis.

The role of the third main economic competency, training people, is different to the other two. Much of it is socially useful. Some technical skills are not just useful but are essential to carrying out work competently. Delusions with the *productivity* role of training come from the wider assumptions of 'human capital theory', which also inclines to privilege training over physical investment.

This thesis took off from the 1960s – Gary Becker[40] was a leading proponent – and is now incorporated in the intangible capital thesis. Calling spending on workers' skills 'intangible investment' while downplaying the role of capital investment again mystifies the production process. Production brings workers and tangible capital together; neither is effective on their own. A machine is just an inert piece of kit until humans activate it. A person can work just with their hands without any tangible capital but their activities will remain primitive: crop picking by hand, or a home-visiting masseur. Not much else is possible for humans without some tools, or premises, or raw materials to work with.

Prioritising the role of human capital can divert from the requirement for much more tangible, innovation-carrying, capital investment. Too little of the latter has been undermining effective production, thereby holding back the productivity of the workers who make up the human capital. People who do not have the opportunity of working with modern technology are not that productive, and most do not have fulfilling work experiences either.

In isolation, training and skills cannot make a business or an economy successful. Mary O'Mahony and Willem de Boer illustrated that relative human capital levels between countries can move in the opposite direction to relative economic performance. They showed that by the end of the 1990s the UK had eliminated its previous small gap with the US in labour force skills, yet over the same period, during the second half of the 1990s, the labour productivity differential between the countries widened, with Britain falling further behind.[41]

Increasing workforce skills are of no value economically in the absence of the capital investment, technology and jobs to use them. Devoting extra resources to training will not produce economic benefits if there are insufficient high-skill, high-productivity jobs for the workforce. A supply of skilled people does not create a demand for them, and skills that are not used are rapidly lost. To be effective, skills need to combine with other factors in production, especially those deriving from adequate amounts of capital investment in innovation.[42]

In conclusion

Astute personal investment advisors warn that 'this time is different' are the four most dangerous words when considering whether to invest in the latest new economic paradigm. It usually turns out to be a bubble. Those concerned about restoring prosperity to the West should similarly beware of 'this time is different' with regard to underestimating the importance of tangible investment for productivity and growth.

It is quite possible to generate a high figure for intangible investment but this has extended the definition of investment to areas of dubious productive value and commensurability. Equating a dollar spent on advertising breakfast cereals with one spent on pharmaceutical research is a specious way even to measure the production of knowledge as the supposed source of innovation.

To finish with a metaphor: renaming eggs as oranges won't change the actual number of oranges. Having more eggs cannot disguise a shortage of oranges, nor can it satisfy the role oranges play for people who want to eat them, or get their vitamin C from them. Likewise, renaming areas of business spending, such as branding or consultancy, as business investment does nothing to change the inadequate levels of productive capital investment.

Spending more on these areas, whatever valuable or superficial role they play, cannot replace the distinctive purpose of investment in better technological processes. Investment still matters, fundamentally. A long time ago Frank Knight wrote of investment's historical significance: without innovative investment humanity risks a return to something like the Middle Ages where 'production methods are a matter of routine … and there is no thought of progress'.[43] A lack of investment represents the abandonment of progress. The failure of investment to revive enduringly over the past four decades shows that the West's economic problems are systemic and structural, not cyclical and transitory.

Part II
The Long Depression

[The] breakdown of the banking system was in part
a consequence of deeper problems. ... A crisis of the
real economy lies behind the Long Slump, just as it lay
behind the Great Depression. (Joseph Stiglitz, 2012a)

FIVE

The problem of profitability

Alongside a belittling of the current role of capital investment, explicit criticisms of investment are heard more often. Some 'activist' shareholders prefer money to be returned to them rather than 'frittered away' on investment projects, while some environmentalists think the material development arising from physical investment is harmful.

Shareholder activists often target undervalued companies, trying to push up share prices by pressuring boards to act differently.[1] Often they oppose investment spending, wanting companies instead to give more cash back to shareholders through higher dividends or share buybacks. These increase earnings per share and push up the share price.[2] Typical is the billionaire Carl Icahn who thinks most corporate boards are made up of lackeys to the CEO: people who typically don't make good investment decisions and shouldn't be entrusted with spare cash.

Making strange bedfellows with short-termist financial investors, some environmentalists are critical of economic growth and of the investment that fuels it. They argue the West has already produced enough things; more production in the advanced economies is unnecessary for decent living standards, while causing environmental degradation.[3]

Although such investment critics are now more prominent and vocal, this doesn't account for the low investment levels of recent times. It would be wrong to conclude that the intellectual case for capital investment has been lost. While the pro case is not usually articulated as passionately as the anti-investment case,[4] the claim from Raghuram Rajan that 'physical capital increases income because it makes everyone more productive' remains the dominant perspective.[5]

Even many financial investors – who are often collectively reviled for their short-termism – recognise the merits of capital investment.[6] With interest rates at historically low levels, some people suggest that there's never been a better time for companies, and governments, to make big capital investments. Even the IMF has reversed its earlier tight-fistedness and taken to arguing that cheap financing justifies stepping up infrastructure investment.[7] Yet, despite the dominant sentiment that investment remains desirable for growth, it remains anaemic. This chapter explores why.

The puzzle of low investment

Mainstream economists are perennially predicting upturns in corporate capital spending. Hoping that economic problems are cyclical, or are due to specific uncertainties that should disappear over time, anticipating a return to the norm of an investment-led capitalism seems reasonable. Yet repeated projections of a sustained pickup in business investment have not come about.

Gareth Williams, from the rating agency Standard & Poor's, captured this juxtaposition between the expectations of investment recovery and the reality of investment stasis. Introducing their 2014 annual investment survey he described how a recovery in corporate capital expenditure remains one of the 'most keenly anticipated trends' in the global economy, while concluding that an investment recovery still seemed 'some way off'. Business investment was 'stuck in neutral'.[8]

For advocates of investment its persistent weakness poses a puzzle, compounded by the presence of many factors that offer good reasons for businesses to invest. Here's how Credit Suisse described the benign environment:

> The fundamentals for US corporate spending look good. Record high free cash flow, near record low leverage, an abnormally old capital stock, an investment share of GDP only slightly above typical

recession lows and a record gap between the return on assets and cost of debt.[9]

Many of the textbook conditions for an investment surge are therefore in place.[10] Corporates enjoy large cash surpluses, easy credit facilities and cheap borrowing. Because investment has been low for a long time there are a lot of ageing capital assets that need replacing, providing further motivation to retool with more advanced technologies. Adding encouragement, corporate taxation has been at low levels, with reduced headline rates and a myriad of concessions, or loopholes, reducing the state's take from profits. The US$64,000 question is why businesses have not been investing more when so many financial and economic factors are strongly supportive.

Cash mountains expand

Rather than being a US$64,000 question, it's the US$3.5 trillion (and counting) question. That was the amount of cash reserves held by the world's 1000 largest nonfinancial, primarily Western-based, businesses at the end of 2013.[11] This establishes that having cash is an insufficient condition for investment. Rather than funding investment, a reverse relationship holds: when investment is low, cash accumulates.

High cash balances are not a recent phenomenon and have been on the rise since the 1980s.[12] They cannot therefore be explained by post-financial crisis caution and the precautionary desire to have a bigger safety net. In 2008, before the financial crash, these companies already held more than US$2 trillion cash. While America's tax laws encourage its companies to keep large amounts of cash overseas, this is an inadequate explanation since high cash holdings are spread across the mature economies. US companies held nearly half, Japanese firms 14%, French 7%, British 6%, and German 5%.

The existence of higher corporate savings is not a sufficient cause either. A major reason for the rise in savings is that companies, especially UK and US ones, have been distributing absolutely and relatively more earnings to shareholders by share purchases (out of their savings), rather than through dividends (paid before the savings figure is measured).[13] Regardless of how profits are distributed to shareholders, it is what is left from the profits after all spending, including capital investment, that is building up in cash.[14]

The common element behind expanding cash balances is sluggish production. Cash grows from companies investing less than they save, making them net suppliers of capital to the rest of the economy. This is a reversal of the previous pattern when businesses borrowed from banks or capital markets to finance the portion of their investment that was in excess of self-generated funds. Well before the financial crash, the corporate sector of the G7 had swung from being a large net borrower to a net lender of funds.[15]

In the four years after 2000 corporates' financial balances – gross savings less gross investment – in the leading developed economies had increased by over US$1 trillion. Over this period Western businesses were adding five times as much to global savings as the contribution from China and all the other emerging economies put together.[16] Nevertheless China's role was what was highlighted in the mainstream discussion of a 'global savings glut'.[17]

While Western businesses have been continuing to make profits – the starting point for corporate savings – they have not been investing much of them back into production. The cash holdings of the top 1000 companies at the end of 2013 were about double the US$1.77 trillion of capital spending undertaken during the preceding year.[18] These companies could therefore have afforded to almost triple their investments without resort to extra borrowing. The *Financial Times'* Lombard column suggests that cash mountains express a long-term cautious shift in corporate attitudes: 'companies have thrown daring to the wind'.[19]

This concurrence of high cash and low investment fuels the real appearance of contemporary capitalism as a predominantly financial undertaking. Financial debt has expanded to keep business activity moving, and businesses' own savings become a source of extra loanable capital. In the absence of organic growth driven by investment and innovation, Western businesses are increasingly being run for short-term cash generation.

When cash becomes king, successful cash-generating firms return some to shareholders, use some for acquisitions and other financial purchases, and keep much of the rest. In a peculiar financial twist, many cash-rich, low-investing companies are *increasing their debt* to build up cash and fund payments to shareholders. Even Apple, one of the world's most profitable and cash-rich companies, has joined this bandwagon.[20]

The result is that financial activities usually take centre stage in discussions of contemporary corporate behaviour.[21] They are better understood as a consequence of the most important feature of business life – the atrophy of productive investment. Declining capital investment, rising cash reserves, and increasing financial activities and spending on financial assets coexist as related features of the Long Depression.

The availability of cheap borrowing

These huge cash balances are relatively concentrated; many companies are cash-poor and would still need to borrow for investment. As well as less cash-generative established companies, these include startups and new ones without time to build up adequate cash surpluses from profits. For these companies the cheapness and availability of capital complements the puzzle over lacklustre investment. Lower cost and easier borrowing by businesses goes back to the 1980s.

The increasing financialisation of the Western economies since then has facilitated its availability. Financial deregulation expanded all forms of finance for business: bank lending, the issuance of equities or bonds, as well as newer sources like venture capital funds. More recently, additional sources of financing have opened up, especially for small companies, in the form of peer-to-peer lending and crowdfunding loans and equity.

Over the 1990s and 2000s debt held by nonfinancial Western businesses rose steadily in absolute amounts and relative to national output. Following the 2008 crash the pace of increase slowed in money terms, with outstanding debts relative to GDP falling for a few years, before rising again in most countries since about 2013.

Britain's corporate sector stands out in experiencing one of the biggest percentage falls, from 86% of GDP at the end of 2007 to 70% by mid-2015. Elsewhere corporate debt held up. In the US corporate borrowing was at 71% of GDP in mid-2015, 1% up on the end of 2007, representing a substantial rise of US$2.3 trillion of debt. In Japan it also rose by 1% of GDP over the same period, and in Germany fell by 1%.[22]

So despite predictions of post-crash deleveraging – paying back debt – by nonfinancial corporations, borrowing across the developed countries has continued to rise in absolute money terms. This debt grew by US$8.5 trillion between 2000 and 2007, slowing to a US$4.9 trillion increase in the subsequent seven-year span between 2007 and 2014.[23] Over the longer term, business debt has expanded steadily across the corporate world, with the main exceptions being the immediate crash-impacted years, and stagnant Britain since 2008.

This continued growth of corporate debt in most places negates another explanation for low investment: that businesses really had been 'deleveraging' and using their profits to pay off debts rather than invest. On the contrary, the relative ease of debt availability has enabled the continued absolute growth of corporate debt with no reversal of anaemic levels of business investment.

Debt is also cheap; its cost has fallen since the early 1980s. The real interest rates banks charge to borrowers have been declining for over three decades (see Figure 5.1). After high and volatile inflation fell away from the early 1980s real interest rates stabilised, before beginning a steady descent to reach recent ultra-low levels.[24] The US shows this clearly – and its rates remain the dominant influence across the mature economies because of the dollar's role as world money. US real commercial bank interest rates averaged about 7% in the 1980s, 5.5% in the 1990s, 4% in the 2000s for the period leading up to the financial crash, and have been below 2% since then.

So most companies have been able to borrow cheaply as well as easily over a prolonged period, yet have not been investing much. It is argued there is one exception to the cheap and easy capital theme: newer and smaller businesses, especially since the financial crash, contributing to their poor investment. Banks

Figure 5.1 Real long-term interest rates

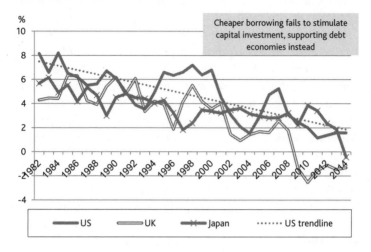

Note: Full data are unavailable for Germany.
Source: World Bank databank. http://data.worldbank.org/indicator/FR.INR.RINR

under the burden of their own debts and facing tougher post-crash financial regulation are said to have been starving businesses of the funding they need to invest. For example, organisations representing British small businesses say that fragile, risk-averse and regulated banks have been deliberately stingy with their business lending,[25] holding back growth from young, promising, creditworthy companies.

Business bank loan figures have fallen since the post-crash recession. The banks contend that lower lending figures represent a lack of appetite for borrowing from businesses: a demand rather than a supply issue. They argue that business caution and other business-driven factors have been restraining demand for new loans.

Both sides of the argument offer genuine instances in support. The overall picture is more nuanced. The official headline data obscure how companies have been repaying loans *and* borrowing at the same time. While banks have continued to lend to both large and small business, businesses have been repaying loans at an even faster rate. Hence, in Britain the amount of bank loans outstanding fell by nearly a quarter between the end of the recession in 2009 and 2014.[26]

The bank lending debate cannot be empirically resolved either by the gross or net lending figures. As the Bank of England notes, disentangling the separate influences of changes in the supply of, and demand for, credit is difficult.[27] However, the fact that the takeup of funds by small business remains languid even when state institutions, such as Britain's Funding for Lending Scheme, subsidise bank lending suggests that the main problem is in demand.

The assessment the Bank of England draws from its regular surveys of businesses and banks seems balanced: the availability of loans has increased steadily since the recession for small, medium and large businesses while demand has remained volatile. It concluded that credit conditions had remained 'easy' for large corporates, and availability had remained 'reasonable' for many small and medium-sized enterprises. This mirrors the Europe-wide conclusion of McKinsey consultants that the cost and availability of financing after the crash has played a secondary part in the reduction of investment.[28]

The role of small businesses should not anyway be overestimated in explaining overall investment levels. Historically, they have collectively contributed only a small proportion to capital investment. Larger firms are the dominant force in investment and have been responsible for about four-fifths.[29] They are also better able to tap the capital markets as an alternative to commercial banks. Understanding investment performance requires looking beyond the small business sector and not giving undue significance to any specific challenges it faces in bank borrowing.

The experience of the Long Depression illustrates that low-priced borrowing is no guarantor of investment. Historically in the developed economies more than 80% of all business capital investment is from retained earnings, not from external sources of finance. Even in normal economic times, therefore, the role of the price and availability of credit for investment should not be overstated. As Charles Goodhart shrewdly observed, the empirical evidence shows capital expenditure to be interest-rate insensitive,[30] undermining a big part of the rationale of modern monetary policy. Barriers other than credit cost and availability are holding back investment and innovation.

Resolving the low investment puzzle

In fact, the easy availability of cash – whether self-generated or borrowed – is not a determinant of investment levels but a consequence of low investment. Analysis of US businesses confirms that rising cash reserves are partly a function of lower capital investment.[31]

Low interest rates are held down by the dearth in investment. The 'global savings glut' explanation for suppressed market interest rates in the mid-2000s mostly ignored investment. The conventional explanation offered emphasised the excess of savings above investment requirements.[32] Not only, as mentioned earlier, did most interpretations miss that the main source of extra savings came from Western businesses – rather than the usual spotlight on China – but it also underplayed the other fundamental force at work: the decay of business investment. The most characteristic feature of recent times has been the unusual weakness of capital investment rather than the unusual strength of autonomous saving.

McKinsey's economists were among a minority who explained that the perceived savings glut was actually due to the declining investment rate. Indeed, contrary to what would be expected in a *savings* glut, they showed that the world's saving rate had not been rising but fell from 23% to 19.6% of global GDP between 1970 and 2002. A 'glut' appeared only because over the same period global investment dropped by almost half as much again from 25.5% to 20.8%.[33]

Low and falling interest rates since the 1980s are consistent with investment demand declining faster than the supply of savings. A depressed economy has reduced demand for capital to invest productively, while produced value is sufficient to maintain an adequate supply of loanable funds, since businesses have less need to use their own profits for capital spending. Capital is cheap and stays cheap.

The sustained fall in interest rates also points to the underlying reason for sluggish investment: falling profitability. This trend has been the main force dragging interest rates down.[34] The market interest rate is the price paid for capital in its money form. The base level for rates is set by profitability, since interest is paid to the lenders of capital out of the profits generated in production. The average market rate of interest is limited by the general rate of profit and tends to move with it. A low rate of profit establishes a lower base for the rate of interest, around which supply and demand factors then work, recently primarily lacklustre investment.

The reason lower interest rates don't generate more capital investment is that the already low market interest rates are ultimately the product of low profitability that suppresses capital investment. Since cheap capital is a consequence of economic slowdown, rather than dear capital being the reason for slowdown, it is not surprising that the even lower interest rates artificially promoted by central bank interventions haven't got businesses investing again.

Falling profitability is the root cause of this curtailed business investment. On a surface level the influence of company profitability is not surprising. A survey of US post-war investment discovered, in line with the earlier analysis, that borrowing costs don't seem to affect business investment much.[35] The researchers S.P. Kothari, Jonathan Lewellen and Jerold Warner found instead that the vast majority of the post-crash corporate investment decline was not specific to features of the financial crisis or the financial markets. They attributed two-thirds of the investment fall by a quarter between late 2008 and late 2009 to the previous decline in profits.[36]

Their analysis of the longer period from 1952 to 2010 established a correlation between profitability and investment: US corporate investment grew rapidly following high profits. They assessed that this could be either due to the availability of 'cheap' internal financing out of previous profits, or the perception of good investment opportunities based on current good profitability, or a combination of both.[37] They went on to show that profitability and business investment both trended down during the post-war boom before entering the era of economic slowdown.

A BIS study investigating anaemic G7 corporate investment also highlighted the importance of profitability, concluding that expectations of future economic conditions and profitability play the key roles in driving investment.[38] But the trend of falling profitability is much more important than its effects on business perceptions. It has a deeper impact on economy-wide investment through bringing on, at some indeterminate point, the economic crisis.

From boom to slump: a crisis of profitability

More than four decades of reduced capital investment account for our prolonged depression. Before this, investment also played a decisive part in its origins. Paradoxically it was the *strength* of investment in the post–Second World War boom that created the conditions for the return to depression.

The roots of economic depression are not in external factors such as the bursting of a financial bubble (the 1929 stock market crash) or in politically motivated oil price hikes (the OPEC rises in 1973). Instead expansions in mature economies exhaust themselves. They hit a self-generated obstruction. Inexorable pressures build up during the good times to bring about economic crisis and a period of economic contraction and torpor.

The post-war boom saw global growth averaging 4–5% a year, driven by rapid technological and value expansion across the developed regions. Diane Coyle describes how improved productivity was a core contributor to this 'Golden Age'. A succession of new technologies and innovations, many of them the fruits of military spending and goals, became available and entered into wide use.[39] In the advanced industrial countries unemployment remained low, business cycle volatility was restrained, and the financial system mostly operated smoothly in the background. Recessions were short-lived and modest. No significant financial disruptions happened.

The state initiated the boom by forcing through wartime restructuring and remained economically active throughout. In levels of spending and in the range of activities, including the expansion of welfare services, the state was more interventionist than it had ever been. While the boom was no expression of 'free market' vigour, the elites felt a great sense of relief following the tremendous turmoil earlier in the century. The British prime minister, Harold Macmillan, caught this mood when he told his Conservative Party in 1957 that 'most of our people have never had it so good'.[40]

Inherent to mature capitalism, the post-war expansion could not last indefinitely and began to show its limits. Britain had the worst of it with a series of 'stop-go' crises through the 1950s and 1960s leading to sterling's shock devaluation in 1967. Everywhere sharp drops in business profitability from the 1960s evidenced the exhaustion of boom-time dynamism. Productive investment declined, productivity growth slowed, and decay emerged in the capacity to create new industries and jobs.

While it is common to link lower profitability with economic decay and languid investment, the direction of causation remains contested. The standard view is that low profits are a symptom, a consequence of economic slowdown – poor sales translate into lower revenues and reduced profitability. Although the fall in business profitability was widely recognised in the 1970s it was conventionally attributed to the mid-decade recession: a weak economy leading to poor profitability.

The prime direction of causation is the opposite: poor profitability leads to anaemic investment and a slower economy. Feedback loops explain the standard perspective, but beneath this surface layer of reality the fall in the rate of profit is the lower-layer reason for the weakening investment that perpetuates the economic depression.

Profit occupies a central role in market economies, both as a motivation for expansion and also by providing its financial means. Individual businesses are driven by the pursuit of profit and securing more value. The criterion for investment is reaping an adequate return sufficiently in excess of the cost of capital, whether using borrowed or internal funds. For existing businesses profit is the direct source of the retained earnings that provides them with the financial means to invest and grow. By undermining business investment, declining profitability is the ultimate source of economic decay.

A few economists have seen through the upside-down appearances of the standard view to suggest that economic weakness has been the result of falling and low profitability. In the early 1980s Dale Allman, from the Federal Reserve Bank of Kansas City, analysed profit rates across the US economy from the post-war boom through to the early 1980s. He showed that before-tax profits as a return on capital were in long-term secular decline from the early 1950s.[41]

This measure of profitability fell from an average of 15% in the 1950s to 11% in the 1970s. Moreover, he showed that the decline in profitability applied across all the main business sectors (with the telling exception of financial services – the spurious character of financial 'profits' probably accounts for Allman's anomalous finding[42]). Given this comprehensive record of decline, Allman dismissed the idea that the fall in profitability could be caused by a business cycle slowdown, or that it could simply recover during the 1980s alongside the economic recovery. His insights were validated by the course of profitability, which has remained low ever since.

Subsequent empirical enquiries have been consistent with the assessment of lower profitability as being the source of economic slump. Some draw out the mediating role of capital investment. One study by Olivier Blanchard (later chief economist at the IMF), Changyong Rhee (later chief economist at the Asian Development Bank) and Lawrence Summers (later President Clinton's Treasury secretary) assessed US investment over the period from the First World War to 1988. They concurred that investment decisions were generally driven by what they called the 'fundamentals' of profit rates. Profitability in the current and previous years represented the main variable determining the annual rate of business investment.

Their measure of profitability mirrored almost exactly the ups and downs of the economic history of the twentieth century. It fell through the First World War years, recovering during the 1920s before falling sharply on the eve of the Great Depression. It rose again after 1932 to reach new highs driven by the Second World War capital restructuring. The current profitability cycle began with a steady decline during the post-war boom from the high of the late 1940s, hitting a low towards the close of the

1960s that marked the end of the boom and the transition into the era of crisis and the Long Depression.

After a brief recovery and stabilisation following the 1973–75 recession, consistent with the partial restructuring that ensued, profitability dropped again from the late 1970s to reach deeper lows in the 1980s.[43] Their analysis showed that business investment rates generally followed these profitability oscillations, sometimes immediately, sometimes with a short lag.

There are lots of ways of calculating from official data the rate of profit, measured as a ratio to the value of the net capital stock.[44] Andrew Kliman, who has spent much time analysing US profit rates, sensibly holds the view that no one particular way of calculating the rate of profit can act as *the* true all-purpose measure of profitability. He concluded that this doesn't matter much as most of the variants show similar trends. Since it is the *trend* in profitability that is relevant here we don't need to pursue the measurement question. On all measures profitability fell during the period of post-war boom reaching new lows in the 1970s and 1980s. With some small ups and downs, it has been trendless ever since.[45]

Esteban Ezequiel Maito, an economist at the University of Buenos Aires, has performed the valuable service of drawing on official statistics from a range of mainly industrial economies to provide estimates for the long-run movement in the rate of profit. Going back to the second half of the 19th century, profit rates in the advanced economies show a clear downward trend.[46] This is evident in an average measure Maito calculated for six leading countries: the US, Britain, Germany, Japan, the Netherlands and Sweden, weighted by the size of their economies (see Figure 5.2).

While the trend is strong, the decline has been interrupted. There are periods of stabilisation and a single substantial recovery in the aftermath of the 1930s slump and into the Second World War. During the Long Depression profit rates have become more stable, and occasionally increased a little. There has been no reversal of the boom-time decline on a par with the late 1930s and 1940s.

This illustrates the much more protracted character of this depression than its predecessor. It is now into its fifth decade, while the '1930s' depression is appropriately described, as it

Figure 5.2 Average profit rate, core industrial countries

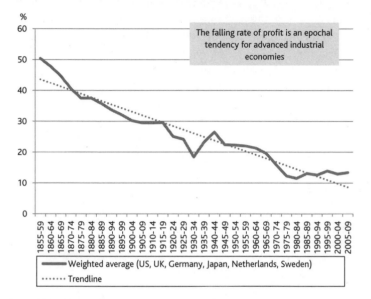

The falling rate of profit is an epochal tendency for advanced industrial economies

Weighted average (US, UK, Germany, Japan, Netherlands, Sweden)
······· Trendline

Source: Maito, 2014, pp 18-19

took about a decade before resolution, and the restoration of profit rates to enable another wave of capital investment. This difference in duration points to the main distinction of the current depression, which is its *containment*. This depression has been neither as destructive nor as turbulent as its predecessor.

It is noteworthy that a couple of much-discussed economic developments since the 1980s that are said to have brought about reductions to levels of capital stock have not had an arithmetical effect in boosting profitability rates, through a lower denominator. Or the effects were insufficient to offset lower baseline profitability.

First, the shift to more service-based economies might be thought to require less physical assets, lower capital stocks and therefore produce higher profit rates. However, we explained earlier in Chapter Four that services are not all alike and some are very capital intensive. Second, the widespread outsourcing of asset-intensive activities like manufacturing to other parts of the world will also have tended to reduce the ratio between output and the assets needed domestically. Without these sectoral and geographical changes the level of domestic capital stock in the denominator of the profit ratio would have been higher over the past three decades – and profit rates even lower than reported.

Drilling down into the profit rates for our group of four economies in Figure 5.3, two other features stand out. First the decline trend is most consistent in the oldest industrial economy, Britain. The longer an economy is expanding, the longer its profitability falls. Second, the deepest declines in profits rates usually coincide with periods of sustained and robust growth. Germany's and America's rapid industrialisation in the late 19th century stand out, as does the post–1945 boom across all four countries.

Figure 5.3 National profit rates

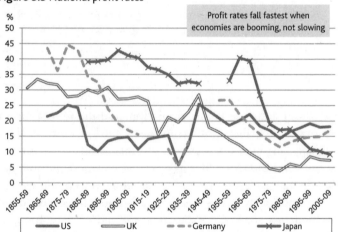

Source: Maito, 2014, pp 18-19

All the features illustrated in these profitability charts – the long-term secular decline, the interruptions and the occasional reverses – are consistent with the analysis made by Karl Marx, presented in the volumes of *Capital*. Before Marx, classical political economy had already recognised the existence of a downward trend in the rate of profit. Smith and Ricardo, among others, had sought to explain why this happened. However, their explanations were either too general (Smith) or too specific

(Ricardo) to be convincing. Smith saw falling profitability as the result of the intensification of market competition, while Ricardo attributed it to the declining fertility of agricultural land that pushed up the cost of food and necessitated rising wages at the expense of profits.

Marx took the explanation onto a different level by identifying that falling profitability was intrinsic to the capitalist process of expanding production. It was not to do with competition in the marketplace, or factors external to industrial production. Distinct to his account, these profitability tendencies existed at the level of capital-in-general, prior to the effects of market competition on individual business units. And while there were always other factors outside of the process of production that could impact on the market economy adversely, these were secondary influences. He presented the tendency of the rate of profit to fall as a systemic law that was specific to capitalism, describing it as 'In every respect … the most important law of modern political economy, and the most essential one for comprehending the most complex relationships. It is the most important law from the historical standpoint.'[47]

Marx discovered that falling profitability derives from the additional capital investments that are necessary to raise productivity. Labour productivity only increases durably as a result of more and better productive capital being employed for each worker. Technically this often takes the form of the mechanisation of work, though it is generically expressed as a greater amount of capital stock for each employee. Productivity-enhancing investments tend to grow the value of the capital invested relative to the amount spent on wages. The consequence is that the accumulated cost of investing in plant and equipment, added to the spending on raw materials and semi-components, rises inexorably relative to the cost of labour.

The operating profit represents the net value produced by this labour, after the deduction of all input costs, including wages, capital depreciation and other operating expenses.[48] The profit arising from the new value created by labour in the production process tends to decline relative to the rising amounts of capital invested in fixed assets and materials. This means that the profit rate measured over *all* capital deployed – in employing people as well as in fixed assets and other inputs – will also tend to decline. This tendency of the general rate of profit to fall follows as a direct consequence of the development of the social productivity of labour, since this is dependent upon increasing amounts of capital investment.

Marx was quick to point out that actual profitability can fall for all sorts of other reasons.[49] Not every fall in the rate of profit is the consequence of rising investment. However, these other reasons tend to be particular, and don't endure for long. They could come from a temporary rise in production's costs (energy costs are especially volatile) or the knock-on effect from disruptions in an important market (maybe due to a financial crash) reducing sales, revenues and profits.

These sorts of instabilities can happen at any time. Secular falling profitability is quite different: a perpetual tendency within the normal dynamics of capitalism that ultimately precipitates economic crisis. It is not an aberration for the modern economy, but its nemesis. As the profitability charts illustrate, the rate of profit tends to fall *during*, not at the end, of periods of economic boom. Profitability declines as a result of the *expansion* of the economy, not its contraction, but then in the end causes it to contract.

This relationship between growth and falling profitability is consistent with another finding in the study by Kothari, Lewellen and Warner: high investment levels anticipated the subsequent contraction of profitability. Although the study's authors rejected a causal relationship because they could think of 'no reason' for one, the correlation they discovered is in accord with the thesis here.[50]

The tendential fall in profitability is an inevitable accompaniment to the *increasing* productivity that is positively associated with periods of investment and economic expansion. The rate of profit exhibits a downward trend not because productivity decreases but because it increases in consequence of innovative capital investment. Falling profitability then becomes a constraint on future investment, reducing productivity growth.

This analysis also accords with another feature displayed recently by the rate of profit: its relative stabilisation since the 1970s. Given that productive expansion drives falling profitability, a more anaemic economy is likely to see the rate of profit flatten out. Just as normal boom-time capital accumulation and growth produce the fall in the rate of profit, so that pressure fades as accumulation weakens after the crisis hits. Since the tendency of the rate of profit to fall is an expression of the increasing social productivity of labour, when productivity stagnates so this tendency is abated.

Because falling profitability is an almost constant feature of expanding capitalism it cannot on its own cause an economic crisis. This appreciation led Marx to reject explicitly any automatic or determinist interpretation of the implications of this 'most important' law. The existence of a falling rate of profit is not in itself an indicator of the current state of economic health.[51] For most of the history of modern capitalism the rate of profit has been falling, yet only rarely and after long periods of time does it manifest itself in a regressive breakdown in production.[52]

The transition from boom to crisis is not triggered because the rate of profitability hits some particular level. Instead declining profitability is important for the onset of economic crisis because it conveys a fall in the overall amount of profit produced *relative* to the amount of capital required for the next phase of investment to raise productivity again. The *mass* of profit, which is normally always rising, therefore plays a bigger role in understanding the arrival of crisis conditions than does the *rate* of profit.[53]

The crisis moment arises from a tension between the amount of profits produced, the size of the existing capital invested, and the even greater amount needed for another transformative round of investment. Raising social productivity across the spread of business sectors requires increasingly larger investments of capital to move ahead. At some point the mass of profit produced and available for the next round of investment is insufficient to make those bigger investments in the next level of technologies. The mass of profit can continue to grow absolutely but may be inadequate *relative* to what is needed for the next stage of accumulation. The profit available will be large but not large enough. Capital reaches a state of overaccumulation.

The Polish Marxist Paul Mattick captured beautifully how the constraint of the rate of profit is fundamentally a *relational* one:

> From the point of view of profitability, the crisis of overproduction represents a situation in which the existing capital is *simultaneously too small and too large*: it is too large in relation to the existing surplus-value and it is not large enough to overcome the dearth of surplus-value. Capital accumulation is thus both the cause of crisis and the instrument that overcomes it.[54]

The amount of profit generated by the existing capital investments is not sufficient to fund the bigger investments need to move the economy onto a higher level.

Dale Jorgenson, Mun Ho and Jon Samuels touched on this dilemma in explaining why productivity-enhancing innovative investment levels have been so disappointing. They suggested that compared to simple replacement, or expansion, investments that use existing technologies, the investment that incorporates innovation 'is obviously far more challenging and subject to much greater risk'. They pointed out that the diffusion of successful innovation requires 'mammoth financial commitments' to fund the investments that replace outdated products and processes and establish the new structures and systems to make use of them.[55]

As a result of the disparity between the resources already produced and the larger amount needed for the next investment round, advance gets interrupted. At an individual business level credit can help to overcome any financing constraints. However, this can't sustain accumulation indefinitely. In practice, debt service payments will have to be paid out of the mass of future profits. What remains would become relatively smaller again, aggravating the shortage available for future investment. Credit in itself is a valuable palliative but it does nothing to boost systematically the rate of profit and overcome profitability constraints.

At a non-predictable point lower profitability undermines the capacity to move society forward. That is what occurred in the switch from the end of the boom to the return of slump in the 1970s. Some specific conjunctural factor brings the potential for crisis into realisation. In the early 1970s, the principal ingredient was the undermining of the value of the US dollar as world money. Mounting domestic economic difficulties in the US, aggravated by the costs of the Vietnam War, broke the Bretton Woods international currency system that had been underpinning the international economic expansion.

The disruptive ramifications of the devaluation of the dollar and the resulting collapse of the Bretton Woods system between 1971 and 1973, including a compensating jump in the dollar price of oil imposed by the OPEC countries, triggered the halt to production. This was expressed through the synchronised recessions in all the mature economies between 1973 and 1975.

Western stock markets started falling in January 1973. By December 1976, the US's main benchmark index, the Dow Jones Industrial Average, had lost over 45% of its value. The deeper symptom of the return to depression was the step-change in productivity growth. Productivity growth slackened as the momentum of technological advance began to decelerate due to reduced investment rates. Joblessness also shot up, and income growth abated.

This productivity slowdown was well recognised among economists, and beyond. Moreover, it was regarded as a matter of social significance.[56] That such attention to the economic fundamentals has recently become less common, especially among the West's political leaders, stands in the way of bringing about a meaningful revival.

SIX

The end of growth

The mid-1970s recession was more than the severe cyclical downturn many saw it as. It marked the transition into an era of decay in the advanced economies' capacity to generate new industrial sectors and enough decent jobs. The West entered an enduring period of atrophy. Edmund Phelps illuminated the impact on America:

> [circumstances are] now quite different from the modern economy that was so scintillating over most of the 19th and 20th centuries. The central dimensions of performance – job satisfaction, unemployment, and relative productivity – make this very clear. Data show deterioration setting in on all three fronts as early as the mid-1970s, with only a temporary uptick in job satisfaction in the last giddy years of the internet boom. A similar deterioration came sooner or later to the rest of the West: … That the deterioration has been lasting suggests that the economy was undergoing a shift of its tectonic plates – a systemic, qualitative change.[1]

Unfortunately, such recognition of the substance of the downturn is rare. Phelps is unusual in assessing the period as 'truly a Second Great Depression'.[2]

The passage from crisis into full-blown depression expressed the failure to restore the conditions for profitable investment and accumulation. Downward pressures were mitigated sufficiently to stave off permanent recession, but the fall in profitability that triggered the return of decay remains unresolved. The crisis turned from a single recession into depression. A depression means both more and also less than economic crisis.

It means more because depression represents a protracted sluggishness in economic activity. Productive capacity begins to corrode. It is not self-healing nor is it easy to fix. Low profitability persists as the principal economic barrier to investment and innovation.

Depression also means less than permanent economic crisis. A depression is not the persistent stagnation of every economic indicator. Even the more intense depression of the 1930s saw episodes of recovery and expansion. This uneven pattern has been more evident during the less disruptive Long Depression. A couple of early sharp recessions and recoveries were followed by an extended period of moderate growth from the mid-1980s. The latter was punctuated with occasional bouts of faster development, including the late 1990s internet boom.

Marx anticipated the resilience of capitalism in times of economic crisis through his identification of forces that offset those represented by falling profitability. He emphasised the existence of counteracting influences to the law of falling profitability, which modify its expression. These counter-effects 'hamper, retard and partly paralyse this fall'. They do not repeal the law, but they alleviate its effects. Otherwise 'it would not be the fall of the general rate of profit, but rather its relative slowness, that would be incomprehensible'.[3]

This is why the law acts as a tendency. Marx never projected capitalist collapse. His counterbalancing factors have become sources of capitalist resilience that offset the forces of decay. They come to the fore during periods of crisis and act as coping mechanisms that keep the breakdown tendencies in check.

Too few of his readers gave sufficient attention to these counteracting influences so that the interrupted, uneven features of the crisis cause bafflement. Marx's critics also usually missed this subtlety. But without an appreciation of the offsetting tendencies, his theory of crisis descends into the rigid soothsaying he warned against, and which is so easy to ridicule. Being perceived as a prophet of capitalist doom, the resilience of capitalism over the last 150 years apparently offered proof of his flaws. Capitalism's survival seemed to justify dismissing his work as that of a misguided revolutionary. Because followers one-sidedly misinterpreted his thesis as one of collapse, the conventional critique of Marxism gained more sway.

In practice productive decay is uneven. The countervailing measures can't restore profitability to enable sustained productivity growth, but they are decisive for many of the ups and downs during a depression. Our analysis of the unfolding of the Long Depression therefore draws more on the coping mechanisms – their positive effects, as well as their limitations – than on falling profitability.

Initially these offsetting forces worked directly either to reduce the value of capital assets, or to reduce labour costs, or to otherwise boost operating profits. As these influences on profit rates become less effective, substitutes emerge that compensate for the shortage of operating profits and keep economic activity going. When spontaneous countervailing factors lose impact, increasingly state institutions have helped to develop support mechanisms. This usually happens more by contingency than by design. Most notable has been the transition to a financialised economy dependent on the expansion of debt.

How the crisis of profitability curtails business investment

The rate of profit under discussion is a society-wide relationship between profits and capital assets. Inadequate profitability relative to the total capital stock previously invested underlies the depression. The dampening effect of lower profitability operates at a high level of abstraction across the whole economy. Slump conditions are not usually perceived by individual businesspeople as a 'crisis of profitability'.

The rate of profit is not the same as a business's rate of return. Businesses do not measure their current profits as a ratio of their balance sheet assets to decide on investment proposals. A rate of return looks at anticipated profits against the outlay on that particular investment project. While there are plenty of instances where the projected returns will be deemed by management to be insufficient to move ahead, this is not how the overaccumulation of social capital generally imposes itself.

More relevant for the profitability constraint is the value tied up on balance sheets in old capital assets deriving from previous rounds of investment. A company balance sheet measures its continued viability; the assets are the firm's material foundation for continuing to operate. But for undertaking major new investments, part of this positive balance sheet becomes a barrier. The existing capital stock that incorporates outdated technologies inhibits comprehensive transforming investments.

Renewing business capabilities with the latest technologies and innovations replaces the old capital, which renders it of limited or nil value. This value writeoff weakens the business balance sheet. This is how Mattick's abstract description of capital being simultaneously 'too small and too large' impacts at the individual corporate level.[4] Businesses can have cash to invest in a major innovation project but its reluctance will be aggravated when it involves wiping out value from their fixed assets.

The effects of depression across the economy reinforce this curb on transformative investments by existing businesses. Depression becomes self-reproducing: a vicious circle that perpetuates itself. Low investment means lacklustre growth. Reduced economic growth limits incentives for businesses to invest. The nexus of low investment → narrow innovation → sluggish productivity → weak production reinforces itself. Investment returns are not guaranteed even in the best of economic times, so the active decision to invest is never easy. In a period of depression businesses are less able to identify suitable opportunities for revenue expansion to justify major investment decisions.

This applies to new businesses as well as established ones. New businesses don't have the deadweight of previous investments holding them back, but they experience the same limiting of opportunities as the incumbents. Starting up also has the additional challenge of creating a new business from scratch. That's why many startups fail: about half of businesses don't reach their fifth anniversary. Sometimes failure occurs because when there is no, or only a very limited, market for their new products it can take years of onerous outgoings before one is developed. Cash can easily run out before then. Or in the meantime a better product arrives, or sometimes one that is just perceived to be better.

When the startup is making an existing product cheaper, it can still take time and therefore much expense to succeed in the face of incumbents with established profiles and financial clout. Existing firms often have the strength and scale to retain market position against the newcomers. This makes it difficult for new businesses to break through, even with the benefit of better production technologies. In times of depression, all the specific challenges facing new businesses become tougher. Market growth is more limited and competition is harsher.

The depressed economic conditions therefore discourage existing and new businesses from expanding and investing. This is why some economic analysts notice that investment is not the lead indicator for economic growth during depressions that it is in boom-times. Standard & Poor's reported that investment spending lags, or is at best contemporaneous with any improvements in revenues and profitability. It concluded that stronger investment is dependent on a better business climate so that capital spending is unlikely to lead economic recovery.[5] This matter-of-fact insight is testimony to the difficulty of escaping depression.

Investment doesn't come to a halt during depressions but the emphasis is on maintenance and replicating types, which are necessary just to remain in business. There is some investment in innovation during depressions, but it is narrow in scope. Transformative activities that are tough to succeed with in a booming economy become that much more difficult in a depressed one. Instead innovations are more likely to be incremental than radical: to add on to existing ways of working than to be a wholesale replacement. Hence the productivity benefits are also more limited.

In practice, it is the larger-scale technology-changing investments that are especially inhibited, and these are the ones vital to driving forward economic and social progress. Radical innovations in a business's processes or products require big investments to redesign or refashion how the business operates. Consider the enormous outlays when manufacturing factories were reorganised in the early 20th century around electricity as a distributed source of power to replace centralised steam power.

Inventions are also still made during depressions, but their full deployment is constrained by inadequate profitability. The prospects of commercial gain are too patchy and uneven to attract the waves of investment needed to maximise their innovatory potential. Take graphene, the atom-thick layer of carbon that is stronger than steel and an efficient conductor of heat and electricity. First isolated in 2004 by Andre Geim and Kostya Novoselov, it is one of the first developed nanotechnologies.

Potential manufacturing applications are enormous, including lighter aircraft, better batteries and flexible display screens. However, existing production companies will find it hard to use in manufacturing partly because this requires writing off the existing assets embodying traditional production methods. Novoselov described the difficulties that are slowing down the faster and more widespread deployment of their exciting new compound.

The investments involved in refitting production, he said, are not worth the return for the existing businesses that are dominant in the potential areas of development. It is very hard to commercialise a new material like graphene and he doubted that big companies are up for such 'big changes'.[6] It was not always this way: recall the innovating role of large companies like General Electric, Xerox, IBM and AT&T during the post-war boom.

Bill Lazonick and Mary O'Sullivan described a shift in corporate practice that occurred around the turn of the 1970s, which illustrates these different investment conditions between boom and depression. They recounted the demise of the 'retain and reinvest' principle that had reigned supreme in the large US corporations since the Second World War. 'Retain and reinvest' described how businesses retained the money they earned from sales and reinvested it in additional capital and for employing and training workers. Since the 1960s 'retain and reinvest' was running into difficulties as large businesses held back from investing so much, symptomatic of the tendency towards overaccumulation.[7]

With large companies not innovating as much during the depression, new companies have become more important for innovating applications from inventions. Pursuing the example of graphene, new companies have made headway in areas like energy-saving light bulbs, false teeth and lighter tennis rackets. The drawback is that they don't have the scale and resources to transform technology and production across the whole economy.

The gap existing between the levels of economy-wide capital-in-general and that of the many individual capital units means that in a depression there are still businesses that appear divorced or immune from the crisis of profitability. During a crisis of profitability most businesses will still make profits and have enough cash to operate. Services and goods continue to be produced, distributed and sold. Some individual companies will thrive.

Particular businesses will be able to get ahead of their competitors and make superprofits. Businesses that have built up strong cash reserves previously avoid experiencing the direct constraints from low profitability. Others borrow to alleviate their own cash shortages. None of these routes though will revive overall investment levels. Investments made by particular companies don't scale up to business-in-totality restoring an adequate overall level of investment.

Society could be lucky and an 'Apple' of the graphene or nanotechnologies world could emerge. But with the depression's restraints on investment the likelihood of this is lower now than 1976 when the original Apple was established. Thoroughgoing economic restructuring, involving the writing off of large amounts of unproductive capital assets, must precede the resumption of a sufficient dynamic of transforming investments.

Investment languishes despite rising individual company profits

Much recent financial and economic discussion has focused on data showing strong corporate profits. This seems to contradict the existence of a crisis of profitability, and adds another dimension to the standard puzzle about low investment. Anaemic business investment seems odd when profits are seen as rising,[8] sometimes hailed as buoyant, or at 'record' highs.[9]

Commentators report that over the past quarter-century profits as a share of GDP have increased in many mature countries to unusually high levels. In the US both in the leadup to the late 2000s crash and again since, the after-tax profit share of GDP hit records for the entire post-war period (Figure 6.1).

Radical, as well as mainstream, economists have highlighted this unusual upturn in reported profits since the mid-1980s. Paralleling the wider puzzlement over low investment, this recovery in profits has also provoked a certain amount of confusion and controversy among left-wing groups.[10]

Figure 6.1 US total corporate profits after tax relative to GDP

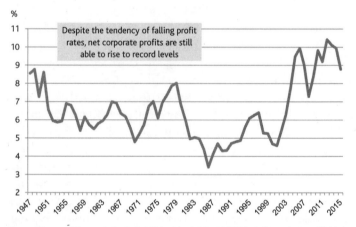

Source: Bureau of Economic Analysis, NIPA tables 1.1.5 and 6.19. http://www.bea.gov/iTable/index_nipa.cfm

However, profit increases, some abrupt, can always happen and should not cause so much intellectual bafflement. Throughout most of the history of capitalism a rise in the *mass* of profits has coexisted with a fall in the *rate* of profit. Both are features of the normal accumulation of capital. As the economy grows, even at modest depression-level rates, private businesses produce and generate turnover and profit broadly in line with the size of the economy. While under depression conditions the rate of profit has stabilised and fluctuated around a lower level, the *amount* of profit continues to grow at most times.

Volatility in the mass of profits is also familiar since capitalism works unevenly at the best of times. Fluctuations around the rising trend in the absolute level of profits are normal, and simply become more pronounced in depressions. Sometimes echoes of the oscillating mass of profits are seen in its rate too; this accounts for the slight 1980s upturn in most rate-of-profit calculations that were so unsettling for parts of the radical left.

Multiple factors influence the absolute level of corporate profits, including the real effects of the counterbalancing sources of resilience. During recessions, revenues and profits are likely to fall away; when resilience kicks in, they recover. Short-term cost-cutting, including staff reductions or wage freezes, will impact on the operational surplus. Total profits are boosted by increasing overseas earnings. Profit figures can also be affected by considerations outside core operations. Alongside revenues from product sales, non-operational income can be included from financial activities, or from selling off assets or business units. Accounting revaluations of inventory stock, of corporate pension funds, or of financial asset holdings can also affect profit measures. Since the counteracting forces have proved unusually effective during the Long Depression – expressing greater resilience than in the 1930s – profit figures have fluctuated more.

After-tax net income is one measure of corporate earnings that has been trending especially high. This refers to what's left after all expenses, including operating costs, depreciation and interest charges on debt, have been deducted. Its trajectory illustrates the impact of two countervailing influences on profitability from outside the production process. Both reflect state policies: cuts in the level of taxation (fiscal policy), and cuts in interest rates (monetary policy). Without any improvements to operational profitability, net corporate earnings are enhanced by reductions in tax payments and in interest charges.

Across the OECD the trend in business tax rates has been downward over the past three decades. The average statutory corporate tax level halved from 48% in 1981 to 25% in 2014.[11] In the aftermath of the financial crash British corporation tax has been reduced to by far the lowest level within the G7. This provides British companies with a valuable benefit – in effect a state subsidy – compared to competitors from other economies.[12]

The US stands out in maintaining a fairly static business tax rate of 39%, reflecting the traditional US preference for emphasising instead low personal taxation. Nevertheless in the US the proliferation of tax loopholes means that the effective tax rate has also been falling from about 35% in the mid-1980s to less than 20% today.[13] These reductions in taxes paid mean that US businesses have also been able to retain a higher share of their profits, trending up from less than 60% of the pre-tax level in the late 1960s to nearly 70% now.[14]

As a result, while pre-tax profits relative to GDP have trended down from 9% to 7.5% reflecting lower social profitability, the post-tax trend has been more resilient and has risen a little (see Figure 6.2). American companies have benefited from lower taxes just as in the other mature economies where headline tax rates have been cut.

Figure 6.2 US pre-tax and post-tax domestic corporate profits relative to GDP

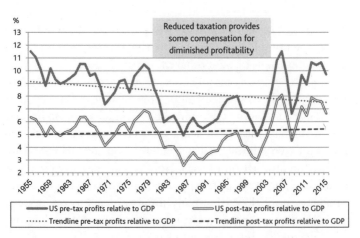

Source: Bureau of Economic Analysis, NIPA tables 1.1.5, 6.17 and 6.19. http://www.bea.gov/ iTable/index_nipa.cfm

Cuts in interest rates have also boosted take-home profitability by reducing debt service costs. In the US, industrial business interest payments on their debts fell from about 8% of GDP in the 1980s to 6% in the 1990s and to a trough of 4% in the mid-2000s (see Figure 6.3). With the introduction of ultra-low interest rates since the financial crash, charges have returned to this record trough.

Figure 6.3 US domestic industrial business interest payments relative to GDP

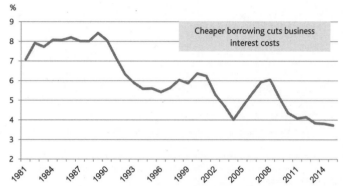

Note: US industry's average interest payments over 1980-89 were 7.8% of GDP. Source: Bureau of Economic Analysis, NIPA tables 1.1.5, 6.15 and 6.19. http://www.bea.gov/iTable/index_nipacfm

The lower interest rate effect has boosted post-tax reported earnings by the same amount: by 2% of GDP in the 1990s compared to the 1980s, and by 4% more recently. This implies that if US businesses had continued to incur interest charges on a par with the 1980s, post-tax reported profits would have been considerably lower ever since: net profits since the start of the ultra-low interest rate policy in 2008 would have averaged about 3.5% of GDP, rather than the 7% reported (see Figure 6.4).

A further significant source of profit resilience during the Long Depression has been the ability to hold down labour costs. We saw in Chapter Two how slowing and flatter productivity growth has undermined continuous wage growth. With the demise of organised industrial activism in all the mature economies, businesses have more easily restrained their wage bills. Lower starting wages for many of the new jobs created and small or negligible wage increases have become normal.

Figure 6.4 US actual and interest-adjusted post-tax profits relative to GDP

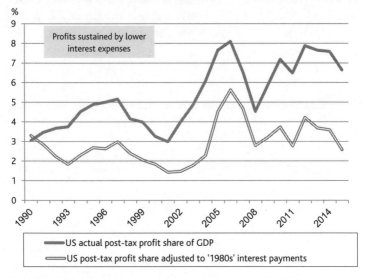

Note: US industry's average interest payments over 1980-89 were 7.8% of GDP.
Source: Bureau of Economic Analysis, NIPA tables 1.1.5, 6.15 and 6.19. http://www.bea.gov/iTable/index_nipa.cfm

This boon to reported profitability is expressed in the breakdown of national income shifting between wages and profits, with workers receiving a shrinking share in recent decades. Across the OECD area the labour share of GDP fell on average from about 58% in the late 1970s to about 53% by the mid-2000s.[15]

The trend is most pronounced in Britain with wages falling from a high of 64% in 1975 to 54% in 2013. The US experience was in the same direction, falling from 59% to 55%.[16] Their biggest labour share drops occurred in the mid-1980s, in the aftermath of the crackdown on the trade unions under Reagan and Thatcher. The decline started later in Germany, from the early 1990s, around the time of its reunification, and later still in Japan, from the early 2000s.

As a consequence of this wage containment the gross profit share calculated by the OECD has been able to increase in each of the US, Britain and Germany by about five percentage points of GDP (see Figure 6.5). In Japan the rise only began from the turn of the millennium and has so far been about half that amount.

Figure 6.5 Profit share of GDP

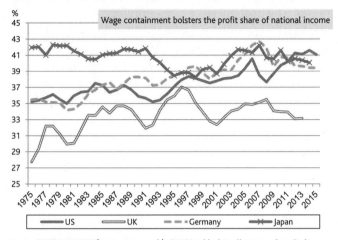

Source: OECD.Stat, GDP (income approach), SNA93 table. http://stats.oecd.org/Index.aspx?DatasetCode=SNA_TABLE1

Research on the British economy drew attention to another change that has tended to support boosted profits: the shift from industry (covering manufacturing jobs in the main) to the financial and business services sectors. In the former, it was traditional for a relatively high share of value to be distributed to workers, while in the latter more value is usually retained as profits rather than being distributed to employees.[17]

Financialisation is therefore another contributor to resilient profitability. High reported profits from financial services companies provided a fillip to domestic corporate profitability, especially during the 1990s and through to the West's financial crash. The collapse of financial sector profits after the crash, and their failure since to regain their previous peaks relative to GDP, suggest their large fictitious component. In the pre-crash period national profitability had been artificially enhanced by the financial services industry reporting profits far beyond those that were simply deductions from the profits made in the productive parts of the economy.

Total reported domestic corporate profits *including* the contribution from financial services were therefore giving an inflated view of profitability relative to circumstances in the nonfinancial, productive part of the economy. In the US the financial sector's share of profits has trended upwards from about 15% at the end of the post-war boom to average around 22% in the 15 years leading up to the financial crash.[18] This 7% increment indicates the useful supplement to overall reported profits arising from the expansion of the financial sector.

None of this analysis of reported profits implies that the measures of profitability provided are disingenuous, or deliberate distortions of the facts. On the contrary, the appearance of strong profitability is real, while remaining consistent with the social crisis of profitability. Arithmetically the US post-tax profit share of GDP is genuinely at record highs for the post-1945 period, even as the national rate of profit continues to languish below the falling levels of the post-war boom.

It is capitalist resilience, not a misleading manipulation of the figures, which enables many businesses to report decent profits and to retain large amounts of cash. This reality neither negates nor trumps the adverse effects for business investment of overaccumulation and the tendential fall in profitability. In fact, the impact of volatility in the mass of profits in sometimes producing fluctuations in the rate of profit illustrates that the declining profitability law is only a tendency; it is not an iron rule that operates without interruption.

The intractability of low profitability

Periodic recessions, by introducing a concentrated burst of counteracting measures, allow for the partial recovery of profit rates. This regenerative capacity has been a characteristic aspect of capitalism and is expressed in the cyclical nature of the market economy. The economy oscillates between periods of recovery and recession, with traditional recessions often destroying the value of enough old capital stock through bankruptcies and corporate takeovers to open the way for a limited resumption of investment and growth.

Kothari, Lewellen and Warner illustrated this business cycle pattern for investment and, especially, for profitability, showing that it had been persistent ever since the start of the post-war boom and into the Long Depression. Profitability rose a little after each recession – enabling some investment recovery – before topping out again mid-recovery, often at a lower level than the previous peak. As profitability fell away again after a few years of economic expansion, investment would also slow and flatten – and sometimes even fall – on the way into the next recession.[19]

The most decisive reversals to falling profitability occur when existing capital values are much more extensively destroyed than happens during a normal recession. A broader destructive devaluation of capital resets the base for profitability. This has happened only once, around the Second World War. It took the barbarism of global conflict and the accompanying forced destruction of capital values before production could be revitalised and the conditions set for the ensuing period of expansion.

This experience testifies that mature profitability-constrained economies can be restructured and renewed. The post-war boom was no mirage or aberration. For over a quarter-century it gave hundreds of millions of people substantial rises in living standards. Unless we come up with a contemporary non-militarised version of this experience, we cannot expect a resumption of such a positive economic performance.

There are plenty of short-term palliatives that offset low profitability and breed political complacency about the economy. But there are no incremental solutions that can take the place of the restructuring of production. Providing more debt, generating a stimulus to domestic demand, lowering a currency to encourage exports, corporate tax cuts: these can all provide temporary boosts to economic activity but they can't overcome the burden of low profitability.

Even what can seem to be more substantial signs of revival, such as spurts to business investment and the accompanying realisation of some significant innovations, are not steps towards an escape from depression. On the contrary, their effects can be self-defeating since the more substantial they are, the more likely they are to trigger another downward step in profitability. It is not coincidental that US corporate profit rates turned down again in the late 1990s following the New Economy ICT investment upturn (see Figure 6.1). Short-term upturns within the broader context of depression reinforce, rather than reverse, the atrophying effects of low profitability.

The intellectual challenge

It is a sign of today's diminished intellectual climate that the Great Depression of the 1930s stimulated a much higher level of debate and thinking about the future of capitalism than the current one has so far done. Most of the big names of 20th century economics, John Maynard Keynes, Irving Fisher, Alvin Hansen and Friedrich Hayek, earned their reputations during that depression. Each made specific contributions to understanding what had gone wrong. Keynes talked of the liquidity trap.[20] Fisher described the debt-deflation trap.[21] Hansen talked of secular stagnation.[22] Hayek argued that the depression was prolonged by the same state-driven artificial credit policies that had brought it about in the first place.[23]

Despite their differences they each picked up on some distinctive feature of what was happening. It was in consequence of these insights that much of the contemporary arsenal of anti-crisis policy measures was developed. Since none of their diagnoses got to the root causes within production, their prescriptions fell short. They could not be effective because they only addressed particular symptoms of the depression. The resulting measures implemented could sometimes provide a short-term stimulus but they failed to address the deeper reasons for the crisis.

This inter-war experience should be an intellectual benefit for today. We could learn from the ultimate failure of their various policy proposals and instead pursue other solutions. This lesson has not yet been learnt. Today's economists mostly repeat what was said 80 years ago. Many still contend that a sufficiently expansionary stimulus of demand (the Keynesian perspective) will be enough to escape from economic slowdown. These include prominently Paul Krugman, Lawrence Summers, Martin Wolf and Joseph Stiglitz.[24] A smaller number from the 'free market' or the Austrian school maintain that an extensive freeing up of markets from rigidities and regulation will revive economic fortunes. These are not such household names, but most follow in the paths of either Hayek or Milton Friedman.[25]

It is futile and counterproductive to call for more of these traditional varieties of economic policy. The essential problem facing investment and production does not come from a shortage of demand, or from an onerous tax and regulatory framework for business. The solution needs to be more radical, going to the underlying conditions within production.

Part III
How we got stuck

The crisis of the year gets all the attention. (Edmund Phelps, 2013, p 310)

SEVEN

Contained depression

A welcome feature of the Long Depression so far is that it has not led to a dangerous buildup of rivalries between the advanced industrial economies. This contrasts with the Great Depression when less than ten years separated the Wall Street Crash of 1929 and the outbreak in Europe of the bloodiest conflict ever, the Second World War.

Although history never repeats itself, it can rhyme, as Mark Twain apocryphally said. When crisis and depression returned in the 1970s it was not outlandish to anticipate a sharpening of inter-nation strains along the lines of 1930s protectionism. Yet more than four decades later the advanced countries continue mostly to cooperate in economic and other areas. Complacency is unwise over the potential rekindling of protectionism in new guises – over trade, or currencies, or cybersecurity, or some other matter – but we should be relieved that tensions until now have been restrained.

This containment of rivalry expresses more than the desire of Western leaders not to repeat the mistakes of their predecessors. Material factors have helped. The subdued features of the economic crisis at home and abroad reinforce each other. The lack of serious disruption in either sphere has made it easier to manage relations in the other.

The domestic consequences of depression have been less damaging and destructive than in the 1930s, which saw huge economic contractions, mass unemployment, widespread impoverishment, and eruptions of social conflict. Between 1929 and 1932 industrial production fell by 46% in the US, by 23% in Britain and by 41% in Germany.[1] A quarter of a million US businesses went under by 1933.[2] Unemployment there increased from about 3% in the late 1920s to 25%, and in some countries it reached 33%. The average family income in America dropped by 40% between 1929 and 1932, and 11,000 US banks, almost one in two, failed by 1933.

Worldwide, economic output fell by 15% in the three years from 1929. In contrast, world output has expanded every year of the Long Depression – with the exception of a single 2% fall in 2009 following the worst financial crash since the 1930s.[3]

The first decade of the Long Depression did share some of the harsher features of earlier capitalist crises. In the 1970s for the first time since the Second World War people became familiar with widespread business closures, wholesale redundancies, and high levels of long-term and youth unemployment. The recessions of 1973–75 and 1980–81 were deep enough to play their traditional role of clearing out some of the weakest parts of economic activity. Jobs and businesses were hit hard.

By the mid-1980s though, economic affairs had noticeably stabilised in most parts of the industrial world, and for much of the time. Recessions still occurred and, occasionally, bouts of intense financial turmoil surfaced. However, these recessions proved milder than before, and the financial disturbances were soon smoothed over.

Even the impact of the sharp national recessions precipitated by the late 2000s financial crash did not come close to matching the collapses of the 1930s. The events of 2008 were a huge shock and the Western world seemed to be teetering on the edge of catastrophe. But at the time of writing, nearly a decade later, and despite an unprecedentedly sluggish recovery, things were a lot better than commentators had earlier grimly anticipated.

Not always and not everywhere of course: capitalism in depression becomes more uneven. Greece and the other peripheral countries in the eurozone were more severely battered by the fallout from its post-2009 crisis. But these were exceptions to the more contained effect felt elsewhere.

Throughout the Long Depression, the destructive tendencies of crisis have been held in check. This has been a slow-drift depression in contrast to the deep slump of the 1930s. Industrial economies remain stuck in productive decay but most have been able to control its destabilising implications reasonably effectively. The prolonged depression exemplifies capitalism's greater resilience now than in the 1930s.

The moderated business cycle

The reduced volatility of the business cycle underlines the containment of the depression's potential disruptiveness. From the mid–1980s until the late 2000s, movements in GDP were less extreme. This is most evident in the US and Britain, but also in Germany and Japan (see Figures 7.1 to 7.4). The dotted lines show the ceilings and floors of economic output changes until the 1980s; the dashed lines mark the reduced volatility that followed. In Germany the muted cycle arrived later because of the volatility brought about by reunification at the start of the 1990s. In Japan it coincided with the shift to lower growth after its late 1980s financial bubble burst.

Figure 7.1 US GDP change, with volatility bands

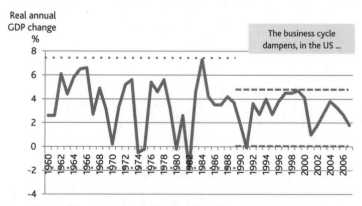

Source: Bureau of Economic Analysis, NIPA table 1.1.1. http://www.bea.gov/iTable/index_nipa. cfm

Figure 7.2 UK GDP change, with volatility bands

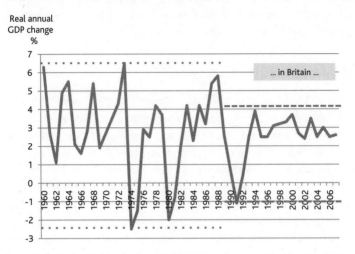

Source: Office for National Statistics, time series IHYP. http://www.ons.gov.uk/economy/grossdomesticproductgdp/timeseries/ihyp/qna

Figure 7.3 Japan GDP change, with volatility bands

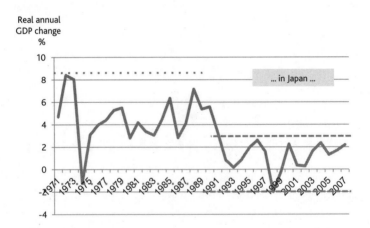

Source: OECD.Stat, GDP (output approach), SNA93 table. http://stats.oecd.org/Index.aspx?DatasetCode=SNA_TABLE1

Figure 7.4 Germany GDP change, with volatility bands

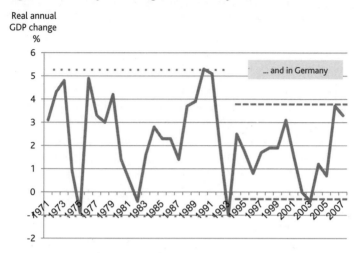

Source: OECD.Stat, GDP (output approach), SNA93 table. http://stats.oecd.org/Index.
aspx?DatasetCode=SNA_TABLE1

Outside Japan, many greeted this dampening of the business cycle as the arrival of a stable, more benign era. Describing this phenomenon in the US, James Stock and Mark Watson coined a phrase in the early 2000s that caught on: the 'Great Moderation'.[4] They attributed the change mostly to 'good luck' in avoiding particularly large shocks. The drop in volatility applied both to GDP and also to investment, consumption, employment, inflation and interest rates.

Soon after, Ben Bernanke popularised the term, a couple of years before becoming chair of the US Federal Reserve.[5] Recognising the lack of consensus on why things had changed, he saw the Great Moderation less as good luck and more as proof of good policy: in particular good monetary policy, and a sign of how well central bankers were managing the economy. Bernanke claimed that the low inflation achieved by central banks since the early 1980s had not only brought about the reduction in volatility, but also significant improvements in economic growth and productivity.

This perception reflected how monetary policymakers had moved from often acting to reinforce the business cycle to instead seeking to moderate it. Earlier central bankers would ease monetary policy when the economy needed stimulating, which sometimes encouraged inflation. They then raised interest rates to curb the inflation, often leading to a recessionary contraction in economic activity. The business cycle was emphasised.

Paul Volcker, the former Federal Reserve chairman, was praised for supposedly breaking from this approach with his aggressive use of monetary policy at the start of the 1980s. This saw the end of high US inflation, and its fall to low single-digit levels. The fact that Volcker's actions actually reinforced the depth of the 1980–81 recession was played down in this interpretation. Subsequent central bankers were following his success in helping to stabilise both inflation and GDP growth. Despite the popularity of Bernanke's argument and considerable research on the subject, mainstream agreement on the causes of the Great Moderation remains elusive.[6]

The 2008 financial crash injected greater economic turbulence again, but this was perceived to be temporary. Before long volatility fell back to pre-crash levels.[7] While the torpid recoveries everywhere became described as the 'new normal', and then the 'new mediocre', these are really different phrases for the Great Moderation, just at an even slower tempo of growth.

The atrophy of economic dynamism

A long period of more stable, modest growth can sound like a good thing. Who wants to live in an unsettled rollercoaster of an economy? But the massive downside of the Great Moderation is the absence of economic dynamism. A less volatile capitalism has also been a more static capitalism, with the creative as well as the destructive aspects of the business cycle subdued. An increasingly anaemic arena of production has accompanied the contained depression, with detrimental consequences for living standards.

The softening of the traditional business cycle was not the sign of a revived and stronger capitalism as assumed by the Great Moderation thesis. On the contrary, less creative destruction undermined the potential for a resumption of economic expansion. The shallower recessions of the early 1990s and 2000s illustrate this trend. They were less destructive and, therefore, less purifying. Business cycle experts Ricardo Caballero and

Mohamad Hammour were initially 'surprised' by this shift,[8] but the arrival of a less destructive form of capitalism is now well established.

The ebbing of creative destruction is not restricted to softer recessions; it is also evident in the lower pace of corporate turnover and specifically the fall in the rate at which businesses have been starting up. In the middle of the last century Schumpeter borrowed from Marx's concepts to come up with the helpful description that expanding capitalism operates through creative destruction.[9] The recent atrophy of this process is the distinctive characteristic of this depression, and accounts for its contained features including, notably, reduced business churn.

In the *Grundrisse* − the notebooks from which *Capital* was written − Marx wrote about 'the violent destruction of capital not by relations external to it, but rather as a condition of its self-preservation', and how through the 'annihilation of a great portion of capital [it] is violently reduced to the point where it can go on'.[10] The devaluation of existing wealth clears the way for the creation of new wealth. Marx stressed that it was often only the *value* of old capital assets that was destroyed when businesses went bankrupt, not their physical destruction. Some assets will be acquired by other stronger businesses at knockdown prices and put to better use.[11]

Schumpeter drew upon these themes within *Capital* in developing his own theses.[12] In the early 1940s Schumpeter wrote:

> The fundamental impulse that sets and keeps the capitalist engine in motion comes from the new consumers' goods, the new methods of production and transportation, the new markets. ... [The process] incessantly revolutionizes *from within*, incessantly destroying the old one, incessantly creating a new one. This process of Creative Destruction is the essential fact about capitalism.[13]

Capitalism needs to be changing and renovating itself continually to be successful and ensure social progress. Businesses and organisations that adopt new and improved processes, products and services grow, displacing those that don't.

Progress directly draws attention to what is novel. But for the new to thrive the old has to be displaced. Mariana Mazzucato has explained that each major new technology involves creative destruction. The steam engine, the railway, electricity, the car, the internet have all destroyed as much as they have created, and in doing so they have led to increased wealth overall.[14] This is the dynamic Schumpeter, and Marx before him, were underlining. The novelist John Steinbeck revealed this essential truth when pondering, 'I wonder why progress looks so much like destruction.'[15]

Following the value destruction of the inter-war depression – and before the physical devastation of war – the 1930s experienced a wave of capitalist creativity. Counterintuitively Alexander Field described this as the 'most technologically progressive decade of the century'. Against the backdrop of business closures and mass unemployment, technological and organisational innovations occurred across the American economy. Chemical engineering (including petrochemicals and synthetic rubber), aeronautics, electrical machinery and equipment, electric power generation and distribution, transport, communication, and civil and structural engineering were among the areas that advanced.[16]

Robert Gordon attributes the rapid growth in productivity in the middle of the 20th century to the devastating effects of the Great Depression and the Second World War. The resulting scale of economic reorganisation ensured that the inventions of the second industrial revolution, particularly electric motors and assembly-line methods, boosted productivity years earlier than might have otherwise occurred.[17]

Creative destruction drives social productivity

Productivity improvement depends upon economic transformation as well as technological innovation. As discussed earlier in Chapter Two, it results from changes within businesses and also from resources flowing between them. Technological advances are introduced either through the internal restructuring of businesses or by the external restructuring brought about through business churn and the disappearance and creation of new sectors and industries. Factors of production – jobs and capital – shift from lower value-adding activities into higher value-adding ones.[18] In this way the innovations that drive up productivity diffuse across the economy.

This reallocation of resources is the prime mechanism by which creative destruction promotes productivity. Ian Hathaway and Robert Litan described the normal non-recessionary turnover in businesses with new replacing old as necessarily a destructive and disruptive process.[19] Caballero and Hammour explained how production units that incorporate the newest techniques and requirements must be continuously created, and outdated units destroyed.[20]

Several studies suggest that previously a substantial share of productivity growth, about a half,[21] has been accounted for by resource reallocation, rather than by in-firm innovation. In some American sectors like retail the movement of resources between businesses has been much more important than productivity gains within existing firms or establishments.[22] In other sectors such as manufacturing the contributions to productivity growth have been more evenly shared across three sources: within-firm productivity; the arrival of new higher productivity firms; and the reallocation of resources to new plants of existing firms.[23]

Analysis conducted for the Bank of England found the relative contribution of the 'between' and the 'within' components of productivity growth are similar in Britain. Productivity improvements within firms contributed just over 40% to aggregate productivity growth. Meanwhile the movement of people between existing firms contributed around 25%, with the net entry of firms adding the remaining third.[24] Hence the reallocation of resources between companies – a manifestation of creative destruction – has previously contributed more than half of the United Kingdom's productivity growth.[25]

Given this substantial contribution, setting up new businesses plays an important role for productivity gain, a point emphasised by labour market economist John Haltiwanger.[26] Although bigger businesses are on average more productive than smaller ones, Haltiwanger reported that some young firms can be more productive as well as faster growing than the incumbents, and therefore contribute substantially to aggregate productivity across the economy. Since they are not constrained by established technologies tied up in existing capital, they can often adopt new, more productive innovations more rapidly than their older counterparts.

Startups also encourage transformative innovation elsewhere, triggering changes within existing businesses to keep up with the new competitors. Shigeru Fujita noted how the invention of a superior technology by a new entrant could encourage incumbent firms to improve their own technologies, creating different jobs for their workers.[27]

The role that new firms play directly in the churning of businesses combined with this restructuring stimulated within existing firms is essential for economic renewal. New businesses operate as the purest vehicles of creative destruction. Haltiwanger concluded they were 'vital to our productivity growth'.[28] Future prosperity is therefore based less on existing businesses and jobs than on the new ones to be created.

An efficient process of moving scarce resources is particularly important for the growth of these firms. Startups need to achieve scale as quickly as possible to cover the fixed costs of entry and begin generating surpluses. A healthy creative destruction process facilitates the experimentation and growth that underpins success, and firm exit in the event of failure.[29]

The paramount economic problem today is that this process has become tempered: the creative destructive tendencies have become muted. As OECD researchers explained, without creative destruction, perpetuating the existing allocation of resources adversely affects productivity levels by blunting the diffusion of innovation.[30] When too many old firms are able to survive, social productivity is impaired. The slower pace of business turnover has compounded the constraints on investment arising from low profitability. A more static business setup has embedded lethargic investment.

The decline in business and job turnover

While the disappearance of old businesses and jobs creates personal insecurity and hardship, society should focus more on what is happening to the business and job creation that can replace them. These could provide decent employment and enhance productivity. In the US there has been a steady decline in business churn since the late 1970s, evidenced starkly in lower levels of business entry. The firm entry rate, measured as firms less than one year old as a share of all firms, fell by nearly half from 15% to 8% between 1978 and 2011.[31] Hathaway and Litan were worried about the implications for growth because they appreciated that in the past these new firms had accounted for a disproportionate share of disruptive and strongly productivity-enhancing innovations.[32]

OECD analysis of business churn across the Western world shows a similar decline in dynamism as expressed in the rate of businesses setting up. The share of startups within all firms has been steadily decreasing across most countries, even before the financial crash disruptions. Unsurprisingly, it found that the post-crash recession had an additional negative impact on startup rates.[33]

Britain experienced a fall of a quarter in both business deaths and business births between the early 1980s and the years leading up to the financial crash. Business deaths fell from about 13% of active firms to about 10%, while births decelerated from about 16% to 12%.[34] Rates of corporate failure and startups remained low, even during recessions.[35] This offers a better picture of the decay in business dynamism than the frequent eulogies to the strength of 'startup Britain'.[36]

Since the financial crash these trends have been reinforced. Alina Barnett, Adrian Chiu, Jeremy Franklin and María Sebastiá-Barriel concluded for the Bank of England that around one-third of the UK productivity slowdown in 2008-11 compared to the half-decade before the crash was due to the slower reallocation of resources between firms. This covered the movement of labour between firms, as well as the birth and death of companies.[37] Parallel research has noted a big increase, starting in the mid-2000s and accelerating with the crash, in the variation or dispersion of productivity across British firms and sectors. The fact that more low productivity firms remain in operation is another symptom of declines in creative destruction and in the pace of resource allocation.[38]

The decay in economic dynamism in the advanced economies is also expressed by the reduced turnover in jobs. With fewer businesses closing and opening, there is less scope for finding new jobs when people leave their existing ones, whether voluntarily or forced by redundancy. The slowing rate of new business creation means more people are working in older firms. Firms no more than five years old accounted for a fifth of employment in 1982, a seventh in 2000, and just over a tenth in 2011.[39]

Transformative investments that embody innovation are a source of job destruction in existing businesses and a source of job creation in new ones. Less investment means less job turnover. While there are more ICT jobs than people would have foreseen half a century ago, most other employment would seem pretty familiar. The other things that might surprise are the higher number of finance-related jobs, and – more dispiriting – the greater proportion of lower skill and lower paying ones.

It is not just how many, or what type of jobs there are compared to an earlier time that are indicative of an economy's loss of vigour. Equally telling is what has been happening *during* the intervening period; how much and what type of change has been going on. The pace of adjustment within the labour market is revealing of the existence of capitalism's renovating creative destructive tendencies and of their more recent curbing. The relative absence of transformation in employment parallels the declining trend in the pace both of job destruction and also of job creation.[40] Figure 7.5 illustrates that the US has been exhibiting a slowdown in both areas.

As was to be expected, job losses peaked following the recession of the early 2000s – though this was so mild that the US failed to meet the conventional definition for recession – and again, following the 2008 crash. It is more striking that the cyclical peaks and troughs in job losses have both been trending downwards. Given the relative depth of the two recessions, the lower rate of job loss after the biggest financial crisis since the 1930s than in the mild recession after the dot.com bubble burst demonstrates the tendency towards less destructiveness.

Analysis of the impact of the post-2007 US recession by Haltiwanger, working with Lucia Foster and Cheryl Grim, confirmed that the intensity of job reallocation declined

Figure 7.5 US private sector gross job gains and losses as shares of employment

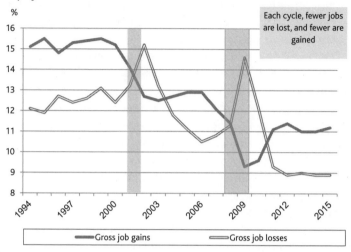

Notes: Shaded areas represent National Bureau of Economic Research defined recession periods (March 2001 to November 2001; December 2007 to June 2009). Data points are annual, March to March.
Source: Bureau of Labor Statistics, Business Employment Dynamics (BED) database. http://www.bls.gov/web/cewbd/anntab2_1.txt

compared to previous recessions. Less cleansing occurred despite the disruption of the crash. In particular, more of the net job reduction after 2008 was due to especially anaemic job creation rather than to what used to be the recessionary norm, a jump in job destruction. Existing jobs were more likely to be retained while there were many fewer jobs from startups. They also found that the reallocation of work that did occur was less productivity-enhancing than in prior recessions.[41]

As revealing about the suppression of creative destruction is the slowing pace of job losses in periods of relative expansion. From annual job losses of over 12% in the late 1990s the pace fell below 11% in the mid-2000s, and reduced further to 9% after 2011. There is less job destruction and churn across the business cycle, in recessions and between them.

In contrast to most other measures of economic decay, which show a secular deterioration, the rate of job losses has been moderating. With a more anaemic production machine, one might expect more, rather than fewer, job cuts. The counterintuitive outcome highlights how unusual is the latest period of capitalist decay: the dampening of destructiveness becoming expressed as a more immobile economy.

The practical consequence has been the increasing preservation of existing jobs, although these can be of sub-par productivity levels. This applies both to the shrinking businesses that remain open, as well as to the reduced employment lost from the smaller number of businesses winding up.[42] Fewer jobs have disappeared in business contractions and, especially, in business closures as more low value-adding businesses have managed to keep going, even under recessionary conditions. This is consistent with the rise of a zombified economy where weaker businesses survive that would have shut down in earlier times.

The other side of this trend has been slowing job creation. In the 1990s expansion in annual job creation averaged about 15% of the workforce, falling to 13% in the 2000s, and to about 11% since the financial crash. This means that about one in six jobs was newly created in the 1990s, falling to one in nine more recently. Since 2000 job creation from new businesses has been especially poor.

There is an exception to the economy-wide feature of falling job reallocation that proves the rule. Consistent with the ICT boom in the 1990s, job turnover rates unusually rose then in certain high-tech industries, before reversing during the 2000s: the pace of job change fell substantially to rejoin the trend in other industries.[43] Steven Davis, researching with Haltiwanger, reported that the high-tech sector experienced a large decline in startups and fast-growing young firms after 2000, reversing the earlier pattern.[44]

Employment growth by decade also expresses the trend towards stagnation. US employment grew by 26% in the 1970s, falling to 20% growth in the 1980s, 15% in the 1990s and only 2% between 2000 and 2010. The consultants McKinsey concluded that the US job creation machine is not functioning as it has in the past.

They highlighted that from 1945 until the 1980s, there had been a tight link between recovery in economic output and recovery in employment. About six months after GDP returned to its pre-recession high, employment would follow. That pattern ended after 1991, when it took 15 months after the GDP peak for employment to return to pre-recession levels. After the 2001 recession, the time was 39 months.[45] After the financial crash, it took until September 2014 for employment to reach its pre-recession high – 45 months after GDP recovered to its pre-recession level in December 2010. This was a half-year longer than in the early 2000s, and over three years longer than before the 1990s.[46]

With each successive recovery since the 1990s, the structural factors hindering job creation have become more apparent.[47] Job recoveries have been correspondingly slower, resulting in the frequent characterisation of recoveries since the 1990s as jobless ones.

Data on the US compiled differently by the US Census Bureau, going back to the start of the depression, show the same trend of declining rates of job reallocation (see Figure 7.6). While both trend creation and trend destruction of jobs have declined, the former has fallen faster. The decay of job creation has been the dominant force in explaining the slowing pace of

Figure 7.6 US job destruction and creation as share of employment

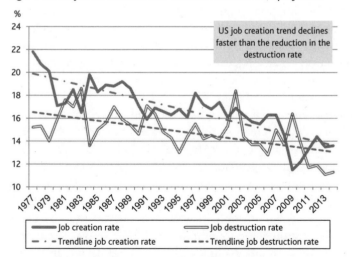

Source: US Census Bureau, Business Dynamics Statistics. http://www.census.gov/ces/dataproducts/bds/data_estab.html

employment growth, with a decline of almost one-third between 1977 and 2005.[48]

In the post-2000 period compared to the 1980s, job destruction was almost a tenth lower. Meanwhile job creation from startups was down by a quarter, and net employment growth was down by more than a half. While relatively more old jobs were being retained, many fewer jobs were being created.[49]

This decay in job reallocation can also be expressed in the way it affects individuals. The overall level of worker turnover, sometimes called *worker* reallocation to distinguish it from job reallocation, adds the everyday churn process of the voluntary and involuntary hiring, quitting and firing of people, *unrelated* to whether a workplace is expanding or contracting. US worker turnover fell sharply from 33.5% of employment per quarter in 1999 to 24.1% in 2010, before rebounding slightly.[50]

For the unemployed, this development increases the risk of long jobless spells. For the employed, it hampers their ability to switch employers so as to move up the job ladder, change careers, or satisfy new locational needs.[51] The less dynamic and the more clogged up the economy, the less opportunity there is for people to find decent jobs, especially young people seeking to enter the workforce for the first time.

For Britain, data on job creation and destruction is still limited compared to that available for the US.[52] However, with the caveat that this covers only a short period, analysis undertaken by Alexander Hijzen, Richard Upward and Peter Wright reveals the same tendency as in the US of slowdown in both job destruction and creation[53] (see Figure 7.7).

Between the late 1990s and the mid-2000s the trend rate of British job creation fell by about one-tenth, from 16% to 14.5% of employment. It is striking that the trend in job creation is downward at all over this period since the latter part was supposedly one of economic expansion. As in the US, the decline in the trend of job creation has fallen a little faster than the decline in job destruction. In Britain too, the decay of job creation is the more influential force on weakening net employment trends. As in the US, the trend decline in British job creation is more evident for new firms than existing ones.

Figure 7.7 UK job destruction and creation as share of employment

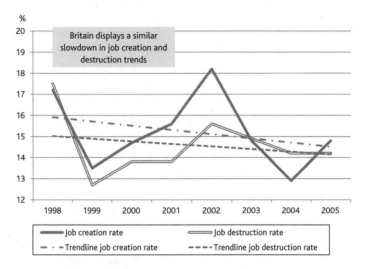

Source: Office for National Statistics Inter-Departmental Business Register, Business Structure Database, cited in Hijzen, Upward, and Wright, 2010

British experience also parallels the American in the markedly nondestructive consequences of the financial crash. Counterintuitively, researchers Bob Butcher and Matt Bursnall found that despite the onset of a particularly deep and long recession after the financial crash, gross job losses did *not* increase between the first half of their study period – the 2004 to 2007 expansion – and the second – the 2008 to 2011 slowdown. In both these four-year periods the average annual jobs lost in businesses that closed down was the same, at 2.2 million, and the numbers lost in contracting businesses only increased marginally from 1.5 to 1.6 million. This relatively stable level of job destruction is significant given the collapse in economic activity following the financial crash.

In fact, they concluded that the main labour market difference from 2008 was not an increase in job losses but was the *reduction in job creation* from new workplaces of about 400,000 a year, down from 2.2 million to 1.8 million per year.[54] The fall in employment after the crash was not therefore primarily the result of many more people losing their jobs, but of lower job creation, especially in new workplaces. The employment problem was not the scale of recessionary destruction but the loss of private sector dynamism.

In both Britain and the US this decay in job creation helps to explain a pronounced labour market feature of the Long Depression: youth unemployment has been rising much faster than general unemployment. Insufficient new jobs becoming available is bound to disproportionately affect those entering the workforce. This is part of a wider phenomenon across the advanced economies. While general unemployment in the developed countries rose from 5.8% to 8.6% between 2007 and 2013, the increase for young people was a much bigger jump from 12.5% to 18.3%.[55]

And young people who do find work are more likely to be involved in 'non-standard' jobs, including temporary employment and part-time work. Evidence shows that a significant part of this increase is involuntary rather than by choice.[56] The incapacity of the Western economies to create any, or meaningful employment for the generation entering the labour market bodes ill for the future. Young people remaining unemployed or entering into insecure, 'precarious' and low-skilled jobs as their first experience of work are likely to be trapped in these conditions. This generational dimension illustrates sharply the human impact of the tendency to decay.

EIGHT

The zombie economy

Although economic creativity is invariably accompanied by the displacement and destruction of the existing, capitalism's destructive tendencies do not automatically revamp the productive machine. Despite what free market advocates claim, the market system will not inevitably generate innovation and good jobs if it is freed from the constraints of the past. The 'market' is meaningless as a force without people and the relationships between them. The creation of a more productive, healthier economy is always an active, collaborative human-led process.

The destructive recessions of the early 1980s illustrate that renewal cannot be assumed. Closures accelerated across many workplaces, especially in heavy industries like steelmaking and shipbuilding, and in areas of manufacturing like cars and consumer appliances. Described as deindustrialisation, 'hollowing out' is more accurate: capitalism in depression revealed its dearth of creativity. Few high productivity businesses and jobs arose to take the place of those that had closed down, confirming that there is nothing spontaneous about creativity following destruction. Being forced to move workplace is never welcome to people, but it is qualitatively worse when inferior, or no, alternative jobs are available.

Replacement employment could have come from within those existing industries, or from new sectors and industries setting up, or, what would have been best, from a combination of the two. The absence of such reindustrialisation was a much bigger problem than 'deindustrialisation'. The 'market' proved unable then to come up with effective solutions to depression.

Even the destruction phase is not inevitable either. Though not a sufficient condition for the creation of newer and better sectors and jobs, the destruction of the old is necessary. With less destructiveness, society is held back by a plethora of less productive activities. The least productive firms keep going, tying up resources and people. Outdated capital assets remain in operation instead of either having their values written off, or the best bits bought and absorbed by other companies.

The flow of resources into new productive areas is restricted. Some economists call this a 'problem of misallocation', but the challenge is much bigger than a technical one of reallocation. Resources are curtailed for potentially higher productivity firms. Their failure to go to where they can be better used impairs an economy's productive potential.[1] Overall productivity growth suffers because the long surviving tail of low productivity firms suppresses the average, and also holds back startups and the restructuring of existing firms.[2] Fewer transforming investments take place.

Less creative destruction

The muting of capitalism's creative destructive tendencies has partly been a spontaneous expression of the moribund features of this remarkably protracted depression. This emphasises that depressions are not periods of permanent collapse and cascading destructiveness. It is one-sided to expect recessions to become more frequent, sharper and more destructive, opening the way for renewal. In practice, the weaker dynamic of investment also restrains the recoveries, and the rate of business change.

This direct effect is complemented by a second order factor of depression. Without a strong investment-led recovery the buildup of pressures precipitating the next recession are also more limited. Over time this tames the oscillations of the business cycle. Consequently the purifying effects of the boom–bust cycle are eroded. Depressions can depress volatility as well as depressing job creation.

This self-reinforcing relationship between lacklustre investment and a moderated business cycle begs the key question: why has this depression been more contained and gone on so much longer than its predecessor between the wars? The main distinction is that the apparatus of state has been playing a more interventionist role this time, and with a particular orientation. This change in the state's focus also explains why destruction, not just creativity, has been unusually tempered by the circumstances of the Long Depression.

The presumption underlying *normal* resource allocation is that market forces induce less efficient firms to restructure their operations or quit, making more resources available to the most efficient firms.[3] This textbook functioning of capitalism has always been hindered in many ways, including by labour and product regulations, by bankruptcy laws, as well as by public subsidies and other state policies. When such practices supporting the status quo proliferate, as has been the case in recent decades, too many of the less efficient firms remain in operation, stunting investment and productivity.

The more subdued character of both destructiveness and creativity during the Long Depression extends an epochal trend. In presenting creative destruction as the 'essential fact', Schumpeter referred to capitalism in an earlier, purer form. As leading capitalist nations matured from the late 19th and early 20th centuries, their essential workings began to become sclerotic. Ageing capitalism lost both its progressive universalising effects and also its spontaneous ways. Creative destruction began to lose its own spontaneity and relied more on state actions to work effectively.

That is evidenced in the rise of state economic intervention during the 1930s and 1940s to help bring about that dramatic creative destructive period of economic renewal. This has a different focus than the standard narrative about the state's role then. The hindsight association of the early part of the 1930s slump with a decisive plan for recovery symbolised by US President Franklin Delano Roosevelt's New Deal is misleading.

Professor Barry Eichengreen has appropriately dismissed the view advanced by many latter-day Keynesians that 'FDR' saved US capitalism from crisis by his commitment to large-scale fiscal stimulus. In contrast to this myth, Eichengreen explains that the president's goal after his first election in 1933 was to 'balance the budget immediately, completely, and, if necessary, on the backs of his supporters'.[4] At that early stage of the depression counter-crisis mechanisms were still in their infancy and were applied reluctantly and haphazardly. Recall too that John Maynard Keynes' classic theorisation for state economic intervention, *The General Theory of Employment, Interest and Money* was only published in 1936.

The pragmatic bouts of increased state spending that occurred in the 1930s had only a limited effect in stimulating economic activity. They brought some growth in output and created some temporary jobs but they strikingly failed to revive productivity or bring about economic renewal.[5] This required something much more transformative.

State economic policies started to cohere from the latter half of the 1930s. Keynes' ideas did begin to gain greater resonance among economists during and after the Second World War, paralleling the adoption of more consistent state economic interventionism by the institutions of the leading warring countries. The economic consequences – in general *unintended*, as they arose primarily from the ardent pursuit of military goals – accelerated the process of creative destruction, clearing out old capital, and paving the way for the post-war boom.

The greater reliance of creative destruction on the state's activism applies also to the partial economic cleansings of the 1970s and early 1980s. The state helped drive these business cycles, not least in pushing up interest rates to catalyse the 1980–81 recessions – Volcker's action as head of the US central bank.

In contrast, the toning down of this shakeup type of state intervention and its replacement by its opposite – as governments seek primarily to stabilise, not energise, economic affairs – has entrenched today's contained form of depression. Through the deployment of a range of state counter-crisis mechanisms, the worst effects of the depression have been successfully ameliorated.

It has been possible most of the time even to maintain an air of economic prosperity, resulting in the appearance of the Great Moderation. With direct and indirect state support, corporations have been better able to sustain themselves, and more than a few have expanded. They have had less need to embark on risky and disruptive rounds of restructuring; it has been easier for them to remain the same than to change. Businesses have been able to rely more on demand for their goods or services being sustained by debt-funded purchases by consumers or other businesses, or directly by government spending and procurement activities.

Corporate cash flows have held up. Notwithstanding the lacklustre state of the economic fundamentals of productivity and operational profitability, business survival has been less of an immediate challenge. The other side of this benign appearance is the gradual ossification of the economy.

The rise of the zombie economy

Throughout the Long Depression Western state institutions have been responding to economic malaise with greater consistency and scope than in the 1930s. But not only has the level of state activity been greater than ever before, since the 1980s it has also gravitated to a novel form qualitatively different from how it had performed previously. While the responses from the various national states have failed to address the root causes of productive decay, they have to varying extents been instrumental in modifying the character of this depression, perpetuating it in its unusually contained form.

Modern states used to balance two economic roles: promoting growth and maintaining stability. In earlier times, some policies expanding growth were seen as consistent with stabilisation, because they were designed to bring actual growth into line with potential growth. However, many pro-growth policies, especially since the Second World War, were more than this. They sought to speed up the growth of potential output by enhancing the productivity of labour. If boosting productivity turned out to be a bit disruptive and destabilising for a time, so be it. These earlier policies for faster growth put the future above the present.[6] The goal of growth often took precedence over short-term stability.

From the end of the boom, and increasingly from the latter part of the 1980s, state institutions have favoured the other aspect of this duality: the stabilisation of capitalism. The return of the economic crisis in the early 1970s brought government attempts to mitigate the effects of the economic slowdown. As the underlying weakness persisted, efforts to *counter* the crisis gave way to its *containment* and the goal of economic stabilisation.

This pro-stability inclination was in accord with the broader spread of a culture of fear and anxiety. A social preoccupation with safety and stability reflected an outlook of lowered expectations.[7] When change is seen as more likely to make matters worse than better, the goal of keeping things as they are becomes attractive. Reflecting these anxieties, the state has become a *conservator state*, working to preserve and protect the current state of economic affairs, while committing less effort, and funding, to the promotion of long-term growth.

The political elites still talk about economic growth but it has become an increasingly hollow commitment. In practice, efforts at stabilisation have been to the detriment of growth, even if that has usually been unintentional. Gordon Brown famously pledged that his economic policies were geared not to expand growth, but to prevent Britain returning to the boom and bust of the past. He told the British Chamber of Commerce national conference in 2000 that his 'vision was of a Britain where there is not stop-go and boom-bust but economic stability'.[8] Since he spoke, Britain, and other mature economies, have experienced an extended period of lethargic growth, unprecedented in modern times – interrupted by a rather destabilising financial crash.

Symbolic of this shift in economic policy priorities are the British Queen's speeches given at the start of each parliamentary session. These are written by the government of the day – not by the monarch herself – and provide a linguistic indication of official economic thinking. In 1995 the economic policy part of the speech opened with a pledge to 'support economic growth and rising employment'.[9] No reference was made to stability in the opening commitment. In fact, 'economic stability' did not feature anywhere in her speech.

Ten years later in 2005 the opening pledge began with 'stability', though it still gave parallel prominence to economic growth: the commitment then was to 'pursue economic policies which entrench stability and promote long-term growth'.[10] Ten years further on in 2015, 'economic growth' had been dropped from the opening sentence. The commitment had become one to 'provide economic stability and security'.[11] Economic growth did not feature in the speech, though nebulous measures to raise 'productive potential' did. Over a period of 20 years, growth has moved from centre stage to become an add-on, while the goal of 'economic stability' has come from an unstated assumption to make top billing.

The state in the advanced economies has evolved an array of mechanisms to accomplish this stabilisation goal by supporting both the economy in general and also its current businesses. Prominent are easier monetary policies that have reinforced the stabilising impact of financialisation. Lower real interest rates underpinned and lubricated the workings of both the financial and also the productive parts of the economy. These underwrote the expansion of private debt – both business and personal – which has been so important to sustaining the economy through the 1990s and 2000s.

The state has also supported the expansion of the financial sector, which has provided all those loans. This included the UK's 1986 Big Bang reforms to a host of regulatory changes, including the eventual full repeal in 1999 of the US Glass-Steagall Act – part of the 1933 US Banking Act which had separated investment banks from commercial banks. As Costas Lapavitsas summarised: financialisation would have been unthinkable without the systematic intervention of the state in the economy. In his view there is little doubt that central banks have been pivotal to state intervention under conditions of financialised capitalism.[12]

The loosening of monetary policy has also operated as a counter-crisis measure when the destabilising features of financialisation occasionally blow up. When the financial markets have taken a big hit and financial prices plummeted, interest rates have been cut and monetary liquidity added in an effort to restore stability. The first major instance occurred shortly after Alan Greenspan became chair of the US Federal Reserve when he lowered interest rates following the stock market crash of October 1987.

The palliative deployment of interest rate cuts continued and was soon adopted by other Western central banks. First, with the US Savings and Loan crisis that recurred in the early 1990s, then the Mexican peso crisis of 1994, the Asian financial crisis of 1997-98, the Russian government debt default in summer

1998 and the subsequent collapse of the ironically named Long-Term Capital Management hedge fund, the 2000 burst of the internet bubble, and the 9/11 attacks. From the early stages of the financial crisis in the late 2000s we have had prolonged historically low levels of interest rates. 'Unconventional' quantitative easing (QE) programmes adopted in the US, Britain, Japan and the eurozone have supplemented the stabilising effects of the low cost of borrowing, by pumping money directly into the economy.

Alongside these monetary mechanisms the state has promoted many other business support measures. These include public-private partnerships, the regulatory and other assistance provided to privatised industries, as well as public procurement policies. The latter provide solid demand for goods and services, not least for the apparently more dynamic parts of the economy such as ICT, pharmaceuticals and aerospace. Legislative changes too have often favoured company survival: for example, curbing the resort to bankruptcy. Even public initiatives with other headline objectives have sometimes unintentionally helped business, such as in-work welfare benefits subsidising employers through the reduced cost of payroll.

On occasions commercial banks have been encouraged to roll over shaky loans and provide other financial support to their ailing corporate customers. With the endorsement of public authorities, Japanese banks took such practices to new heights during their 'lost decades' starting in the 1990s.[13]

State policy measures generally favour existing companies at the expense of the new firms that could help drive productivity higher.[14] Regulations usually favour current businesses over new ones. Product market regulations tend to help incumbents and impede firm entry.[15] Environmental regulations also often side with established businesses.[16] Ironically, even some pro-innovation policies can work to the disadvantage of startups. Since many young innovative firms typically make losses in their early years they do not benefit from the R&D tax incentive programmes that help established companies which have profits to offset.[17]

Governments have brought about a corporate dependency that is as debilitating for the economy as the welfare dependency they have created for individuals.[18] The state and the market economy are now so thoroughly integrated it is impossible to disentangle them. The result of this reorientation in state economic intervention is the development of a zombie economy: an economy dead in productive dynamism that is being propped up to ensure the semblance of life. This interferes with the process of creative destruction with the result that new sources of growth are stifled and aggregate productivity suppressed. Both the within and the between sources of improved business productivity are curtailed. The state has therefore become a barrier to, not a driver towards the necessary restructuring of production.

Contemporary forms of state intervention impede the pressures towards business change that were already dampened by the depression. Stabilisation policies are an extra barrier to value being released from productively backward firms. As Chris Watling, chief market strategist at Longview Economics remarked, QE has 'held back the long-term health of the economy as we have not seen the normal pattern of business deaths that is part of the creative destruction process'.[19] The effect of these official conservation efforts has been to blunt further the enfeebled tendencies towards creative destruction.

This brings an accumulation of zombie businesses that are dead in their capacity to expand value but which keep going artificially with the direct or indirect assistance of the state. Rather than go bankrupt as they soon would if reliant only on their independent means in normal conditions, they continue to operate, employ people and produce things. Keeping the less productive producers afloat means they are able to sell their goods and services at market prices despite making below average profits or losses at these prices. These get in the way of more productive businesses.

In Britain after the 2008 crash a higher proportion of businesses than usual were unprofitable and making losses, but fewer went bust. As the Bank of England's Ben Broadbent described, firms are being kept in business, and retaining their employees, despite making relatively low returns.[20] The headline figure of company liquidations remained lower in the recession following the financial crash than it had been in the early 1990s recession, despite the 6% GDP collapse being about three times as deep.

The annual rate of company liquidations was 17,000 from 2009 to 2012, lower than the 21,000 experienced from 1991 to 1994. This was also not much of an increase on the average from the mid-1990s to the mid-2000s of 14,000, contradicting any notion that this was an especially destructive recession.[21] The absence of a leap in business failures occurred despite a post-crash jump in the number of loss-making firms from about a quarter of businesses in the 1990s to more than a third since the crash.[22] More businesses were losing money but fewer were closing down.

This higher survival rate of unprofitable firms after the crash was primarily due to the record low level of interest rates, which has helped keep down corporate borrowing costs, complemented by the extension of other government support schemes. In addition, bank 'forbearance' on business debts helped reduce company failures.[23] Forbearance is the practice of giving material support to business customers who are struggling to meet their debt obligations rather than letting them go bankrupt.[24] Joao Pessoa and Van Reenen suggested that political pressures were exerted, speculating that the British government promoted forbearance to avoid small business closures and rising unemployment.[25]

In Britain other explicit official support came from the tax office's time-to-pay scheme. The number of companies it gave extra time to pay their Value Added Tax (VAT) – the main UK sales tax – peaked at 118,000 in 2009, representing around 5% of VAT-registered businesses.[26] Such recession-time relief measures are always welcome since businesses and employees are able to remain working as a result. However, when they are part of a broader and persisting package of state expedients that sustain a zombified economy, productivity and employment both eventually suffer.

A Bank of England review of bank forbearance activities estimated productivity among small and medium businesses being helped was 40% below the norm. Such forbearance doesn't help the longer-term prospects of these lower productivity operations, and is bad for the economy overall. The suppression of productivity levels reinforces the slow growth environment that is a further deterrent to innovative investments by new and existing businesses. Illustrating this, in Britain firm entry rates have fallen most in industries with the highest levels of bank forbearance that were helping to keep unprofitable businesses afloat.[27]

Zombification is more serious than the proliferation of zombie businesses. It fosters a broader zombie economy that is an impediment to economic restructuring. State measures to boost economic output artificially and maintain higher employment levels obscure the urgency for restructuring, and also block the potential allocation of resources to more productive ends. Capital has become less 'mobile', to use the term applied by Broadbent to describe the British business environment.[28]

Moderately profitable businesses are also assisted to cope. They continue to operate commercially, though innovation investment remains unappealing for them, and even replacement investment is put off as long as possible. Most importantly for future economic prospects, the stronger businesses with access to funds – internally or borrowed – are held back by zombification too. Although better able to afford the writeoffs that come with major transformative investments, the lacklustre economic conditions can't provide the revenue growth needed to make investments sufficiently profitable.

Accepting more dependency on state intervention to cope with sluggish economic conditions becomes the default position for individual business. This takes over from engaging in the risk and disruption involved in carrying out their own technological revolutions. Better to prosper in an environment of silent corporate dependency on the state, than risk all on a new entrepreneurial venture.

Individual businesses and their workforces may enjoy the immediate benefit of stability and continuity, but over the longer term the economy and all the people who rely on that economy for their livelihood and incomes will suffer. A zombie economy becomes a black hole that sucks in and dampens all activity, and frustrates creative impulses. It represents a 'trap', as Stephen King called it, reducing the 'profitability and income' of more efficient companies so that the growth rate of the economy inevitably atrophies.[29]

It is often claimed that the modern state does a lot to make life *difficult* for businesses, especially through too much controlling regulation. This is made worse by the incessant regulatory tweaking which forever complicates business life and becomes an extra deterrent to a long-term business perspective. However, the 'opposite' less noticed aspect of conservator state activity is more significant. Making it *easier* for particular businesses and for the economy as a whole to cope with the effects of the depression puts a block on economic renewal. Ironically it is not the anti-market but the pro-business orientation of state intervention that is the bigger barrier to economic renaissance. By acting to save what exists, contemporary state interventions have increasingly had the consequence of preserving economies that are essentially stagnant.

The Japanese experience during its 'lost decades' illustrates that the rise of zombie businesses is associated with falling levels of restructuring. Investment and employment growth for healthy 'non-zombie' firms there fell as the percentage of zombies in their industrial sector rose. Zombification depressed business investment by between 4% and 36% per year, depending on the sector. In those with the most zombie firms, job creation was especially weak, while those where zombies became more important had the worst productivity growth.[30]

The distortions identified in Japan included depressing market prices for their products, raising market wages by hanging on to the workers whose productivity at their current firms declined, and, more generally, 'congesting' the markets where they operated. Caballero, in conjunction with Takeo Hoshi and Anil Kashyap, explained how the normal competitive outcome whereby the zombies would shed workers and lose market share was thwarted. The resulting artificial oversupply that lowered prices and raised wages reduced the profits and collateral that new and more productive firms could generate, thereby discouraging their entry and investment.

The congestion caused by the zombies put off the implementation of more productive projects and the entry of more productive firms.[31] The existing perceived risks of business investment and expansion were exacerbated. The artificial maintenance of oversupply made it more difficult both for the stronger incumbent businesses and for new ones to adopt more advanced production methods. Markets crowded by zombies will limit the scope for other businesses to sell enough to build up the financial resources that can allow them to innovate and expand in the future.

The new stabilising form of state intervention has created a double dilemma for the prospects of restoring social progress. First, the actions of the conservator state have been effective in muddling through many of the day-to-day difficulties arising from production's decay. But for as long as the sources of decay are unresolved, it festers and deepens. The shelving of the underlying problems does not make them go away. They will return and reappear in everyday life, most likely in larger episodes of turmoil and hardship.

Second, the conservator state is shunning a potential role as the *collective actor* necessary for bringing about the economy's restructuring. The objective barriers to restoring the material basis for prosperity cannot be overturned by market forces alone. This can only come about as a collaborative social activity; individual piecemeal efforts soon get dissipated. Market forces do not have the self-healing powers attributed to them by free market ideology. Some type of collective institution will have to facilitate restructuring by allowing and even encouraging the old parts of the economy to go, while sponsoring the development of the new higher productivity replacements.

Far from pursuing such a transforming economic policy, the governing elites have instead displayed complacency and evasiveness in the face of depression. While a seemingly easier position to take, it is one with enormously retrograde consequences for economic and social progress. The institutions of state have engaged in a style of intervention that is diametrically opposed to the goal of economic renaissance, perpetuating the Long Depression.

Unintended outcomes

The state's stabilisation actions aren't deliberate, calculated policies to embed a zombie economy, but that's their effect. Governments are mostly just attempting to keep the economy on an even keel. Often measures are stumbled upon to meet an immediate challenge, and then are maintained, or become permanent ways of operating. Zombification is being promoted unintentionally.

Take ultra-low interest rates, introduced as an exceptional step. As Andrew Haldane, then the Bank of England chief economist noted, the stickiness in interest rates at these levels has surprised both policymakers and financial markets. After they hit their floor in response to financial turmoil, market data implied official rates were expected to unstick in 6 months in the US, in 10 months in the UK, in 13 months in Japan, and in 14 months in the euro area. But in the middle of 2015 they still remained stuck: in Japan for over 20 years and in the US, the UK and the eurozone for over 6 years.[32]

Similarly, the QE that was introduced as an emergency measure in the aftermath of the financial crash has endured much longer than anticipated. Nearly seven years later it was either still being expanded – in Japan and the eurozone – or had not yet begun to be reversed - in the US and Britain. In an emergency, calling the fire brigade is appropriate. But if the fire brigade is still at the scene many years later, this is a sign of futile desperation. Talk of recovery is bogus when all economic enterprise has been so dependent on artificial liquidity.

Overall the impact of the various pro-stability measures has been to exacerbate the atrophy of production. The Caballero, Hoshi and Kashyap study of Japan's zombie economy concluded appropriately that there has been more than a simple credit crunch story at work during its depression.[33] The same is true for the rest of the mature economies. Explaining the unprecedentedly sluggish recoveries since 2009 as due to dislocation of the financial markets misses the deeper causes.

The explicit stagnation features since the crash represent more directly than before the moribund nature of capitalism. The further tragedy is that the crash precipitated more intense state interventions that have reinforced the zombie economy. The objective constraints arising from previous, now outmoded, capital investments are perpetuated. Lethargy is brought to the fore. As a result more people are recognising that economic life in the advanced industrial world is a lot tougher than it seemed before the crash.

A contained depression is no better than its predecessor

At first a *contained* depression sounds better than the alternative experienced in the inter-war years. In the here and now it is. Most of the mature world has escaped the more acute hardships of the Great Depression when output collapsed and unemployment soared. Of course that is not unheard of today: in Spain and Greece during the eurozone crisis unemployment exceeded 25%. But most people in the mature industrial countries have been spared the adversities and suffering so many more experienced in the 1930s.

However, over the longer run a contained depression is just as economically and socially regressive as the previous instance. A slow drift to economic obsolescence replaces the sharper collapses of the 1930s. The recent revival of the pre-war idea of 'secular stagnation' highlights both the same reality of decay between the two periods as well as the differences.

This depression has taken much longer for economic conditions to present themselves in this way. In the Great Depression less than a decade elapsed before Hansen coined the 'secular stagnation' term in 1938. In the Long Depression it took 40 years until Lawrence Summers resurrected the phrase in 2013. The road to recognisable decay has been longer and more uneven this time around, but ultimately the same destination has been reached.

While a less destructive capitalism initially seems a preferable thing, it comes at the cost of a more static economy that can't produce enough decent high productivity, well-paid jobs. While propping up old businesses might sound to be good news for the employees concerned, it is only a stay of execution.

And when the closures eventually happen, workers have been trading down in employment into worse paid and less secure jobs. While any jobs provided by a zombie economy may seem better for people because at least they are in employment, these are precarious jobs.[34] Working for a loss-making business does provide a salary. But, including for many profitable businesses today, it is often not a generous one, nor one that can be expected to last for long. People and their families suffer from the shortage of expanding firms and sectors of growth to provide secure, productive well-paid employment.

Perpetuating a zombie economy trades the prospect of decent, better paying jobs in the future for keeping people in worse paying, more unreliable jobs now. It puts one form of pain – including growing economic insecurity and hardship in work, punctuated by periodic and severe recessions – over the other form that comes from losing those jobs through economic restructuring, but with the opportunity of obtaining new and better ones. There is no alternative to the disruptive part of economic renewal, but there are ways of collectively mitigating the human cost through assisting people into better jobs. This presumes though that those good jobs in new sectors and industries are being created.

In preventing a business cycle shakeout the policies of government and central banks are not strengthening the economy but making it more depressed. Tolerating a contained depression is to put up with contained economic pain. It is to accept the persistence of a more impoverished life than society could technologically provide. While not doing away with hardships today, it also builds up sources of disruption in the future. We have already lived through the damaging effects of one serious financial crash. A contained depression brings no end to this dual scenario: persisting austere, though not disastrous times today, with more disruptive episodes in the future.

In one other crucial way, the contained depression has been more stable: politically. This is notwithstanding the rejection of the values of technocratic governance demonstrated by some recent popular votes, such as the outcome of Britain's EU referendum and the election of Trump. These responses have yet to turn into a positive and comprehensive political alternative, though the possibility remains.

Despite deindustrialisation, the extent of the decay in productive capability has been mostly obscured. For long periods the economy has seemed to function reasonably well for many people. Because it is contained, this depression has become even more difficult to escape from, politically as well as economically.

The answer to this conundrum of productive decay coexisting with reasonable social cohesion lies in the unusual conditions that have developed for bringing out and maximising capitalism's resilient qualities. The next three chapters address the peculiar political and cultural circumstances that have made this possible since the 1980s. In doing so they describe the transition from the more conventional earlier years of this economic crisis.

NINE

The intellectual crisis of capitalism

The reorientation of state institutions from growth to stabilisation is mostly implicit. Governments continue to pay lip service to the objective of economic growth. Doubtless many establishment politicians would like to have *both* stability and a bit more growth. However, there is a big gap between this latent attachment to growth and embracing the level of social dislocation needed to bring it about. In practice the policy inclination towards stability is at the expense of sustained growth. Economic dynamism is not restorable except through disruptive destabilisation involving the widespread destruction of old capital values.

The precondition for escaping the Long Depression is to challenge and overturn the conservator activities of the state. In the Sun Tzu *Art of War* spirit of knowing your enemy, the next three chapters explore how this shift in the role of the state has come about. There are three interrelated strands to the new conditions informing the emergence of the conservator state: the intellectual, the political and the economic. Together they have fuelled the rise of this type of state intervention and account for the successes of its muddling-through approach.

The intellectual retreat from change

This chapter examines how intellectual developments through the 20th century culminated in an outlook amenable to rebalancing state activities towards stabilisation. It describes the retreat from the traditional values associated with economic and social progress so that national leaderships now lack much sense of long-term purpose. Elites have become disenchanted with the themes previously proudly associated with capitalism: materialism, wealth and making profit.

This shift reflects a self-reinforcing lowering of expectations. When aspirations are downsized, the results are diminished. Modest outcomes confirm the good sense of lowering horizons in the first place. And so the circle of contraction continues. A loss of belief in the progressive potential of human intervention is self-fulfilling in the way it stunts progress. In this climate the conservator focus of state intervention seems appropriate, while its results seem to justify cutting back on ambition.

An earlier enthusiasm for the Enlightenment values of openness to experimentation and risk-taking has been replaced with a gloomier perspective on making change. Society views change gingerly. The state's adoption of a preservationist emphasis both expresses and also ingrains discomfort with human-led transformation.

The elite's unease with change reinforces a reluctance to restructure in favour of state activities that seek to stabilise capitalism. The Japanese experience under the 'three arrows' of economic policy launched by Prime Minister Shinzō Abe in 2013 illustrates this. It is telling that the third, disruptive arrow of structural reform has made the least headway. This contrasts with the other two of monetary and fiscal stimulus, which, though unable to restore economic vitality, better fulfil a stabilising mission.

The ubiquity of business uncertainty

Today's social discomfiture with change is manifest in the reversal of perspective on uncertainty within the economic and business worlds. Uncertainty is now widely regarded as a constraint on the economy. In fact, the *perception* of uncertainty is more important for what it says about the intellectual climate than for the economic one.

Viewing uncertainty as detrimental represents a turnabout in social attitudes. For most of the history of capitalism, uncertainty was regarded neutrally or positively: it was sometimes embraced as an opportunity for gain and advancement. Businesses in the past were not deterred by future uncertainty, but accumulated capital to secure increased means to control the future. The classic financial investment advice to 'buy when there's blood in the streets' revelled in periods of acute political uncertainty.[1]

In contrast, it is now a cliché to say that business and markets 'hate uncertainty'. It sneaks into commentaries about almost any piece of disappointing economic news. Some responsibility for economic atrophy is invariably attributed to uncertainty over ... take your pick: the US budget negotiations, the eurozone crisis, oil price movements, China's prospects, climate change effects, or the outcome of the next election or referendum.

The uncertainty factor also comes into explaining those cash mountains described earlier. Anxious businesses are said to build up cash reserves as a comfort cushion against a more uncertain future. Thomas Bates, Kathleen Kahle and René Stulz claim that the increase in the cash-to-assets ratio of firms is related closely to precautionary motives. Firms with higher uncertainty about their cash flows hold higher cash-to-assets ratios.[2]

Business leaders, as well as many pundits, attribute uncertainty as the reason for putting off investment decisions. A frequent survey finding is that business is not investing because of its lack of confidence in the face of an uncertain future.[3] Marcel Fratzscher, president of the Berlin-based think tank, DIW, reports that Germany's managers have long blamed the high uncertainty in the business environment as the main reason for low investment.[4] Similarly, the rating agency Standard & Poor's explanation for low capital investment highlighted the role of 'expectations and confidence about future returns (so-called "animal spirits")'. Uncertainty, especially around levels of demand, was holding back investment.[5]

William White, the frequently insightful chair of the OECD's Economic and Development Review Committee, focused on the role of uncertainty to explain the puzzling lack of Western investment despite the favourable financial conditions. Top of his list he put the 'environment of ever growing uncertainty' about a number of key issues. These were the future of domestic demand due to uncertainty about job prospects; future foreign demand given uncertainty about exchange rates and protectionism; and uncertainty as to how fiscal restraint and possible public debt reductions might affect the corporate sector.[6] Others emphasise the restrictive impact of heightened credit risk – a borrower failing to make required payments on a debt – and liquidity risk – not being able to sell assets for cash. Adding a metaphysical tone, Professor John Kay claimed that we are in a world characterised by 'radical uncertainty', in which not only the probability but the nature of future outcomes is unknown.[7]

Geopolitical crises in places like the Ukraine or Syria are said to be examples of a new era of systemic disorder. It is often said nostalgically that the Cold War was dangerous but at least it was stable. The unwinding of Cold War assumptions has instead 'created a world that is dangerously unpredictable'.[8] Meanwhile, the extension of international business operations has elevated the importance of 'country risk': the uncertain things that can go wrong when business is conducted across borders. Country risk specialist Mina Toksöz has written an illuminating treatment of this phenomenon.[9]

On top of these international sources of political uncertainty, domestic politics intrudes too. It is often argued, especially since 2008, that domestic political risk has intensified, interfering with business decision making. The leading British business organisation, the CBI, reported a survey finding that an overwhelming 96% of firms said political uncertainty was discouraging investment.[10]

'Regulatory uncertainty' has also become a common complaint. For example, US Senator Susan Collins introduced a bill to put a moratorium on all new regulations. She claimed businesses have not only blamed weak employment expansion largely on a climate of uncertainty, but most notably the uncertainty created by new federal regulations.[11]

The contemporary focus on uncertainty is an extension of an older 'lack of business confidence' explanation that commentators fall back on to account for economic slowdowns. 'Spending is low because of a lack of confidence.' A greater sense of uncertainty about the future is another way of expressing low confidence.

Keynes gave authority to the economic role of confidence when he explained that business investment was subject to 'animal spirits'. The volatility of investment, he claimed, followed businesses' swings in mood.[12] When animal spirits were dulled, when businesses were pessimistic about the future, as many were during the 1930s, underinvestment resulted. Ever since then, business pessimism in recessions has been linked to a dearth of animal spirits.[13]

The mechanism for uncertainty's impact on investment is straightforward. Superficially it can seem sensible: if business is uncertain about the future, it won't know how its next set of products or services would sell, so best to hold back from expanding. Why commit to large investment expenditure when the future is unknown? Academic studies have backed this notion of an adverse connection between uncertainty and investment.[14]

Uncertainty-based correlations with economic sloth find empirical evidence because they genuinely describe the business mood. But this does not make them explanatory. When businesses aren't investing, their leaders often don't feel confident and exhibit uncertainty about the demand for their products. But this tells us nothing about the original source of the economic circumstances about which people feel 'uncertain' or 'unconfident'. It does not account for why and how tougher economic conditions arose in the first place.

Theories about low investment based on animal spirits mistake effect for cause. Non-investing business leaders are likely to express uncertainty, while investing ones will be less focused on it and more concerned about making their investments work. Recessions can drain the confidence of business leaders. But that does not establish the reverse relationship: businesspeople feeling bad brings about, or perpetuates, stagnant conditions.

Correlation is not causation. This is why longer-term studies are more sceptical of the uncertainty factor – even some published recently. The analysis of post-1945 US investment trends by Kothari, Lewellen and Warner found no evidence that an increase in uncertainty reduces aggregate corporate investment.[15]

The issue is not the direct impact of uncertainty on business decision making but what the pervasiveness of the perception of uncertainty says about contemporary anxieties over the future. Business leaders do not exist apart from society but reflect the ideas that prevail more generally. Business executives do not live in their own bubble segregated from the world. Their ideas are shaped by the broader sociocultural sentiments that now view uncertainty as a negative factor.

Shifting views on uncertainty, the future and change

The future is always uncertain because it has yet to be written. It unfolds based on what we do. Businesses, households and policymakers have invariably been making their decisions under uncertain conditions. Therefore there can be no determinate economic effects of uncertainty: it coexists with times of slump *and* of boom. *The lack of certainty has not inhibited the business investment accompanying economic and technological progress in the past.* Previously, innovating business changes and the follow-on gains in productivity have powered ahead despite the constant reality of uncertainty.

It is frequently asserted that we live in peculiarly uncertain times. Yet historical illustrations indicate that things are not all that different today from the past. In some respects things are *less* uncertain today since society has gained greater technological mastery over the effects of natural forces like storms, floods and famine.

The epoch-making advances of the first industrial revolution in the 18th century took place against the deeply uncertain backdrop of revolution, war and the threat of war. The huge investments in plant and factories that accompanied the invention of the steam engine, the spinning jenny and the cotton gin happened despite these uncertainties. These times covered the unstable aftermath of England's Glorious Revolution of 1688. There was an ongoing potential of war between Britain and France. America fought a war for its independence. And the French shocked Europe with their 1789 Revolution.

The second industrial revolution of the 19th century saw even more business investment in an equally uncertain era of mounting domestic struggle and international turmoil. The costly expansion of the railways, the increasing investment in factory machinery, and the first investments occasioned by the development of electric power and telephony all occurred alongside the uncertainties of those fast-changing times. A spate of republican revolutions began in Sicily in 1848 in the aftermath of capitalism's first systemic crisis, which spread to France, Germany, Italy and the Austrian empire.[16]

From the Tolpuddle Martyrs in the 1830s this period saw the first stirrings of working class militancy in response to the impact of capitalism on people's lives. America was racked by its own bloody civil war in the 1860s. A few years later at the start of the 1870s the Franco-Prussian War transformed Europe: French defeat catalysed the unification of Germany, and brought the revolutionary Paris Commune of 1871. On the other side of the world Japan was beginning its economic climb to unsettle further global power relations. These were far from a stable and 'certain' setting for the huge commitments business made to drive the ascendancy of industrial capitalism.

The context for the next wave of industrial expansion and business investment was no time of certainty either. We noted earlier Alexander Field describing the 1930s as the most technologically progressive decade of the century. He made a strong case that the most rapid era of innovation in all of American history was not the roaring 1920s, nor the dot. com bubble of the 1990s. Rather, it was the time between the Wall Street Crash of 1929 and the attack on Pearl Harbor in 1941.[17] Notwithstanding that period's wretched uncertainties, business investment played no small part in making era-defining technological changes happen.

The third industrial revolution of the 1930s and 1940s brought tremendous industrial advances in the chemical and pharmaceuticals industries, jet travel, nuclear energy, computerisation and the beginnings of space rocketry. This took place alongside the Great Depression and the global warfare that ensued. These were not times of low uncertainty. There was social unrest on a vast scale in the slump-ridden nations, combined with inter-imperialist tensions, and a spate of local wars in Manchuria, Ethiopia and Spain. This all culminated in the Second World War when democracy was in mortal combat with fascism. Yet business didn't let such minor sources of uncertainty put them off investing for long.

And before the dust had settled after the Second World War the Cold War broke out, bringing the possibility of nuclear annihilation. Yet this extended era of existential uncertainty provided the backdrop for the most impressive economic boom ever in human history. Business investment during the post-war economic expansion was as vigorous as it had ever been since the dawn of capitalism. The risk of all that new capital stock being vaporised with only a four-minute warning didn't deter enterprising business leaders.

Previously, therefore, uncertainty and investment were far from being mutually exclusive. A century ago Frank Knight explored the relationship between the two in a very different way to today's discussion. In his classic 1921 book *Risk, Uncertainty, and Profit* he reflected the common view then of uncertainty as being constant and ubiquitous.

Knight is best known today for making a precise distinction between *uncertainty* and *risk*. He defined uncertainty as referring to an event whose probability cannot be known, unlike risk whose probability can be determined, and therefore potentially insured against. In other words, risk is quantifiable while uncertainty isn't. This was not some semantic difference of interest only to the insurance industry, or to probability statisticians. For Knight it underpinned how capitalism worked. He explained that uncertainty was an essential feature of a functioning capitalist society. It represented an opportunity for profit from investment.

His thesis was that entrepreneurs earn profits as a return for putting up with uncertainty. Knight could not envisage the market working without it. As Mazzucato later put it, echoing his sentiments: 'Without uncertainty there would be no point in even trying to form competitive strategies.'[18] If everything were predictable there would be a limited possibility of gaining competitive advantage. Uncertainty provides the terrain for individual businesses to make superprofits, when they risk their capital to get ahead of competitors by deploying the latest innovations and cutting prices.

Uncertainty was for a long time recognised as the basis for markets to function. This refutes the assertion that markets 'hate uncertainty': they need uncertainty. Or, to be more precise, since 'markets' do not have an independent power of their own: the motivations of people operating *through* markets are informed by the uncertainties implicit in competition and fluctuating prices.

Despite today's conventional negativity about uncertainty, the way capitalism works means a few contemporary observers still find it difficult entirely to relegate this economic role.[19]

Knight made a clear link between uncertainty and entrepreneurship. In business the function of intelligent decision making resides most acutely in the classic risk-taking entrepreneur. This is someone who has no choice but to operate in 'the fact of ignorance' and necessarily has to act 'upon opinion rather than knowledge'.

Today not only is there an unfavourable view of uncertainty but there is also a more ambivalent view of entrepreneurship and especially of the risk-taking that used to be intimately associated with it. Although the self-employed are often flattered as being 'entrepreneurs', and 'social' entrepreneurs are feted, risking all on a business idea that could transform production is often seen as rash, if not dangerous.

Traditional business risk-taking is castigated as reckless behaviour that can incur unacceptable economic or social costs. Some business-bashers use the word 'risk' as a slur that connotes imprudence, foolhardiness and even immorality. The standard narrative of the West's financial crash as an excess of irresponsible risk-taking carried out by bankers and other financial players illustrates the negative attitude to risk and risk-taking.

Even Knight's key distinction between uncertainty and risk has become a casualty as society seeks to minimise them both. Businesses recategorise more areas of traditional uncertainty as risk – political, market, credit and so on – and devote increasing resources to trying to manage them as quantifiable risks. The consequence is to further ossify economic activity under the weight of ever-extending risk management practices, a tendency we'll return to in the next chapter.

What has changed society's, and therefore business's, attitudes to uncertainty and risk so dramatically? It reflects more negative views about the results of past progress. Fundamentally, there is scepticism about the scope for human agency – the capacity of people to act independently and to make their own free choices – and greater anxieties about the future. Today's heightened concerns about uncertainty reflect not greater levels of uncertainty but society's *more equivocal views of the future*. Underlying the outlook that the world has become more uncertain is the sense that we are less in control and less able to make a positive difference. The future is perceived to be more uncertain and unpredictable because society feels less able to handle what it brings with it.

Going beyond the issues of competition and entrepreneurship, Knight went on to claim that 'Without uncertainty it is doubtful whether intelligence itself would exist.'[20] What he meant was that a society without uncertainty would be a predictable and staid place where thinking, and acting on these thoughts, could have little consequence. To be 'certain', life would be following a predetermined script. A certain life would be a life without the prospect of human agency changing things for the better.

In earlier modern times, as reflected in Knight's writings, humanity aspired to obtain greater control of the world as the best antidote to uncertainty. The computer scientist Alan Kay, who developed the Graphical User Interface that went on to inspire the Apple Macintosh, succinctly summed up this perspective on human action and control in 1971: 'The best way to predict the future is to invent it.'[21] Now there is much less faith in our abilities to do so. Humanity's earlier enthusiasm for progress has cooled considerably. This is a seismic shift with far-reaching implications, not least for society's responses to the Long Depression.

Knight had seen 'change' as primarily a human activity: change does not usually just happen, he wrote, but is largely itself the result of human activity.[22] He pulled together the inherent connectedness between uncertainty and the human venture of social progress. '[Progress] involves uncertainty in a high degree',[23] and stressed that uncertainty is indeed an 'inevitable concomitant of progress'.[24] Knight concluded that 'uncertainty is dependent upon change, and in fact largely upon progressive change'.[25] Progress would itself bring about unpredictability, not least when based upon invention and innovation. 'It is a commonplace fact that one of the chief sources of uncertainty in business life is the improvement of technological processes, methods of organization, and the like.'[26]

With these assumptions about human activity Knight's writings still reflected the influence of the classic Enlightenment view of the relationship between progress and uncertainty. Since the 18th century reasoned change had been embraced as enabling the improvement of the lot of humanity. Social progress provided the means for controlling uncertainty, as well as resulting from successfully dealing with it.

Equally, the uncertainty of the future is both alleviated and also aggravated by making change. Changes were made by society, and by business, with the goal of controlling or limiting some uncertainties. Meanwhile, the very act of making these changes necessarily changes the future. This emphasises that it is impossible to be certain about what will come next. While uncertainty about the future could never be eliminated, the humanist goal of gaining mastery over uncertainty became one of the drivers of progress.

Now this Enlightenment perspective on change has been reversed. Rather than uncertainty propelling change, human-directed change – not least that geared to economic development and growth – is increasingly seen as contributing to unnecessary uncertainty. It should therefore be limited. This reflects a shift in the sociocultural zeitgeist, characterised by *discomfort with change*. It is better that humanity seeks to conserve than to change.

The ebbing of Enlightenment values

Today's greater anxieties about uncertainty are driven by a loss of belief in the benefits of progress and of humanity's ability to make a better world. Since the 2008 crash more commentators have highlighted the draining of confidence from the establishment,[27] but this is the end of a much longer journey. Over the course of the past century there's been a growing discrediting of the cardinal Enlightenment idea of human progress as being good for society. Instead humanity's interventions have been increasingly regarded as making life worse. The political commentator Janan Ganesh epitomised the contemporary sentiment when he claimed that 'the status quo is superior to many plausible alternatives. Things can be made worse not just better by well-meaning politicians.'[28]

The humanist pursuit of progress is now seen by many across the political spectrum to cause problems and, sometimes, to be downright destructive: socially, environmentally, materially, and morally. Of course in practice progress has frequently been accompanied by mishaps. In fact the next steps ahead are often forged out of the lessons learnt from previous misfortunes and setbacks. It can be a case of three steps forward, one step back. Making progress is neither fully predictable nor orderly. Nevertheless it is overwhelmingly a 'Good Thing' for humanity.

In contrast, late 20th century society has increasingly reacted against the uncertain and disruptive aspects of progress. Human-driven progress, in parallel with other core Enlightenment concepts – humanism, individualism, freedom – are seen as in some way contributing to, if not responsible for, the West's descent into a moral and political malaise. And, as well, making a mess of the natural environment.

A century of setbacks

This trajectory in thinking had been bubbling away throughout the 20th century, at least since the terrible intellectual shock represented by the outbreak of the First World War. The sheer brutalism of its fighting had an impact way beyond the direct combatants. The calamity and horrors of this conflict were a huge blow to the self-assurance of the Western elites. The late 19th century and the earlier years of the 20th century had already seen an incipient loss of purpose, especially within Britain. But the impact of the war catalysed a deeper and wider intellectual crisis.

At the end of the Cold War the political scientist Francis Fukuyama highlighted how the First World War had been a critical event in the undermining of Europe's self-confidence.[29] The sociologist Frank Furedi cogently established that this war had more than the usual unsettling outcomes associated with a military conflict. He described how it called into question the self-belief of the political and cultural elites of Western societies: 'it disrupted and disorganized the prevailing web of meaning through which Western societies made sense of their world'.[30]

The experience of the 'Great War' set in motion a loss of confidence in progress that continued to intensify through the remainder of the century. Oswald Spengler's *The Decline of the West*, published in 1918, captured this developing mood of unease with the values of Western civilisation and the gnawing disillusionment with modernity. Society was witnessing the last season, the 'wintertime', of civilisation.

The subsequent inter-war turmoil – the market and banking collapses, and the hardships of the 1930s slump – and the Second World War, with its associated horrors from the Holocaust to Hiroshima, took a further toll on the confidence of the elites. The failure of the European economies to resume forward movement after the First World War did little good for the belief in capitalist values. As Furedi noted trenchantly: it was difficult to celebrate a system of production that appeared inherently unstable and prone to economic malaise.[31]

The work of Schumpeter well expressed the loss of faith in the capitalist model by the late 1930s. As a supporter of markets, he highlighted the widespread 'atmosphere of hostility to capitalism' and that it was then normal to be anti-capitalist.[32] The thesis in his tome *Capitalism, Socialism and Democracy* published in 1942 was pessimistic for the future of capitalism. Asking himself 'Can Capitalism Survive?' he answered bluntly, 'No. I do not think it can.'[33] He anticipated that a socialist form of society would inevitably emerge from the equally inevitable decomposition of capitalist society. Capitalism was tending to self-destruction.

Schumpeter described a bourgeoisie that was losing not just its wealth in the economic crisis but also its sense of purpose. He drew attention to the evaporation of 'the will' to go forward.[34] In this assessment he was as much describing his own self-doubts as those of others around him. Reflecting these qualms he reinterpreted the rise of Marxism in the late 19th century as stemming from a lack of faith in capitalism. Marxism, he thought, had been better able to appeal to the rationalist and positivist frame of mind.

By the time the Second World War ended, even the benefits of science and technology were in dispute. The destructive way science had been put to military service in the atomic bomb added tremendously to the sense of unease. This reinforced anti-modern sentiments. By the end of this three-decade span of economic and political instability, book-ended by periods of massive human slaughter, capitalist elites had become gravely defensive. They doubted the merits and possibilities of their system and questioned the progress it had hitherto brought about.

This despair was not limited to the established elites. The intellectual crisis of the right was mirrored among their critics on the left. As the prospects for radical social change faded, the left too lost their belief in progress. The cumulative impact of regressive developments in the Soviet Union was devastating for many. The USSR failed to live up to the liberating potential of the 1917 Russian Revolution. Instead it descended into the mayhem of working class repression and economic disarray.

With the emergence of fascism in Italy and Germany and of Stalinism in the Soviet Union, left-wing intellectuals were sometimes the most overt questioners of Enlightenment rationalism. Reason, they surmised, had lost its positive potential in a mass society where people seemed to be susceptible to emotional persuasion. Democracy too became suspect.[35] In the closing stages of the Second World War the Frankfurt School philosophers Theodor Adorno and Max Horkheimer wrote the *Dialectic of Enlightenment*, which became a seminal influence on parts of the left. The brutal and authoritarian experiences of fascism and Stalinism represented the failure of the Enlightenment: 'Myth is already enlightenment', they wrote, 'and enlightenment reverts to mythology.'[36]

Questioning the very possibilities of human emancipation and freedom, their defeatist perspective subsequently informed the thinking of many from the left. By the 1950s, crystallised by the invasion of Hungary in 1956, the Soviet experiment in transcending capitalism had turned into a symbol of the hubris of trying to create a better world. Subsequently the left was re-energised by the social changes of the 1960s and the turmoil emerging from the imminent demise of the post-war economic boom. However, it was now a pale imitation of the progressive influence it had exerted in the earlier part of the 20th century.

At the end of the millennium the author Michael Ignatieff effectively summarised how the intellectual attitudes to progress had mutated over the previous century. While people were now 'living' the benefits of progress, he described how they were intensely unsettled by it: 'in the 50 years since 1945, we have lived with a deep ambivalence about progress'.[37]

Temporary relief

Following the Second World War two factors had temporarily alleviated the elites' crisis of confidence. The first was the unexpected arrival of the Cold War. As a by-product it provided a new sense of purpose for the Western elites. They had been through a demoralising and unsettling half-century. Now they could justify their system again: as being better than the repressive alternative offered by their new foe, Stalinism.

The negative example of the Soviet way of life helped Western politicians to dodge the question of what they really stood for. The Soviets may have had a big military machine and lots of powerful missiles, but the West won hands down when it came to personal liberties and living standards. This theme was brought out by the 'kitchen debate' in 1959 between the Soviet leader Nikita Khrushchev and US Vice-President Richard Nixon.

The two leaders were viewing an American exhibition stand in Moscow. Showing off US colour television sets to Khrushchev, Nixon prompted an outbreak of verbal jousting between the two about their country's respective ways of life. Whoever won the ensuing war of words, the Western sense of superiority was symbolised by the backdrop in the news pictures. The debate was shown in front of a 'typical' American kitchen featuring the sort of mod con appliances and gadgets of which Russians could only dream.[38]

The second mitigating factor was the equally unexpected return to strength of the West's economies. By the late 1930s many commentators had been anticipating a continuation of depressed economic conditions. Hansen's concept of secular stagnation portrayed the gloomy scenario of stalled living standards far into the future. The post-war boom was therefore not just a return to crisis-free times. It was a surprising and welcome relief.

Lasting from 1950 to the early 1970s this era became talked about as the 'Golden Age of Capitalism'. The advanced economies grew faster over a longer period than had ever happened before. Between 1950 and 1973 American output per person expanded at over 2% a year, consistently faster than over the previous century. On the other side of the Atlantic Britain also had the reassurance of expanding at a similar rate to America though more unevenly, and for a shorter period into the early 1960s. Yet this was double its growth performance of earlier in the century. The absolute and relative growth rates in Germany, Japan and a host of other mature economies were even more impressive.[39] The French with an annual 4% per person growth rate exaggerated the boom's length only a little in referring to it as 'Les Trente Glorieuses', the 30 glorious years.

For Western elites who had been so unnerved by their pre-1945 experiences, this genuine material advance provided a huge comfort. Capitalism seemed to be back in working order. Perhaps all those grim memories could be dismissed as an unfortunate nightmare.

However, by the end of the 1980s everything changed as both the supportive developments fell apart. First, the economy hit the rocks again: from the 1960s for Britain, and across all the industrial countries by the start of the 1970s. The end of the boom rattled faith in capitalism, as well as in the progressive impact of state intervention. Within another two decades the 'reprieve' of the Cold War was also over, even more unexpectedly than its outbreak.

By the early 1990s the West had to rely on its own resources again. Economic conditions were bleak. The opening years of the decade had seen another recession, followed by a modest and jobless recovery. The elites' earlier doubts about capitalism and human progress were rekindled. They subsequently evolved into a more acute crisis of confidence, of meaning and of purpose.

Enemies evaporated

The irony is that it was not the *strength* of alternatives to capitalism but their *demise* that eventually crystallised the elite's intellectual crisis. The return to depressed economic conditions had already put the establishment on the defensive. But capitalism's self-confidence took its next blow not from the vehemence of anti-capitalist attacks but by the reverse. Opposition withered away, not just the Soviet Union as its international enemy, but the domestic challenges from the left and the organised labour movement.

During the early part of the depression, dealing with protests from the radical left and with the resistance of the trade unions and labour movement provided some focus to the elites' day-to-day endeavours. Even that went along with a good dose of dithering on both sides of the Atlantic.[40] In early 1981, for example, Thatcher's government had buckled and retreated in the face of a threatened national miners' strike.

However, through the recession of the early 1980s the political elites firmed up a stronger confrontational stance. Old industries were shaken out. Millions of people were forced out of work across Western countries. Restrictions were imposed on infrastructure investment and welfare spending to limit the effects of rising taxation eating into spending and profitability. Conflict with the unions helped cohere this transition to a more combative posture.

To this day the reputation of the 1980s administrations under Reagan and Thatcher rests primarily on their association with taking on those regarded as the enemies of capitalism. Their standing as effective, even history-changing governments comes from the forceful tactics pursued against domestic labour movements, as well as internationally against the Soviet Union.[41] Throughout the whole Long Depression, the 1980s remains a high point of capitalist self-assurance. The right seemed to have won the 'economic war' in favour of capitalism and markets.

The triumph was rather overstated, as it was a victory primarily by default. The opposition had more given up than been defeated. While the return of crisis in the 1970s had sparked a revival in industrial militancy and radical left activism, this was the swansong for the labour movement and the left. Working class organisation was not as strong as it might have seemed on the basis of the increased level of strikes.

The US sociologist Mark Mizruchi noted how organised labour in America began to experience a series of setbacks even from 1977, during the more sympathetic administration of President Jimmy Carter. Opposition had grown to the anti-union Taft-Hartley Act that had become law in more fractious times, shortly after the Second World War. However, despite a Democratic president and Democratic control of both the US

Senate and the House of Representatives, the labour bureaucracy proved unable to achieve the passage of a bill weakening it.[42]

As a symptom of failing strength, the density of trade union membership fell steadily from the 1970s throughout the industrialised countries. The trade union movements on both sides of the Atlantic were finished off during the 1980s with staged confrontations. In Britain the 1984 miners' strike and the 1986 print workers' strike were defeated. In the US the 1981 air traffic controllers' strike was crushed with 12,000 sackings. The outcome of these conflicts was never in much doubt, not because of the strength of the establishment position, but because the organised labour movement was only a shadow of its former self.

These events made explicit the outcome of the longer-term political decay of working class contestation. Labour strife and industrial disputes fell away across the Western world never to recover (see Figures 9.1 and 9.2). Mizruchi rightly concluded that by the end of the century the US labour movement had been 'consigned to irrelevance'. The situation was little different across Britain, Japan and Germany.

The collapse of labourism was presented for a time as a vindication of the market system and proof of the futility of socialist and labourist alternatives. But it also meant that the Western elites had lost an arena where they could summon some purpose. No longer with a domestic class enemy to fight, the establishment felt emptier. In Britain, it was not long before

Figure 9.1 US and UK working days lost due to industrial action

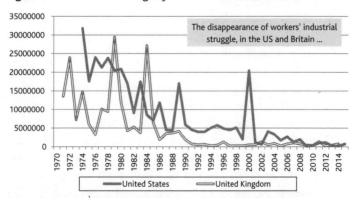

Source: International Labour Organization ILOSTAT, Strikes and lockouts. http://www.ilo.org/ilostat/faces/help_home/data_by_subject?_adf.ctrl-state=96vv1z9gc_695&_afrLoop=16746432664984#!

Figure 9.2 Germany and Japan working days lost due to industrial action

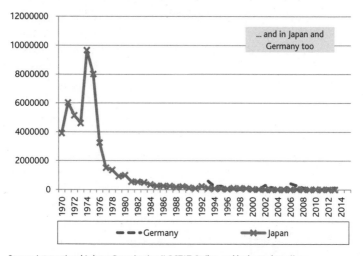

Source: International Labour Organization ILOSTAT, Strikes and lockouts. http://www.
ilo.org/ilostat/faces/help_home/data_by_subject?_adf.ctrl-state=96vv1z9gc_695&_
afrLoop=16746432664984#!

the stabilisation of political life after the 1984 defeat of the
miners exposed the weak moral and intellectual foundations of
elite authority. The mission that the Thatcher government had
displayed evaporated soon after the enemy had been defeated.
Thatcher's third electoral term from 1987 was a mishmash of
policies with little coherent direction, including the introduction
of the unpopular poll tax. After 11 years her premiership ended
in 1990 with the ignominy of an internal party coup.

This duality that accompanied seeing off the domestic foe
– the initial sense of triumph, succeeded by a loss of purpose
– was even more evident with the winding up of the Cold
War. Through the 1980s the Soviet system was falling apart.
As with the demise of the labourist and socialist alternative at
home, this disintegration was for internal reasons rather than as
a consequence of pressure from the West. The Soviet Union's
inability to drive up productivity eventually took its toll. The
collapse of oil prices and rising debt levels in the Eastern Bloc
brought matters to a head. In November 1989 the Berlin Wall
was breached, and the breakdown of the rest of Stalinist Eastern

Europe soon followed. At the end of 1991 the Soviet Union disintegrated into 15 separate countries. The Cold War was over.

However the resulting jubilation of the Western elites rapidly turned into a nostalgic yearning for the apparent simplicities of this earlier political era. Now that both international and home-based adversaries had all but disappeared, market capitalism was left unchallenged *and* simultaneously exposed. Capitalism had to stand on its own merits, but very few were able to make a *positive* case for capitalism and market relations.

The idea that capitalism was a successful system because it was better than either the Soviet Union or the models proposed by its domestic critics was always only a *negative* endorsement. Capitalism had been presented as better than alternatives that were easy to vilify: trade unions for 'holding the country to ransom'; social democratic politicians for their association with discredited tax-and-spend policies; a Soviet system known for its austerity and its denial of freedoms. When those alternatives fell away, the pro-capitalist premise was immediately less compelling.

Efforts have been made to substitute these old enemies with the new ones of 'fundamentalism' or a 'war on terror'. After some particular atrocity – such as the 9/11 attacks in the US, the 7/7 bombings of the London transport system in 2005, or the Paris attacks in November 2015 – these attempts have elicited some popular resonance. But they have never gained the same grip and cohering power of their predecessors.

The disintegration of Western triumphalism at the end of the Cold War expressed the return of an old question that haunted the Western elites: 'what do we really stand for?' As Furedi explained, once the Berlin Wall had fallen and the Soviet Union followed it on to the scrapheap of history, the Western elites could no longer answer: 'We are defined by our hostility to Communism.'[43]

Nor was the acclaimed revival of free market values popularly associated with the governments of Reagan and Thatcher able to attain a firm intellectual or cultural hold on society. And this was even before the arrival of the West's financial crash in 2008. Market capitalism came under attack from the 1990s – mainly from within. Free market ideas failed as a positive endorsement for capitalism. 'Anti-capitalism' became a normal stance again, just as it had appeared to Schumpeter in the 1930s.

This time it was both a feebler, more 'pretend' form of anti-capitalism, but also one with a different focus. In the 1930s anti-capitalist movements had sought to replace capitalism with another way of running society. Today anti-capitalism leaves capitalism as a mode of production essentially unchallenged. Rather it expresses a greater unease with and retreat from the negative consequences of market activities. It seeks to restrain not overthrow capitalism.

Anxieties about widening inequalities, self-serving business leaders, and environmental damage have become ubiquitous. These are no longer just campaigning issues for nongovernmental organisations and the remnants of left-wing groups. They have come to preoccupy mainstream thinking and overwhelm an appreciation of the benefits of growth. One-sided discomfort with the unattractive aspects of economic life embodies a critique of the values traditionally associated with capitalism: progress, dynamism and risk-taking. The irony is that the passing away of a small revolutionary anti-capitalist movement has coincided with the emergence of a broader 'anti-capitalism' that has backing within sections of the establishment.

Critics of business, many of whom come from within the business elite, desire a less turbulent, milder and caring form of capitalism. Competitive capitalism is denigrated in favour of a less confrontational capitalism. Reflecting the changed zeitgeist, the Enlightenment economist and philosopher Adam Smith has been reassessed as an apostle for responsible, caring capitalism, rather than as the original advocate of free markets. We are encouraged to read his *Theory of Moral Sentiments* as revealing the real, sensitive Smith, rather than restrict ourselves to the self-interested capitalism of *The Wealth of Nations*.

The diminishing of the human

The elite's resumed crisis of meaning brought to the fore and enhanced the earlier doubts about Enlightenment values and the benefits of human progress. As a society we have become reluctant to validate and promote the active, positive side of humanity to change things for the better. This represents a turn against a central Enlightenment perspective: seeing man as rationally capable of making a better future. Instead individuals these days are frequently presented as weak, sometimes irrational, and often requiring restraint from above. The humanist essence of Enlightenment thought has lost its appeal. The potential for meaningful, purposeful human intervention is frequently doubted and questioned.

Hence, the disposition for extending regulation, not just of the economy, but of all areas of human life. This regulationist bent is underpinned by the urge to control what man does and to contain what are perceived as the frequently problematic consequences. The expansion of regulationism is not just a quantitative matter of imposing more and more regulations. It is also informed by a less flattering, increasingly misanthropic view of humanity.

Humanism arose in response to the fatalism of medieval times and propagated the idea that people were not just the objects of change, but also the subjects of change.[44] Now, in contrast, many claim that people do not comprehend their own interests and are prone to acting irrationally. Man cannot be trusted to act in his own best interests. This charge was evident in the elites' anti-democratic reactions to the Brexit decision and to Trump's election; in both of these situations the rationality and aspirations of voters were dismissed.

The enlightened humanist view of the relationship between the state and the public has become reversed. The state is no longer an institution that needs to be controlled by people. It is now the state's role to judge what is good for people, to raise public awareness, and to socially engineer people to do 'the right thing'. The earlier emphasis on the importance of human agency has been replaced by an emphasis on human vulnerability and powerlessness. And because people are so powerless and vulnerable this is seen to justify that we need the support of public institutions.

State intrusiveness is rarely presented in overt authoritarian terms. More usually it is posed in the language of providing caring and therapeutic support. The social critic Christopher Lasch already identified this paternalistic tendency in his 1979 book *The Culture of Narcissism*. He shrewdly explained that whereas earlier liberals 'assumed the primacy of rational self-interest' in man, later ones rejected this and 'installed in its place a therapeutic conception of man'.[45] The objective of regulating people, both in their work and private lives, Lasch suggested, is to bring the 'whole man' under control. The tendency to exert state control *of* man is an outright reversal of the earlier sense of the control of society and the state *by* man.

The economic impact of Enlightenment values

The Enlightenment concepts of reason, humanism and freedom are invaluable to society. They are fundamental for individual autonomy and a healthy public life. They are not justified by any instrumental benefits, economic or otherwise.

Nevertheless, as a fact of history, the flourishing of the Enlightenment spirit has had huge economic consequence. For hundreds of years before the development of industrial capitalism, humanity's living circumstances barely budged. The renowned economic historian Angus Maddison estimated that world output per person was US$467 in the year 1 AD, falling slightly to US$453 1000 years later, and rising to only US$615 by 1700.[46] That's an average annual growth rate over 17 centuries of 0.02% – effectively zero for influencing people's life experiences.

Output per person only began to grow markedly in the industrialising countries from the latter part of the 18th century.[47] With the emergence of a future-orientated enlightened perspective, industrial capitalism enabled the leap to sustained productivity growth. British output per person increased by a half between 1700 and 1820 – a modest one-third of 1% annual growth per person during the first stages of its industrial development. It then accelerated to average about 1% a year over the next 40 years to 1860.

Subsequently productivity went up a further gear. Despite the interruptions of the 20th century's world wars and the 1930s slump, real output per British person quadrupled in the 100 years through to the 1960s, an annual average of nearly 1.5%. Across Western Europe the performance was similar. In America the annual average was a bit faster at just below 2% a year.

Industrial capitalism could not have taken off without the intellectual backdrop consistent with the age of the Enlightenment. Productivity growth relied on openness to experimentation and change. Ronald Bailey explained that industrial and technological development provides the necessary *means* for economic growth. However, the series of industrial revolutions since the 18th century were inexplicable except as a product of the core Enlightenment contribution of liberty. Liberty brought with it a relaxation of the social, cultural and economic strictures on innovation and experimentation.[48]

This is also the thesis advanced by Joel Mokyr in his book *The Enlightened Economy*. He explained that economic change in all periods depends on what people believe. We cannot understand industrial revolution without recognising the importance of the intellectual sea change represented by the coming of the Enlightenment. Economic change does not happen without human intervention. Beliefs inform reasoned human activity. As a movement that celebrated 'social progress and the improvability of mankind', the Enlightenment encouraged the application of reason and observation to bettering the human condition, including its material foundations.[49]

Similarly, George Magnus related Western economic strength and durability for most of the 19th and 20th centuries to the specific cultural features that are associated with the Enlightenment. He explained that the institutions that embodied this culture had helped the West 'to adapt, to be creative and to reinvent' itself. They also inspired humanity 'to challenge the status quo, undertake structural reform and innovate'.[50]

A cultural aversion to restructuring

In recent decades and especially over the past 25 years these strengths, capabilities and ambitions have been much less in evidence. Their intellectual and moral foundation has been crumbling. The ebbing of Enlightenment values has mediated the evolution of the Long Depression.

Just as the ascent of Enlightenment ideas informed the economic advances of industrial capitalism, so the reverse applies with today's slow-drift capitalism. Discomfort with change is antithetical to the business dynamism that the market system relies on to move forward. Cultural uneasiness with disruptive change runs counter to the creative destruction that is essential for capitalist growth and economic progress. This discomfiture informs the mainstream political inclination for stability over disorder.

At a rhetorical level it is still recognised that economic growth depends upon innovation and investment, and that these rest on an adequate commitment to science and research activities. The political elites are occasionally forced by circumstances to address real economic challenges like stagnant productivity. In response they still pay lip service to the importance of long-term investment, to the benefits of dynamic economies and to the worth of high quality science and innovation.[51] The reason these platitudes remain hollow is less due to the government's financial constraints – real or self-imposed – than their unease with change. This has drained the elites' capacity to undertake genuine programmes for economic change at anything like the scale required.

Paul Ormerod highlighted that growth can't happen without openness to change and disruption. The absence of this outlook brings a reluctance to engage in innovation and transformative investing. Crucial to research and the subsequent innovation is the 'willingness of a country to embrace, rather than resist, change'.[52]

With regard to government, the cultural unease with disruptive change mainly operates through an act of omission, of what is *not* taking place. The elites are loath to promote, never mind lead, the economic shakeup that is required to recover the West's economic mojo. This failure to restructure and deal with the inevitable upheavals of letting the old go has been critical in perpetuating the Long Depression.

In conclusion, discomfort with change, a subjective feature of contemporary times, has become an objective barrier to renewal and progress. This is now institutionalised with the emergence of the conservator state. Bringing about economic change will depend on achieving a revolution in the dominant cultural perspective. As a consequence, ending the Long Depression is initially an intellectual and a political challenge. The prime objectives are to restore a positive endorsement of the benefits of change, and to rescind the ossifying forms of state intervention.

TEN

Discomfort with change

Unease with change resonates through ideas and movements that have gained widespread endorsement in recent decades. Three are reviewed here: a heightened fixation on risk in business; greater anxieties about the impact of new technologies; and the rise of sustainability as a business principle. Each of these gets in the way of transformative investment and economic development. They also sustain a climate agreeable for state economic policies that favour stability over growth.

Heightened fixation on risk

In 2013 Ben Casselman, then a reporter for the *Wall Street Journal*, wrote a feature on the loss of US economic dynamism. For years companies had been adding jobs more slowly. Venture capitalists had been putting less money into new firms. People had been starting fewer businesses and been less inclined to change jobs or to move location for new opportunities. Casselman concluded that the US had turned 'soft on risk'. A fading of America's famed risk-taking spirit underlay its more sluggish economic recoveries since the early 1990s.[1]

This insight applies in other Western societies too. The consultants McKinsey describe the 'bias against risk' across international business.[2] There are always some individuals and business leaders willing to break the mould. But when society is unfavourable to change, then the barriers mount to businesses in general making risk-taking investments.

Uncertain businesses turn more to risk analysts and risk management tools for guidance. Some, notably financial businesses in the aftermath of the financial crash, have appointed chief risk officers to their executive teams and company boards.[3] The common business justification is that embedding risk management practices builds capabilities for better dealing with and taking advantage of an uncertain future. In practice, this more often has the debilitating effect of institutionalising risk-averse behaviours. Even when a businessperson's instincts suggest a bolder approach, the risk management regime is there to counsel caution. 'Think more of what might go wrong.'

Elevated risk consciousness has been reinforced by the financial crash but it goes back long before. When James Poterba and Lawrence Summers looked at the declining competitiveness of US companies in the 1990s, they noticed signs that business leaders were overly cautious in approaching investment decisions.[4] The hurdle rates of return being used in capital budgeting exercises were often higher than standard cost-of-capital analyses suggested were appropriate. Poterba and Summers concluded that these more risk-averse firms were turning down projects that could be profitable. European businesses were being similarly overcautious in pushing up target rates of return.

Another McKinsey report on investment spelt out how the bias against risk worked. Managers would fear the potential losses more than value the potential gains, leading them to reject too many investment proposals as being too risky. Echoing Poterba and Summers, businesses would frequently add an arbitrary 'risk premium' on top of the previously agreed cost-of-capital in an attempt to compensate for risk. This risk premium was seldom 'fact-based' but embedded 'opaque assumptions' about the risk of the investment. The study found it 'difficult to isolate and scrutinize' them, and concluded businesses were failing to pursue many promising investments.[5]

British businesses have been exhibiting the same timorous approach with the addition of chunkier risk premiums. As mentioned earlier, bank loans have been unprecedentedly cheap, with interest rates on lending to businesses falling from about 6-7% in the early 2000s to 3% since the financial crash. Regardless, research showed companies were setting even higher return hurdles due to the perception that the external economic and political environment made investments riskier than ever.

Prior to the crash, finance directors would approve investments that looked likely to pay back over a period of six years. By 2012 this period had shortened to around four years.[6]

An increase in the required rate of return from an average of about 9% to 14% has constrained investment. This applies especially to the critical transformative investments: the 'irreversible' ones necessary to improve productivity. Heightened fears over things that do not actually occur have been adversely affecting the growth of activity, investment and productivity for some time.[7]

Andrew Haldane concurs that an increase in business caution has inhibited investment going back for at least the past two decades. He noted that the precautionary trend by companies to 'invest' more in passive assets such as cash than active ones such as physical capital had blossomed since the 1990s. 'Dread risk' describes this elevated perception of risk in the face of uncertainty.[8]

The inexorable trajectory of risk management is that there will always be additional risks to identify and seek to control. Once the premise is accepted then you can never have too much of it. Because the future is unknowable, things are bound to happen that are not predicted. These 'known unknowns' become justification for more stringent risk management processes and systems. When existing risk processes prove ineffective to prevent another corporate crisis then the conclusion drawn is that the processes must be deficient. The institutionalisation of risk management extends.

For instance, the financial crash appeared to establish that pre-crash risk management mechanisms were inadequate and needed to be supplemented. The third instalment of the Basel Accords from the Basel Committee on Banking Supervision were agreed over 2010–11 to enhance risk control procedures for the world's banks. Since Basel I and Basel II didn't work to prevent the crash, a stricter 'Basel III' was seen to be needed to make up for earlier deficiencies in financial regulation. Basel IV is already being talked about. No doubt there will be further instalments after future financial crises.

Post-crash, this trajectory in risk management was further sanctioned by the emergence of the 'black swan' perspective.

Black swans are low-probability and low-frequency, but high-magnitude and high-impact upheavals. A key feature of Nassim Nicholas Taleb's original theory – which is often overlooked – is that these events are theoretically predictable, just as the existence of black swans could have been anticipated without ever seeing one. Taleb's argument is not to attempt to predict black swan events, but that more effort should be applied to building 'robustness' against inevitable adversities.

Taleb argued that the existing 'value-at-risk' models popular with financial institutions were not good enough. They were naïve in using 'Gaussian normal distribution' bell curves which tended to exclude the very extreme events that they were supposed to be safeguarding against.[9] More robust tools would be needed.

Others drew the same conclusion from the way the crash unfolded, especially from its cross-border repercussions. A catastrophe in one part of the world affects the sourcing, manufacture, shipping and sale of products locally. Moreover, the interconnections of global financial, economic and political networks ensure that the effects of such events 'ripple around the world'. Standard enterprise risk management (ERM) tools could not cope.

The usual suggestion is not their replacement, but to *add* extra layers of control. The ERM approach remains relevant for managing 'run of the mill' business risks across 'strategic, operational, financial, and hazard' risk categories. But black swan 'high-magnitude, low-frequency disrupters' call for the complementary commitment of more resources towards risk management 'disrupter analysis'.[10]

Even ahead of the capital investment projects that are being put off, the greater attention to risk has undermined innovation's foundational research. Early-stage R&D activities occupy the extreme end of entrepreneurial risk-taking. They are not just risky but are intrinsically uncertain in outcome. R&D exemplifies 'Knightian' uncertainty in its original sense. Not only are the financial returns unknowable but also much R&D is likely to have *no* return at all, as was described in the earlier chapter on innovation.

Mazzucato describes how R&D not only takes years to materialise into new products, but most fails. In pharmaceuticals research projects can take up to 17 years, cost about US$403 million per drug, and have an extremely high failure rate. Only 1 in 10,000 compounds reach market approval phase, a success rate of only 0.01%.[11]

Risk-taking and speculation are absolutely necessary for innovations and transformative growth to occur. Mazzucato concluded that nothing less than 'bold courage' is required to delve into this world of uncertainty.[12] In a climate where such activities are deemed rash and reckless there will be less commitment to long-term R&D, expressed in the falling share of research within overall business R&D we noted earlier.

Business risk-taking is never easy. There is always the potential of loss, which can even threaten survival. Without risk-taking, though, business dynamism suffers, and the possibilities of economic progress too. The indecisiveness and paralysis that follows from today's greater fixation on risk stifles individual businesses. It thereby reinforces slow-drift capitalism.

The ascendancy of techno-pessimism

Discomfort with change and fears about the future are also manifest in growing anxieties over the impact of technology. Technology as the vehicle for economic development has become regarded more ambivalently than in the past. Increasing attention is drawn to its dangers.

This hasn't stopped technology advancing: most of us remain keen to use it. We love our electronic gadgets that gain additional functionality year-by-year. They are such an indispensable part of our lives that earlier fears about mobile phones making us ill or stupid are confined to the box: 'too awkward to worry about'.

However, when it comes to the generic applications of technology then anxieties are openly expressed, including from many established areas. A team from Oxford University's Future of Humanity Institute assessed the top 12 gravest risks with the potential to wipe out humanity. What was striking about this particular piece of catastrophist speculation was that most were not natural events over which we have little control, such as an asteroid impact. Instead, the top risks came from existing human-led economic and technological developments. Instances that could go horribly wrong included synthetic biology, nanotechnology and artificial intelligence.[13]

Klaus Schwab, founder of the World Economic Forum that runs the annual Davos gatherings, argued that the pace of technological change means there has never been a time of greater potential peril. Dangers arise from the unequal division of the spoils of technological advances; from the threat of mass unemployment; as well from the potential abuse of robotics, genetic engineering and cyber weapons.[14]

Some attribute bouts of financial instability to technology too. Jaron Lanier, one of the pioneers of virtual reality technology, argued that the internet underlay the financial crisis. Cheap computation and networked information 'did drive or at least amplify and accelerate' the whole thing. It wasn't just financial engineering that led to the crisis, but *computational* financial engineering.

No bank could have sliced-and-diced, assembled and sold on those supposedly low-risk portfolios of questionable mortgages without the aid of network access to global information.[15] ICT has certainly enabled modern-day financialisation. But what is symptomatic of the pervasive culture of technological anxiety is how attention focuses on these technological levers, instead of the underlying economic drivers of financial turmoil.

Lanier explained that computation made it possible to keep track of all the details needed to 'manufacture the deception'. Characterising the crash as a 'deception' by financial practitioners shows the misanthropic bent that often sits alongside techno-anxieties. Destabilising technological advances are regarded as products of human arrogance.

Technology is also anticipated to provide humanity with its just desserts. People create the technologies, which then cause humanity harm. Nemesis can take the form of technologies killing us: by drones or robots escaping from human control. Even human survival might be imperilled by technology.

Professor Stephen Hawking warned that with 'near certainty' technological advance is endangering the planet. Artificial intelligence could spell the 'end of the human race'.[16] Hawking also reflected that humanity is not as powerful and pre-eminent as had been thought. Man is really quite limited in his capabilities.

While thinking machines could redesign themselves at an ever-increasing rate, humans lack that capacity: 'Humans are limited by slow biological evolution', and 'couldn't compete'. In time they 'would be superseded'. Man is hubristically destroying the planet with his technologies, while these technologies could also destroy man himself.

Elon Musk, the technology entrepreneur who runs Space X and the electric car producer Tesla, shares Hawking's misgivings. He also called artificial intelligence 'our biggest existential threat'.[17] Bill Gates has echoed these concerns. He thinks something resembling the science fiction *Terminator* films is feasible if the perilous potential of artificial super-intelligence is not taken seriously.[18]

Lanier, Hawking, Musk and Gates are not innate cynics or pessimists about technology. On the contrary, they have built their reputations from within the world of science and innovation. They have all pushed forward technological frontiers, and some still are. That they are prominent worriers indicates how extensively the technology-anxious mood has spread.

On a more mundane level technology is blamed for joblessness, now and even more threateningly for the future. Mass unemployment beckons as the machines take our jobs: white-collar as well as blue-collar. Some suggest the digital economy is itself the driver of secular stagnation.[19]

In his award-winning book *The Rise of the Robots*, Martin Ford argues that as technology continues to accelerate machines will begin taking care of themselves. Fewer people will be necessary in work. He thinks artificial intelligence is already well on its way to making good jobs obsolete: many paralegals, journalists, office workers and even computer programmers are poised to be replaced by robots and smart software.[20] Professor Lynda Gratton shares the view that technology is hollowing out work and shrinking the number of intermediate-level jobs.[21] She admits it is hard to build a positive narrative about the future of work.

The idea that machines are taking away our employment is, of course, not a new one. Since Luddism in the early 19th century, technology has been blamed for people losing jobs. In fact, many of the original Luddites were positive about machinery and were technologically savvy. Their protests were not an attempt to turn back the technological clock. Rather, they were motivated by the dehumanising aspects of the rise of industrial capitalism.[22] However, new technology *was* replacing people, so the anti-technology reputation stuck. A century later, in the early days of the Great Depression, Keynes coined the phrase 'technological unemployment' for the way machines would replace workers.

Whenever unemployment jumps during economic crises, technology is usually offered as one main explanation. This is false. The driver of joblessness is not the loss of jobs due to rising productivity but the failure of a depressed economy to create enough *new* sectors and good *new* jobs. What is important is having a breadth of invention and innovation that provides the replacement sources of employment for the future.

Decent jobs, including mid-skilled ones, began to decline as a share of employment from the 1970s,[23] paralleling the slowing in accumulation throughout the Long Depression. Timing alone undermines the ICT-attributed thesis. Good, well-paying private sector job creation has been lacking as a symptom of the weakness of productive innovating investment. This is what has prevented the unemployed and young people trying to join the workforce from getting decent jobs.

Some claim that this argument is now superseded because of the growing 'intelligence' of machines. Erik Brynjolfsson and Andrew McAfee acknowledge that technology has in the past been a net plus for jobs: but things are different now with the rise of smart machines.[24] Today's machines are increasingly able to perform tasks with human-like capabilities. These newest technologies, combined with the globalisation they facilitate, bring a decline in jobs that require moderate levels of skill. Further technological progress, they think, will threaten jobs that had seemed safe, both higher up and also lower down the skill spectrum.

The contention is that computers will move on to 'analysis'. This is thought to herald a nightmarish future when an ever-decreasing number of professions is immune from robotic and algorithmic encirclement. Carl Frey and Michael Osborne, no doubt with the assistance of computers, assessed that almost half of US and one-third of UK current employment is in occupations that are at high risk of being automated and disappearing over the next two decades. This includes roles like legal secretaries, financial accounts managers and tax advisors.[25]

But this prospect doesn't change the source of persistent joblessness as being an insufficient creation of jobs. Current and future generations of robots and software are still essentially a form of automation. Just like the textile looms, they will replace labour. But just like that first industrial revolution did, the next one will create many new sectors and new areas of employment.

A conceptual difficulty adds to the misapprehensions over technology and employment. It is much easier to imagine how familiar existing roles can be replaced by automation than it is to anticipate what might replace them. It is much more difficult – even impossible – to imagine all the new jobs, new sectors and industries which could be generated by productive investment in the years and decades to come.

No one at the start of the 20th century could have accurately forecast all the types of occupations people were doing 100 years later. Not just workers in the ICT sector, but all the new roles that make use of computerisation: from shop-till cashiers to electronic commerce to call centres. Or the additional services enabled by the surpluses and higher living standards from previous productivity growth: from entertainment to fitness gyms and personal trainers, to fast food shops, to international cuisine. Or consider today's healthcare system. It would be unrecognisable in scale and scope to anyone transported from the year 1900.

Deep pessimism about technological unemployment forgets that jobs and occupations would always be changing in a dynamic economy. Labour market turnover in industrialised economies is much higher than we often imagine. Only a small proportion of the people who leave their jobs each year is due to technological displacement.

Such churn is not a problem when there are enough good quality jobs to take up instead. In more vibrant times extra jobs replaced the ones displaced by automation. For instance, over the past 150 years agricultural output has rocketed while millions of farming jobs have disappeared. The consequence was not continuous mass rural unemployment because other industries started or expanded to provide employment for these technologically displaced workers.

New technologies bring about new economic environments. They inspire further innovation. In the process this creates a lot of work to be done and makes employment. Technological advances themselves create all sorts of new occupations: areas such as aerospace, pharmaceuticals and energy over the 20th century.

Technology takes and gives employment. Air travel reduced employment in passenger shipping. But it created many more jobs not just in flying, but in maintaining planes, in servicing air passengers at airports, and in air traffic control. It also helped create a mass tourism and travel industry. This employs even more people arranging holidays, and then providing the hospitality services at their destinations.

Just as many people have roles now that were not invented 100 years ago, the same *should* be true 100 years hence. It is a wonderful thing, not to fret over, when machines take over the drudge work not just of manual routine labour, but also of mental routine labour. This opens up the space for new sectors where people have more scope to use even more of their creative potential.

In conclusion, stronger employment needs more technology, not less. Higher productivity generates higher living standards and provides more means to invest in new areas and expand economic activities. The problem of joblessness arises when not enough surplus is being productively invested to generate new employment. The irony is that persistent unemployment arises not from an excess of technology and productivity growth, but from the dearth of technological advance that would open up more industries and sectors to provide many new jobs. We need more and better robotics, not risk-averse restrictions on its development.

Technological change, the primary means for economic and social progress, has been corrupted into an argument for stasis and even for regression. The social barriers to capital investment are being exacerbated by fear of the change that is inherent in technological transformation. Technology's potential is being strangled by the social mores that see development as dangerous and damaging.

The mantra of sustainability

Today's anxieties about economic progress only occasionally translate into an explicit rejection of the need for growth.[26] For a long time though, and increasingly since the 1960s, critical commentators have focused on the problems that come alongside growth and development.

Ezra Mishan's *The Costs of Economic Growth*, published in 1967, caused a stir by highlighting the 'external diseconomies' of growth, such as urban traffic congestion, smoke and noise pollution. 'We have paid dearly for the material plenty and for the technological toys bequeathed to us by science.'[27] A few years later in 1973 E.F. Schumacher published *Small Is Beautiful: A Study of Economics As If People Mattered*, arguing that the modern economy was not sustainable, not least because of natural resource depletion. Schumacher put forward a philosophy of 'enoughness'. He condemned the notions that 'bigger is better', and that 'growth is good'.

Overt claims that the world had grown enough were minority views then. It was too evident that the 'third world' remained mired in a state of poverty that could only be overcome with more economic development. In the industrial economies many people did feel, correctly, that they were better off than ever before. For most, though, this did not seem like an age of abundance, of having 'enough' material comfort.

Half a century on, explicit rejections of growth are still unappealing to many. People around the world aspire to higher living standards for themselves and for their children. Few question that rapid economic growth has confirmed its social value in helping lift hundreds of millions of people out of poverty in South and East Asia. Even in an advanced country like Britain, a housing shortage exemplifies that pressing concerns of material want remain.

Instead discomfort with progress has entered the mainstream through the rise of environmentalism. Changes that are most sanctioned these days are those that seek to limit or reverse man's impact on the environment. Reducing carbon emissions has widespread endorsement as the way of addressing climate change. Less development is favoured over more development to combat and adapt to global warming.

Modern environmentalism began to take off during the 1960s. Initially, as with Mishan, concerns focused on pollution and the damage being inflicted on the natural world. Rachel Carson's *Silent Spring* (1962) is credited with sparking the contemporary interest in environmental issues. She drew attention to the detrimental effects on wildlife arising from pesticides. In its wake, membership of organisations such as the World Wildlife Fund rocketed.

Ten years later the Club of Rome, an international think tank founded in 1968, published *The Limits to Growth*, which became the best-selling environmental book ever. It pulled together all the issues that had become more prominent in the intervening decade. The environmentalist agenda broadened from pollution and overt despoliation to emphasise natural resource depletion as well. This was timely. Only a year later the Arab-Israeli war focused attention on the uncertain supply of one essential resource: oil. Anxieties over resource dependence and possible depletion have never subsided.

Although the gloomiest environmental predictions from the 1970s have not come true, the idea that there is a trade-off between environmental aims and economic growth has lasted.[28] By the mid-1970s Daniel Bell described with some surprise how growth had become 'held responsible for the spoliation of the environment'.[29] More than a coincidence, the discrediting at the same time of Keynesian fiscal policies designed to stimulate growth was consistent with the increasing scepticism that more growth was beneficial.

A follow-up Club of Rome publication in the early 1990s drew out the misanthropic tendencies of the anti-development perspective. Responding to the end of the Cold War its authors thought that the sudden absence of traditional enemies meant that 'new enemies have to be identified' to provide social coherence.[30] Noting that pollution, global warming and water shortages would fit the bill as common enemies, they cautioned though not to mistake symptoms for causes.

They recognised that in their 'totality and their interactions' these ecological phenomena constituted a common threat which 'must be confronted by everyone'. But they emphasised that all these dangers are actually caused by *human intervention in nature*. 'The real enemy then is humanity itself.'[31] The report called on humanity to curb its aspirations and engage in more benign, nondestructive forms of economic activity.

Uneasiness with human progress has translated into the notion that growth has many downsides. Mishan, Schumacher, the Club of Rome and others identified growth's 'negative externalities'. Combatting these costs was seen to require the exercise of human restraint. Daniel Ben-Ami shrewdly explained this shift in attitudes to growth through the category of *growth scepticism*: a 'conception of growth with limits'.

Growth remains an acceptable goal to have, but only until it runs up against some type of limit. These limits may be social or moral or, most popularly, environmental. Once these limits are reached further growth is seen as damaging. This is not outright hostility to growth; it is simply sceptical that its benefits outweigh the costs.[32]

The sceptical perspective puts society on guard against the destructive consequences that come with economic change and development. In this spirit some people even welcome lower growth rates because this minimises the detrimental side effects. The ideal sought is stable, or, as it is often called, 'balanced' growth. An ambiance is created that is hostile to quite ordinary development that requires extra infrastructure. This is easy to see in increasingly vehement protests against plans to build new roads, railways, dams, power stations, pipelines, airports and runways – and even houses.

Growth scepticism translates into precaution trumping economic progress. The *precautionary principle* institutionalises this, stating that 'if an action or policy has a suspected risk of causing harm to the public or to the environment then this takes precedence to guide us not to act or to stop doing something'. The burden of proof that something is *not* harmful falls on those wanting to act. Caution counsels doing nothing.

The first major international implementation of this principle was in 1987 with the UN Montreal Protocol on Substances that

Deplete the Ozone Layer.[33] This justified the phasing out of the production of substances that were deemed to be responsible for ozone depletion. Since then this principle has become a regular component in international climate change declarations and protocols.

The adoption of the precautionary approach leads either to state decisions or to self-regulated behaviours that restrain development. EU directives ban genetically modified foods. The US places restrictions on stem cell research. The principle also spawns strictures on fracking and horizontal drilling technologies (mostly in Europe), nuclear power (led by Germany) and fossil fuel extraction (worldwide, but especially in wilderness areas like the Arctic).

The main expression of growth scepticism is the ill-defined concept of 'sustainable development'. The impulse for restraint and stability has been given substantial social force through the sustainability agenda. This had its roots within environmentalism. Initially the idea of 'unsustainable' growth meant that it so damaged the planet that it destroyed the means to enable further growth in the future. From these foundations in a sustainable natural world the concept broadened to become a warning against the damaging effects of growth on social as well as ecological phenomena.

One of the first promotions of sustainability came in a 1972 article, 'Is growth obsolete?', by two eminent Yale professors William Nordhaus and James Tobin.[34] They were exploring the more ambivalent views on economic growth being aired by people like Mishan during the 1960s. On balance, they concluded, growth was still necessary, distancing themselves from the 'anti-growth men' of the 1960s and 1970s. However, in doing so they were among the pioneers of growth scepticism.

Their arguments against the growth critics were pragmatic, rather than offering a positive case for growth. They thought, for example, that the idea of zero economic growth was simply too blunt an instrument for a goal like cleaner air. It would be 'prodigiously expensive and probably ineffectual'.[35] While accepting the notion of inherent tradeoffs, they were unwilling to abandon growth when the counterarguments failed to convince.

While answering the question posed by their title in the negative, Nordhaus and Tobin incorporated some of the assumptions of the anti-growth brigade and were among the first to advance a sustainability approach to economic growth and development. They saw gross national product type measures of growth as limited and over-materialistic. In their place they developed one for 'sustainable economic welfare'.

The notion of justifying growth only as long as it was sustainable both epitomised, and subsequently evangelised, the sceptical message about growth. Through the 1990s the accepted wisdom across most of business became the pursuit of only 'sustainable' growth. But what does this qualified type of growth include, and what does it exclude?

Growth that gave no consideration to the consequences for the survival of employees, or suppliers, or to a grossly polluted environment would be literally unsustainable. Economic growth that wiped out all its workers and suppliers and destroyed the planet would grind to a halt. However, instances of such fantastical forms of activity exist only in the fiction of anti-corporate novels and movies, not in the real world.

Contrary to the presumptions of sustainability, the social development that comes with economic growth actually provides the best antidote to such self-destructive behaviours. History illustrates that one of the benefits of economic development is the way it enables the phasing out of more primitive forms of production that are more likely to have adverse social and ecological consequences. Industrial capitalism curbed its own antisocial activities. These range from 19th century restrictions on child labour and the length of the working day, to more recent controls on industrial pollution and the ban on asbestos in building construction.

The measures currently being undertaken to clean up health-damaging smog in Beijing and other large Chinese cities would not have been possible without the gains from decades of double-digit economic growth. 'Sweatshop labour' in the least developed countries can be eliminated not by international protocols initiated by the richer countries but by those countries' own further economic development.[36] That's the way these conditions have been largely overcome in the developed world.

Unfortunately the sort of sustainability that is being promoted today, because it is inimical to dynamic economic growth, is more likely to sustain reactionary production practices than get rid of them.

The notion of sustainability now goes way beyond any literal meaning. In 1987 the World Commission on Environment and Development under the leadership of the former Norwegian prime minister Gro Harlem Brundtland produced its *Our Common Future* report. This extended the definition of sustainable development to that which 'meets the needs of the present without compromising the ability of future generations to meet their own needs'. Sustainable had become extended to mean non-damaging, because anything that was damaged could be seen as a loss for 'future generations'. Sustainable growth has become growth that not only does not damage the ecology or the direct means of production or damage the customers, but is not damaging to almost any feature of life.

For example, the UN Conference on Sustainable Development held in Rio de Janeiro in 2012 set the world 17 sustainable development goals including reducing inequality, empowering women, healthier lives and providing inclusive education, as well as overt ecological objectives. Jeffrey Sachs, director of The Earth Institute at Columbia University, has motivated their connections in his 2015 book *The Age of Sustainable Development*. Growth is now therefore deemed unsustainable if it accompanies growing income or wealth inequality, a lack of gender diversity, or deteriorating health. With the precautionary principle in operation, there is no obligation to provide proof of any causal connections between growth and these phenomena. It is up to others to disprove the claimed adverse impacts of growth.

In conclusion, the problem with the sustainability perspective is that its conservatism sanctions efforts to preserve capitalism as it is. It institutionalises the cultural backdrop for state institutions to promote stability. Mostly unintentionally, 'sustainability' becomes consistent with the curbing of capitalism's creative destructive tendencies. Strict adherence to sustainability denies the case for disruptive economic restructuring.

ELEVEN

The appeal of muddling through

In Britain the parliamentary Public Administration Select Committee scrutinises the running of government. An investigation into the lack of national strategy heard from witnesses lamenting the absence of strategic reflection in government. David King, a former government chief scientific adviser, described the poverty of long-term thinking across government departments. He emphasised that this reached into the heart of government in the Cabinet Office.

Patrick Carter, chair of the National Health Service Co-operation and Competition Panel, similarly recounted the absence of 'an overall strategic plan for the domestic situation', adding that 'a succession of governments have never felt the need' for one. Nick Butler, the chair of the King's Policy Institute, diplomatically declared it was 'regrettable' that these deficiencies had left Britain without 'a National Strategy for the economy or for the future of the country'. The select committee endorsed these concerns and contrasted the absence of a coherent, strategic approach with the tendency of successive governments to adopt a 'muddle through' style instead.[1]

This characterisation captures important features of contemporary government activity extending across the Western world: myopia, pragmatism, reactiveness and indecision. In Japan, the two 'lost decades' since its financial bubble burst have seen persisting failures from its political elite to act decisively to restructure the economy. In the US, governments have become stuck in near paralysis over economic matters, stumbling from one congressional gridlock to the next. The American propensity to muddle through is often attributed to the separation of powers between the executive and legislative branches. However, it is unreasonable to explain this change in governing practice from a constitutional framework in existence since the country's foundation.

On the other side of the Atlantic, managing the eurozone crisis since 2010 has been a protracted exercise from the EU and from national governments in 'kicking the can down the road'. *Der Spiegel* dubbed this *die Philosophie des Durchmuddelns*: the philosophy of muddling through.[2] Time and again a 'pretend and extend' approach was applied to sovereign indebtedness among the weaker eurozone economies. The eurozone's institutional dysfunctionality has been ignored, however close it has come to collapse.

Leaders of the West's governments seem reluctant to act in the face of problems. As the founder of Apple, the late Steve Jobs knew about having purpose. He captured the irresolute inclination among politicians after a dinner with President Obama. 'The president is very smart, but he kept explaining to us reasons why things can't get done. It infuriates me.'[3]

The depoliticisation of economic intervention

A reluctance to intervene decisively is only part of the failure to fix the depression. The state has over the past four decades in fact become *more* active in the economy, as in other areas of life. Economic policy brings hesitancy and scope together in an extensive range of reactive interventions. Whenever problems become too pressing to ignore, action is taken to muddle through in an effort to retain or restore economic stability.

The conventional perspective that the state has been receding into the background behind a neoliberal revival of market freedoms is a myth. There has been no 'rolling back the state'. Contrary to those who see a neoliberal resurgence starting under the Reagan and Thatcher regimes, in both the US and Britain state economic activities became more comprehensive. The decayed condition of Western production made state intervention more necessary and pervasive than ever.

More public money has been spent, ratcheting up with each slowdown. Regulation has increased. Easy monetary policies have been the rule. The divide between public and private has blurred as state support for market activities has proliferated. Many businesses have become increasingly dependent on the operations of the state.

As state intervention spread, it has at the same time become less democratically accountable. Chapter Nine described how the end of the Cold War removed a mask disguising the exhaustion of left-right politics. The establishment's more evident lack of mission and focus produced an erosion of democratic norms.

Without purposeful programmes, the links between the elites and their constituencies broke down. Politicians estranged themselves from their electorates. The gap widened between the state and its citizens. The resulting loss by the political class of its public legitimacy and moral authority was a significant factor behind Britain's vote to leave the EU and the election of Trump as US president. The subsequent anti-democratic reaction by cultural and political elites to these votes had itself been foreshadowed by the previous weakening of democratic accountability for economic (and other) policies.

The muddle-through process has operated increasingly outside traditional political arenas. The decline of domestic political contestation enabled politicians to avoid difficult issues. Responsibility for handling them is transferred to technocrats. Governance has thus become less democratically accountable to people. More and more the state operates through arms-length bodies whose members are not elected or open to democratic recall.

State economic activity has become depoliticised. The underlying economic problems of production are much less debated within mainstream politics. Public spending, taxation and fiscal deficits are still discussed, frequently, in parliaments. But this illustrates the debasement of debate over alternative economic visions into the detail of national bookkeeping. The challenges of reviving economic growth are rarely discussed in the chambers of representative democracy. This is not to romanticise the quality of economic debates of earlier times, but alternative ways of promoting growth were on offer. Since the 1980s most state economic interventions have operated away from the accountability of political debate.

The depoliticisation and bureaucratisation of public life have been among the most important features of the post-Cold War world. Corey Robin, the political theorist, noted the trend when explaining that the new class of political elites has little contact even with the business community. The primary experiences outside of government have been in academia, journalism, think tanks, or some other part of the culture industry.[4] Anthropologist David Graebner also picked up on this, not least in the US. Final victory over the Soviet Union had not led to the expected domination of the market but cemented the dominance of 'fundamentally conservative managerial elites'.[5]

The discrediting of state economic policies

The route to the depoliticisation of economic policy began with the collapse of the post-war mixed economy 'Keynesian' model. Labelling it with his name was a little unfair to Keynes. He had died in 1946 before the economic boom got going. His theory, from which post-war economic practice drew legitimacy, had been developed for the different circumstances of economic depression.

Even during the war Keynes had been prescient in noticing that others were extending his ideas into a more routine justification for state economic intervention than he had intended. Hence his acerbic comment after attending a meeting of American economists that he was the 'only non-Keynesian there'. Nevertheless, it was his slump-time theories that provided the intellectual justification for the extension of post-war state interventions by politicians of all persuasions.

The return to crisis in the early 1970s shocked governments across the Western world. Political leaders had got used to the calmer conditions of the boom. Their disorientation was reinforced by the unsuccessful attempts in the 1970s to deal with the effects of slowdown. Out of this malaise, one idea began to gain ground: that activist state economic policy was not only ineffective but was becoming counterproductive. The left-right consensus around the Keynesian perspective hit the buffers, to be replaced by a shared intellectual disillusionment with interventionist economic policy.

In the early stages of the crisis demand stimulus had been tried, including by governments from the right. In 1971 the Republican president Richard Nixon announced an expansionary budget to try to keep the American economy moving. The right-wing Nixon was happy to declare, 'I am now a Keynesian in economics'.[6] Other countries followed suit. In Britain a year later the Conservative government tried the same approach when the chancellor Anthony Barber announced a tax-cutting, deficit-expanding 'dash for growth'.

These policies failed to get the economy moving. Instead they seemed to produce 'stagflation', a new combination of inflation and continued economic stagnation. The misery of mounting unemployment was compounded by rising prices and higher public sector debt. The anti-Enlightenment presumption that human intervention made things worse seemed to be endorsed by the failures of fiscal policy and its unravelling in rising prices.

Soon social democratic governments were also renouncing the fiscal spending that they had earlier become so passionate about. In Britain, Labour Prime Minister Jim Callaghan famously told his party conference in 1976 that it wasn't possible to spend your way out of crisis. 'We used to think you could spend your way out of recession and increase employment by boosting government spending.' To shocked delegates he declared,

> I tell you in all candour that that option no longer exists ... and in so far as it ever did exist, it only worked on each occasion since the war by injecting a bigger dose of inflation into the economy, followed by a higher level of unemployment as the next step.[7]

Keynesian economic intervention was not simply ineffective. It was condemned for creating economic problems.

The following year, West Germany's Chancellor Helmut Schmidt, also from the leftist Social Democratic Party, likewise repudiated Keynesian economics. He argued that the German economy had only avoided the levels of inflation incurred elsewhere by resisting the fiscal temptation others had fallen into. The same anti-state spending lesson was drawn. Schmidt declared that the time for Keynesian economics is past because the main global problem was now inflation.[8] Enthusiasm for using state spending to stimulate the economy was cast aside almost everywhere.

The reputation of state industrial policies fared no better. Their discrediting was made easier by how they were being applied: not to help build new industries but to prop up crisis-hit ones. Britain's industrial policy gave support to firms in declining industries, such as steel, shipbuilding and cars. Presented as a programme of 'picking winners', it was ridiculed as shoring up a series of 'lame duck' losers.

Most of Britain's troubled steel industry had already been nationalised in 1967. Over the next three decades despite continued state support plant after plant closed down. The surviving parts were returned to the private sector in 1988.[9] In 2016 Tata Steel that owned half of the remaining industry announced it wanted to pull out of steelmaking in Britain.

In 1975 British Leyland, representing much of the domestically owned car industry, also had to be part nationalised. The industry never regained competitiveness and eventually went bust in 1986.[10] Meanwhile the declining shipbuilding industry was reorganised by government in the early 1970s before full nationalisation in 1977. After the few profitable yards were sold off privately during the 1980s, British Shipbuilders closed its last shipyard in 1989. Such failures undermined support for anything called industrial policy.

President Reagan summed up the new scepticism of state economic policies in 1981: 'Government is not the solution to our problem; government is the problem.' The writer on intellectual history Angus Burgin described how by the 1980s debates in the Anglo-American sphere were permeated with the assumption that the workings of the free market should be protected from government attempts to intervene.[11] The following decade, the nominally left-wing President Clinton declared that 'the era of big government is over'.[12]

TINA and the rise of technocratic governance

This broad consensus ensured economic policy stopped being an openly political topic. As early as the 1980s, debate over economic problems was withering. Despite Thatcher's later reputation as breaking the mould, her policies were not that original or distinct. They were part of a common bipartisan international trend. At the time the *Financial Times* astutely identified the erosion of political difference. In November 1984, at the height of Thatcher's prime ministerial authority, it wrote that: 'Thatcherite economic policies are not very different from, or better or worse than, those to which other European governments, whether called conservative as in Germany or socialist as in France, have found their way.'[13]

Thatcher articulated better than most the new consensus developing. One of her favourite phrases, 'there is no alternative', encapsulated it. There was no alternative to capitalism as an economic system. Its acronym, TINA, became an international rallying cry for the advocacy of pro-market policies and a smaller economic role for the state. By the end of the 1980s the TINA mantra was emboldened when the implosion of Stalinism removed the most established alternative.

Fukuyama's celebrated 'End of History' thesis highlighted how the dissolution of oppositional forces marked the end of credible replacements for the market.[14] Across the political spectrum the market – whatever its admitted deficiencies – was perceived to be the only reasonable way of running a modern society. More than ever the market was regarded as the natural order. Like the weather, it was not susceptible to successful human intervention.

China's adoption of market mechanisms to drive its economic development offered further corroboration. The whole world had lined up behind the merits of the market system. The core economic question – whether the market was positive or negative for society – was no longer an area of political difference. Elites everywhere, from Washington to London, Frankfurt, Moscow and Beijing acknowledged the market economy.

Government leaders, including those from socialist traditions, gave up on competing visions for a better economic future. They adopted a more technical and managerial approach to economic life. This was coherently expressed in the 'Third Way' projects of the 1990s espoused both by Clinton and British Prime Minister Tony Blair. More recently Emmanuel Macron, then the French economy minister, extended this in his proposal for a new bipartisan political movement 'En Marche' ('Forward').[15] The 'third way' transcended the counter-position between socialism and free market fundamentalism; it was deemed appropriate for post-political times.

The new consensus around the market, in tandem with growing reservations about the benefits of growth, meant that politicians were relaxed, even desirous to take a backseat in economic policymaking. Although coping practically with the consequences of depression necessitated a more extensive scale of economic intervention, in the absence of contestation these state activities lacked their previous politicised form.

Political elites have embraced a technocratic and managerial orientation through which they attempt to present themselves as reliable, apolitical forces for stability. Blair personified this when claiming that 'nothing matters more to me' than the ability to 'manage the economy'. He went on to declare his belief that 'stability is sexy'. The appropriate government strategy was 'steering a course of stability in an uncertain world'.[16]

In parallel with seeing themselves as pragmatic managers rather than visionaries, governing politicians have been outsourcing their authority on economic affairs. They have delegated their responsibilities to the non-elected experts who populate an array of unaccountable institutions, task forces and commissions. Contracting or commissioning the provision of public services from technocratic quangos and quasi-state private agencies takes the place of direct government intervention. This has separated more state activities from political discussion and democratic accountability. Economic decision making gets relocated from representative assemblies to unaccountable national or supranational institutions.

Almost everywhere 'independent' central banks have adopted the prominent role in trying to manage market fluctuations. The monetary policy that has become today's most important area of economic policymaking is in most instances formally separate from the democratic accountability of governments. One of the first acts of Blair's New Labour government in 1997 had been to declare the Bank of England 'independent'.

Appointed individuals and bodies now take most of the day-to-day economic policy decisions in Britain. These include not just the Monetary Policy Committee of the Bank of England, but also the Competition and Markets Authority, and the many official regulators. They oversee tracts of business, covering large parts that used to be under direct public authority.

When pushed to account for decisions ministers invariably defer to the outside experts. So in August 2015 when the British government was criticised for the timing of the sale of some of its shares in the Royal Bank of Scotland that it had bailed out during the financial crash, ministers passed the responsibility to others. The Treasury justified its actions by saying that they were only following the advice of the financial advisory group Rothschild and the governor of the Bank of England.[17] Buck-passing by politicians has become routine.

The anti-democratic tendency in policymaking has been most explicit in European matters. Here the outsourcing of responsibility by national politicians has given impetus to the ascendancy of EU institutions in running economic and other affairs, unaccountable to the demos, the democratic populace. Even Pope Francis lamented how the great ideals that once inspired Europe have been replaced by the 'bureaucratic technicalities of [EU] institutions'.[18] The EU is more a symptom than a cause of national depoliticisation, but it does sharply express the anti-democratic tendencies. The trends being described here are therefore not just problematic for perpetuating slow-drift capitalism. They also strike at the heart of society's democratic freedoms, fuelling, for example, Britain's referendum decision to leave the undemocratic EU.

During the eurozone crisis unelected governments were installed in Italy and Greece. In 2011, under pressure from EU institutions, the economist and former European Commissioner Mario Monti was named prime minister in Italy, while the former central banker and vice-president of the European Central Bank Lucas Papademos was appointed as Greece's prime minister. The Monti government was fully technocratic and contained not a single MP or member of a political party.

Technocrat government at national levels was introduced as a mirror to technocratic decision making at the supranational pan-European level. The justification offered was the technical and anti-democratic one that only non-political governments divorced from electoral pressure could carry out the painful reforms necessary. In practice both these governments simply pursued more of the same muddle-through policies. They narrowly focused on attempting to reduce state budget deficits, but now without democratic accountability. The eurozone crisis continued to bubble away.

Resilience enhanced ...

Another aspect of the exhaustion of Enlightenment politics has facilitated the muddle-through approach to economic management. The demise of challenges to capitalism gave more scope for coping effectively with the decay in production. The absence of working class pressure at home and the expansion of market relations internationally have helped Western capitalism to extend existing ways, and find new ones, to offset the effects of depression. This greater ability to draw on more sources of resilience has reinforced the peculiar character of this depression as being contained as well as protracted.

... at home ...

Industrial strikes have become much less frequent than over the previous 150 years of capitalism. When they do happen they lack the earlier element of combative class struggle. The absence of much social conflict has made it possible for political and business elites to withstand and then work through the economic challenges in a less pressured way than in the past.

Without needing to deal with social opponents head-on, governments and their outsourced partners-in-state have been able to pursue their muddle-through coping measures without having to concern themselves much with what the masses – the public – are doing or thinking. These less confrontational times make it easier to realise those conservative impulses of limiting the amount of disruption and maintaining stable economic conditions.

For example, the long record of easier monetary policy since the late 1980s has been helped by the flexibility arising from the less polarised domestic environment. Central bankers are today less concerned – rightly so – about the potential for inflationary takeoff when they set or review interest rates. Prior to the mid-1980s, when there had been more prospect of upward pressure on wage levels from a stronger labour movement, a 'fear of inflation' had more sway in tightening interest rates sooner rather than later.

It does not matter that their understanding of the cause of inflation saw things upside-down. Rising prices during the early part of the Long Depression were primarily a business response to the consequences of lower profitability. Businesses pushed up market, including consumer, prices in a self-defeating attempt to boost profit levels. Workers collectively fought back for compensating wage increases to offset the impact on living standards.

Today the greater ease with which the economy and most businesses have been coping with low profitability has been a much bigger counter-inflationary factor than powerless trade unions. However, perceptions matter. A genuinely weaker workforce that is less able to pursue higher wages encourages the application of easier monetary policies.

The more quiescent and less political industrial relations climate has also helped business more directly to moderate the effects of depression. With the disappearance of most militant trade unionism wage growth has been easier to contain. Moreover, corporate cost-cutting has been transformed into a near permanent business strategy. Change management programmes to whittle down operating costs have been easier to implement.

In the aftermath of the recession in the early 2000s John Philpott described the '3Rs' phenomenon: the simultaneous *Reorganising*, *Recruitment* and *Redundancies* happening within the same organisation. The average company was then reorganising itself once every three years. And in between these major programmes, smaller changes were being made to work practices. Businesses were changing their organisational structures all the time, both losing and recruiting people whatever the economic conditions. This contrasted with the previous era when redundancies were predominantly for recessionary times.[19]

Explaining this practice of continuous business change, Robert Gordon developed what he called the disposable worker thesis. Weaker workers were increasingly being treated as 'disposable commodities'.[20] Firms were reducing employment and hours with impunity. Gordon suggested that the unusual degree of corporate cost-cutting provided an explanation for the upsurge of US productivity growth in 2002–03. Hours of work were reduced more quickly than the decline in output. He quoted *The Wall Street Journal*'s assessment that the mildness of the recession masked a ferocious profits crunch that had many chief executives slashing jobs and other costs.[21]

Gordon concluded that it has become easier since the late 1980s for businesses to cut costs repeatedly in response to profit pressures. Cost-cutting is no longer only a recessionary phenomenon but continues throughout the business cycle. This allows more firms to survive economic slowdowns and staves off the need for wider economic restructuring.

This disposable worker pattern was evident during the 2008–09 recessions. The US experienced a disproportionate rise of involuntary part-time employment as well as a significant fall in the employment rate. With predictions of an economic calamity on a par with the 1930s businesses 'tossed every deck chair overboard', slashing employment as well as fixed investment.[22]

Cost-cutting in the context of a more individuated workforce is consistent with analysis from Oliner, Sichel and Stiroh. They discovered that the American industries that experienced the steepest declines in profits from the late 1990s to 2001 also tended to post the largest declines in employment and the largest increases in productivity in the early 2000s. This led them to conclude that reported productivity growth after 2000, at least until 2004 when it fell away again, had been boosted by industry reorganisation and cost-cutting in response to profit pressures.[23]

Consulting firm McKinsey described the 'relentless' pursuit of efficiency in the late 2000s recession too. Facing much less collective employee opposition, two-thirds of American companies, and three-quarters of the largest ones, had reorganised their operations to reduce the number of workers needed.[24]

With less conflict at work, businesses have been able to find these more immediate ways to meet their earnings goals. This lets them avoid inevitably unsettling bouts of transformational investments. Better to persist with frequent internal workplace reorganisations that whittle down costs and boost profits.

... and through internationalisation

Due to the spread of market relations around the world, Western economies have also found substantial *external* support to help them muddle through. Globalisation became the defining buzz phrase of the current era when the failing socialist countries adopted market forces. This began with China's 1978 opening up under the influence of Deng Xiaoping's market-friendly reform policies. Subsequently, from 1989, the Soviet bloc in Central and Eastern Europe, and satellite countries around the world, also adopted capitalist ways. Although results were mostly less impressive than in China, international trade and investment shot up.

The international division of labour jumped stages when hundreds of millions more wage labourers joined capitalism's global labour market. George Magnus calculated that the world's effective labour force increased fourfold between 1980 and 2007.[25] This step-change extension to the global capitalist economy helped the mature economies offset their tendencies to stagnation.

The revenues and profits from foreign trade have helped Western countries through their domestic economic difficulties, not least the stronger exporting nations of Germany and Japan. Exports to the emerging markets boosted revenues. Imports cheapened supplies. Low-priced imported goods, from China especially, have been a blessing in helping keep business costs down and alleviating pressure for wage rises by boosting individual spending power. This has also suppressed inflation further, facilitating the West's easy monetary policies.[26]

The demise of the East–West confrontation has also made it easier to manage international economic tensions. National or regional outbreaks of economic and financial instability have been contained with less international disruption than hitherto.

And just as the disappearance of class conflict at home broadens the elite's room for manoeuvre in economic management, so diminished inter-nation conflict has been a boon for muddling through.

As geopolitical tensions fell in anticipation of the end of the Cold War, the 1989 Brady Plan from the US Treasury Secretary Nicholas Brady illustrated the greater scope for smoothing economic affairs internationally. The plan sought to remove the burden on capital markets of the high levels of debt built up by a number of developing countries in Latin America, and others in Africa, Asia and Eastern Europe. Cutting the debts in exchange for less onerous Brady Bonds benefited the Western banks that had made the loans. Debtor countries could go back to the markets to fund their further economic development.

Such enhanced international flexibility has been replicated many times since. From the Mexican peso crisis in 1994 through the East Asian, the Russian and the Argentinian financial crises, collaborative interventions have been generally effective in mitigating the destabilising global effects they could have had. The potentially devastating repercussions from the 2008 crash were also alleviated by the existence of a more interconnected global economy. As requested at international economic gatherings, less impacted parts of the world, notably China, were able to provide global stimulus.

The areas of productive dynamism in the South have offered a huge new source of value creation in the world. The mature West has been able to draw on this to help itself. Businesses have moved there directly for their own production facilities: relocating, or outsourcing, parts or all of their production to these thriving areas. This gets around domestic profitability constraints. The returns generated from this capital export through foreign direct investment have been a sizeable benefit for all the advanced industrial economies, not least Britain and the US. Ruchir Sharma of Morgan Stanley Investment Management estimates that the share of US corporate profits from overseas operations has risen from about 17% in the late 1990s to 27% by the mid-2010s.[27]

Capital flows *into* the West have been another huge assistance for countries having to live with domestic decay. Financialisation is far from a domestic affair. Its pervasiveness and effectiveness have been greatly enhanced by the international capital inflows since the rise of the emerging markets, and especially China's opening to the capitalist world.

British and US state institutions have gained greater room to manoeuvre with their easy money measures and with other state activities that rest on financialised debt. This operates in four main ways: financing the external deficits that accompany the expansion of debt; a backstop against destabilising currency falls; funding government deficit spending; and suppressing market interest rates.

Funding external deficits

Capital imports have made debt-fuelled spending affordable. In effect capital flows, much of them from emerging economies, have financed external deficits in some mature ones. This reliance on foreign capital prompted Bank of England governor Mark Carney's warning, at the start of the EU referendum campaign, about Britain testing the 'kindness of strangers'.[28] In the circumstances of the debate this was loaded language since external financial dependence long preceded the referendum discussion and the vote to leave. Britain has been running a current account deficit since 1984. The US's deficit began even earlier, in 1982 – with only a tiny surplus in one year since: recessionary 1991.

On a global level an arrangement akin to vendor financing grew. US and Britain ran persistent expanding trade and current account deficits because these societies were living beyond their self-generated means and purchasing stuff made abroad. Foreigners lent the money to make this possible.

This arrangement can be seen operating bilaterally between China and the US. There is no technical necessity for bipartite flows of trade and capital to balance, but it is striking that both grew together. As the US's trade deficit with China grew – with all those cheaper 'Made in China' goods retailed across the US – China emerged as the biggest overseas buyer of US debt. It was in China's interest that the US could afford to buy its exports, so it helped provide the funding.

There is one significant difference to traditional vendor financing. This is often a financialised means by troubled producers to boost sales artificially. Less competitive producers offer credit to possible buyers. In the Chinese-American relationship the shoe is on the other foot. China as the ascending value producer is in the position of strength. It can determine how much of its capital goes to the US, or to other Western countries, or to other developing countries. China has already been redirecting more value from its production to uses other than supporting the US. More is staying in its domestic sphere to boost its home market. More is going into other emerging markets in Asia, Africa and Latin America, including its 'Belt and Road' initiative.

Insurance against currency collapses

Capital inflows have supported Western currencies, especially the dollar and pound, and offered a safeguard against the potential for disorderly falls that easy money policies might precipitate. Although over the longer term exchange rates tend to move in line with relative productivity changes, other factors can trigger bouts of unwelcome currency volatility. Easy money policies bring this possibility as they make it less attractive to park value in a country's low interest-bearing assets.

In practice, lower value currencies have been one of the silent goals of these monetary policies, and in particular of quantitative easing. 'Silent' because memories of 1930s protectionism still make everyone reticent about currency wars. A lower currency is often welcome in helping exporters to be more competitive. Indebted governments, again in silence, also actually like some inflation from costlier imports to reduce their real debt burdens.

However there are downsides from lower currencies. Higher import prices can curb consumption, offsetting one of the goals of financialisation to boost domestic spending. Funding external deficits can be more difficult. A lower exchange rate also makes it more expensive to do anything abroad, from travel to foreign direct investment.

Floating currency levels are never easy to manage and these attempts at financialised manipulation can produce volatility and the risk of going into a disruptive free fall. The resulting turmoil would probably incite central banks to push up official interest rates to protect the exchange rate, especially for countries like the US and Britain with large overseas deficits to fund, robbing them of their cheap money prop.

The availability of capital flows into the US and Britain has curbed the potential for currency collapse. Incoming capital has sustained exchange rates higher than would otherwise have been the case. Although exchange rates under financialised regimes have not been stable, without foreign capital imports currency falls could have been more extreme and erratic.[29]

Supporting government deficit spending

Foreign capital helps fund not just external but, specifically, public spending deficits in the industrial countries. Higher state spending alongside depressed tax revenues produce near permanent deficits, adding to the national debt. Foreign governments have taken on an increasing amount and proportion of these public debts.

For the US, foreign ownership of its Treasury bonds expanded from about 15% at the start of the Long Depression to 35% by 2000, peaking at over 60% in 2008. Although under QE the Federal Reserve has emerged as a significant holder of its own government debt, foreigners still retained about 50% in 2013. Outstanding US Treasuries nearly tripled between 2008 and 2013 from US$3.6 trillion to US$9.8 trillion; the amount owned by foreigners more than doubled to nearly US$5 trillion.[30]

Foreign ownership of UK government debt increased from about 19% in 1996 to peak at 36% in 2008. As in the US, QE purchases of government bonds by the Bank of England reduced overseas ownership, to about 30% in 2013. It is striking though that the volume of foreign holdings still doubled over this period, rising to over £400 billion in 2013.[31] Foreign capital inflows have been imperative in funding US and British government deficits, enabling these states to continue to perform their coping and stabilising activities.

The China relationship has also been at the forefront of foreign ownership of US government debt. In 2008 alone, China lent the US government more than US$400 billion – equivalent to more than 10% of Chinese GDP. This was a tremendous stabiliser for the US government during the crash. It offset the possibility feared by some of America experiencing a sovereign bond crisis.

Lower interest rates

Rising foreign ownership has also had the additional benefit of keeping down government debt service costs. Financial investors – whether domestic or foreign – have to be persuaded to buy government debt as attractive financial investments. High existing debt can make this more difficult. This prompts concern not just that it will ever be repaid, but also how little the repayment might then be worth due to currency declines. Potential investors demand a much higher rate of interest in order to offset the perceived riskiness of purchasing.

The availability of large foreign capital inflows to buy public debt has been beneficial for government finances in keeping interest rates lower than they otherwise would have been. An IMF study found that on average an increase in the share of securities held by non-residents by 10 percentage points is associated with a decline in yields of 32 to 43 basis points, or between a third and nearly a half of a percent.[32]

By suppressing market interest rates capital inflows also support easy monetary policies. Chapter Five explained that low interest rates are a reflection of reduced profitability within the mature economies, reinforced by weak levels of productive investment and the corresponding high level of corporate savings. Much of these savings flows into financial assets, including bonds. The greater demand for bonds pushes up their price, with the inverse effect on interest rates since the coupon interest rate is paid on the original nominal price of the bond regardless of the higher actual price.

Foreign capital flows into the West's public and private debt create another strong tailwind to help suppress interest rates, short and long term. This downward impact became apparent in the US in the early 2000s when the central bank found its attempts to drive up long-term US interest rates for business and household borrowing ineffective. Alan Greenspan, then the Federal Reserve's chair, dubbed this a 'conundrum'.[33]

Long-term interest rates had trended lower even as the Federal Reserve had raised the target federal funds rate. This was the opposite of the normal pattern. The answer to the conundrum – alongside the domestic corporate savings discussed earlier – was that China and other emerging economies were buying up so many bonds that they were holding down market interest rates. IMF analysis later confirmed that foreign official purchases of US Treasuries contributed significantly to the decline in real interest rates in the first decade of the 2000s.[34]

While this blunted the efficacy of Greenspan's monetary tightening, this was a small price to pay for the other benefits of the foreign funding of debt. Anyway, the Federal Reserve's usual penchant has been for easing, so at most times capital imports have helped to reinforce the easy and cheap money policies of financialisation. Since the Long Depression began foreigners have bought an increasing share all US long-term debt, both public and private. From about 5% in 1974, since 2007 they have held over a quarter of it.

Enrique Mendoza and Vincenzo Quadrini have analysed the connections between financial globalisation and the rapid expansion of US debt. They calculated that since the mid-1980s *more than half the rise* in net borrowing by US nonfinancial sectors – that's borrowing by businesses, people and government – was financed by foreign lending. Foreign capital flows have contributed significantly to the 'surge in debt'.[35]

This feature of capital flows also facilitates the workings of the symbiotic debt-trade mechanism between the US and China. Chinese official lending went mainly to the US government rather than directly to US households. However, it was the low interest rates and the easy credit markets that Chinese capital inflows helped maintain that sustained American consumer spending on Chinese products.

In conclusion, post-Cold War internationalisation has significantly buoyed the durability of the West's expanding debt economies. Capital has flowed from the emerging economies in Asia, as well as Middle Eastern oil producers, to the depressed ones. Less capital inflow would have meant higher domestic interest rates in the West, and probably a slower expansion of debt. Domestic economic activity, living standards and GDP would all have been lower.

The fashion for blaming West–East imbalances as one of the causes of the crash[36] condemns a decisive force that has kept Western economic activity going. Capital imports from the surplus countries enabled economic life in many parts of the West to appear as healthy as it did before 2008. Without that steady source of foreign demand the continued expansion of debt, especially of government debt, might have spooked financial investors and precipitated an earlier financial crash.

The combined intellectual, political and economic circumstances, domestic and international, since the 1980s have favoured a muddling-through state approach. The enhanced range of measures for better coping with the effects of the depression provides the material basis for today's slow-drift capitalism. They have effectively alleviated the worst features of decay. Can this continue?

TWELVE

The limits of muddling through

Since the mid-1980s, and especially until the 2008 crash, economic life seemed all right for most people living in the West. Output grew moderately most years. Recessions were modest affairs. The financial crash changed things but not that much. Following its deep recessions, economic conditions have disappointed with their sluggishness. Yet great personal hardship has remained the exception. There is now pessimism about a return to strong growth, but still little sense of impending doom.

This relatively benign state of economic affairs is testimony to the success of coping in being able to draw upon capitalism's resiliencies. So why can't we continue to muddle through forever? If interventionist, stabilising state institutions have been so effective, what's wrong with relying upon them? Why should anyone worry about the decay in Western production? These reasonable questions indicate that the political challenge from muddling through arises less from its limitations than from its effectiveness. Fair stability justifies the continued procrastination over fixing the broken economy.

False comfort

The successes of muddling through in stopping things falling apart have maintained a false sense of wellbeing within the elites. The pressure on political leaders is tempered. Muddling through works and becomes self-justifying. The urgency for deeper, radical changes to revive the economy is disguised. Society's unease with the disruptions inherent in change has spawned a deep *conservatism* within the establishment. The resistance to economic reorganisation coexists with complacency that economic life is really not that terrible.

Buoyed by the material effectiveness of muddling through, elites are oblivious to how deep-seated the problems are. There is a *great evasion* from facing up to economic atrophy and from recognising the need for wide-ranging restructuring. An IMF official captured this reluctance to act, describing politicians rejecting suggestions for change with the shrug: 'There isn't a crisis, there isn't a recession, so why is there such a need to act?'[1]

The philosopher Julian Baggini sagely advised that if you find yourself 'drawing on your resilience a lot' then you really ought to ask yourself why you keep hitting the floor.[2] That personal advice can be equally directed at the Western elites. If economic life is so dependent on resilience, they should ask why we need to draw on it so much. Instead, the great evasion has persisted.

Even when the crisis intensifies, complacency about the scale of problems within the productive sphere has survived. The financial crash, for instance, was viewed primarily as a *financial* matter. Financial cleansing helped settle anxieties and pave the way for financialisation to resume, but very little cleansing of production occurred. The crash itself did little to expose that the previous appearance of prosperity was spurious.

The wrong lessons were drawn. Discussion focused on the antics of financial practitioners and the failings in the financial markets. Instead of seeing the crash as a symptom of productive decay that needed fixing, the dominant response blamed greedy bankers, gullible borrowers and ineffective regulators. The crash was another wasted opportunity to recognise the seriousness of the depression. Maybe the shock of the popular votes during 2016 in Britain and the US will stimulate some new thinking. However, a progressive outcome relies upon a successful contest of ideas over the current state of affairs and what to do about it.

This chapter explains that the complacency of the great evasion is also myopic. Coping measures of recent decades cannot be effective forever. Their limitations are relative, not absolute. The level of debt, or public subsidy, or the amount of QE undertaken, never hits a hard ceiling. But the extra debt, subsidy or monetary easing will never quell the original forces causing decay.

While limitless in themselves, the effects of muddling through are limited. This will not appear as a final collapse of muddling through. But over time the benign appearances resulting from coping will become dimmer, and be interrupted by sharp crises. Primarily this is because productive decay is not an event; it is a process with regressive consequences that build up over time.

Coping with economic decay brings three predicaments: perpetuation, exhaustion and destabilisation. While the coping mechanisms can manage the underlying tendency of decay, they don't negate it. Reactions are ultimately weaker than the force of decay that brought them into play.

Decay persists and its ramifications worsen. In addition, most coping tools tend to become less effective the more they are used. Some also introduce their own problems and create additional sources of instability. The financial crash demonstrated these three limitations. The continued extension of debt didn't stop decay spreading. It didn't prevent a deep economic recession. And the financial bubbles that debt caused created huge turmoil.

These limits are comparable to the effects of medical treatment for some disease. A palliative drug could be the right thing to administer to relieve symptoms and allow the body to get on with healing the initial problem. But in some conditions, the drug might simply be disguising the underlying ailment and letting it fester: *perpetuation*. The uplifting effects of the treatment might lessen over time as the body's immunity grows: *exhaustion*. This can be compounded by the drug's adverse side effects in creating extra acute conditions: *destabilisation*.

Eventually the root cause of the disease will need to be addressed. As Greek tragedian Aeschylus wrote, there is no avoidance in delay. And because the underlying medical condition will be further advanced when it is eventually addressed, treatment will most likely be more invasive and disruptive than if applied earlier.

Perpetuation

With effective coping, the Long Depression has more time to permeate more deeply and widely in ways that ultimately make it less controllable. When opportunities for change are postponed, assets may be lost forever. The symbolic crumbling of 40-year-old buildings[3] and collapsing bridges in the US[4] suggest what is to come. In Germany, too, bridges across the Rhine are showing the decrepitude of age. Medium-sized vans have been banned from using the major A1 motorway bridge in Leverkusen.[5]

Prolonged decay rarely brings actual collapse. Steady deterioration and atrophy is the norm. By muddling through the depression, countries can stay reasonably rich. However, they slide steadily to the margins of the world, consigned to a less productive and less influential future. As Fareed Zakaria declared, the primary danger for the West is not economic death but sclerosis.[6]

The narrow results of coping through financialisation exemplify the perpetuation of decay. Financialisation's essential shortcoming is that its impact is limited to the spheres of finance and exchange. Financial expansion can boost share and house prices, and borrowing can stimulate consumption. They are ineffective, though, in producing a revival of capital investment in productive assets. Even Adair Turner, a former chair of the UK's superseded Financial Services Authority, challenged the orthodox presumption that loans are extended mainly to fund new business investment. Only about one-fifth of bank lending finances capital investment. Most credit in advanced economies finances either household consumption or the purchase of existing assets.[7]

Easy finance can't renew a moribund productive sector. Financial mechanisms operate based on taking value from elsewhere: from other places where values are generated, and especially through borrowing, which in effect takes value from another time: the future. Financial and debt expansion can artificially sustain demand in the economy. They do nothing to transform the circumstances in which things are produced. That must come from what the producers do. Developments in the financial arena, however innovative, or however well regulated, can't resolve what's gone wrong within production.

Monetary policy exemplifies how financialisation perpetuates rather than reverses decay. This policy is frequently described as the 'only game in town'.[8] However, the scope of this game is restricted to purely financial affairs. In spite of the most accommodative monetary policies on record, the Western economies have been experiencing their weakest post-recession recoveries since before the 1930s, perhaps ever. The policies that adjust how easily and at what price people and businesses can borrow money are merely administrative levers. Central banks don't invest or produce or build anything. They don't generate any new wealth, nor can they determine how others produce wealth.

Central banks head a financial totality that is unproductive of new value. Costas Lapavitsas made the essential point that however complex and apparently independent the modern financial system is, the key economic relations that provide content to finance – value production – do not lie within its own realm. These exist within the rest of the economy.[9]

The central or commercial banks can create more money but this could only influence production supply conditions if businesses take up that money for transformative investments. Nor can cheap money make businesses invest. As discussed in Chapter Five, low interest rates are a symptom of weak investment and economic slowdown. Costly capital is not the cause of lethargy, so cheaper capital is not the solution.

Official interest rate setting is like the impact of a tailwind or a headwind on an aircraft. It can speed the plane up or slow it down, but it can't change the direction of travel. Ultra-low central bank rates following the financial crash were a tailwind pushing down already low market interest rates. The Bank of England's 0.5% base rate was the lowest its official rate had been throughout its more than 300-year history.[10] The previous low was 2%. Over the US Federal Reserve's shorter history of 'only' 100 years, its official interest rates have also never been as low, when they were cut to the zero to 0.25% range in late 2008. Yet this cheaper capital courtesy of the central banks has failed to kick-start business investment. Instead, low state-maintained rates have reinforced the atrophy cycle of more borrowing perpetuating poor productivity.

The paradox of monetary policy is that the state banks have great formal authority and a significant influence on financial markets, but very little power over the value-making part of the economy. Central banks are the key institutions of the *financial* economy and have become revered institutions in comparison to the discredited political class. Yet they have minimal *economic* clout.

As a central banker, Mark Carney emphasised that his institution had limited powers over real phenomena. 'We're not going to build a single house at the Bank of England. We can't influence that.'[11] He's right: easy money policies can sustain or boost house prices (which can appear positive for people who already own their homes). But those same policies do nothing directly, or automatically through house builders, to ensure new homes are constructed for society to enjoy.

That would be genuine wealth creation. The former governor of the Cypriot central bank Athanasios Orphanides similarly explained that central banks couldn't ensure the formation of high-quality jobs. Monetary policy cannot substitute for the structural policies needed for sustained growth.[12] Decay continues undisturbed.

Exhaustion

Over time even the surface-level benefits from coping measures fade. This is not immediately apparent because the exhaustion of uplifting effects rarely leads to the particular support mechanism being openly abandoned. On the contrary, it usually prompts more of the same treatment. Efforts are redoubled on the presumption that there has not been enough of it.

State financialisation since the crash illustrates the exhaustion limitation too. The diminishing effectiveness of monetary policy for preserving even an appearance of returning normality is expressed by the adoption of increasingly 'unconventional' forms. It is further shown by how emergency measures were still being applied more than half a decade later.

Following the Lehman Brothers' collapse, the standard lowering of interest rates in times of slower growth became the application of ultra-low rates. With recovery still lacking, quantitative easing came next with the massive expansion of central bank balance sheets. While the first use of QE in the US in November 2008 helped to relieve panicking markets from freezing up completely, its continuation in order to promote economic recovery never worked. Rounds two and three had much less positive results.[13]

Proponents of QE rested much of their claim for its effectiveness on confidence: making people and business feel better. The *Financial Times* summarised: 'buying government debt was like a confidence trick'.[14] It was hoped that the 'wealth effect' from higher asset prices would boost consumer spending, and increase confidence among businesses, encouraging them to spend and invest.[15] QE's failures showed the fruitlessness of such hopes. As Jonathan Davis put it: 'Whatever else the history of QE programmes has shown, it is evident that it does nothing in itself to generate economic growth.'[16]

Some central banks then experimented with the more unconventional policy of *negative* interest rates. In Europe, the first region to adopt them, around half of all government bonds carried sub-zero yields in early 2016, led by Germany, Finland and Switzerland. What was once considered an improbable theory was also adopted by the Bank of Japan at the end of January 2016.[17] Such desperation affirms the dwindling effectiveness of monetary policy.

The exhaustion of muddling through is also shown by the lessening impact of increasing debt levels for sustaining economic activity. Comparing expansions between the post-war boom and the Long Depression across the advanced economies, the ratio of loan to output growth increased from 1.5 times to 1.9 times. While per capita real output grew by an average 4.2% in the post-war years and lending grew by 6.2%, these rates fell to 2.6% and 4.9% respectively after the collapse of Bretton Woods.[18] As the pace of economic growth fell, the 'credit intensity' of growth increased. This intimates a diminishing economic bang for each buck of debt, consistent with moving from value-led to debt-led eras of growth.

The relationship between debt and production has become even more stretched as the depression has aged. Over the two decades prior to the financial crash Adair Turner found indications that the credit-to-output growth ratio has been widening.[19] Other studies confirm that the rate of expansion of debt-to-GDP ratios accelerated in the period 2000–08 compared to the earlier stage of the Long Depression.[20] Turner suggested a 'second derivative' effect: the extent to which private credit growth has to exceed output growth is increasing over time.[21]

Aggregating all forms of debt – from the capital markets as well as banks – the increase in credit intensity is still more marked. John Mauldin and Jonathan Tepper described this as the 'diminishing marginal productivity of debt'.[22] A unit of debt buys less and less GDP growth as time passes.

This trend exists at a global level too: between 1990 and 2009 debt grew on average about 2.3 percentage points a year faster than global GDP.[23] However in the latter part of this period from 2002, the debt-to-output gap widened. Global debt grew faster at an annualised rate of approximately 11%, while annual output grew at about 4% a year. Global debt growth outstripped GDP growth by nearly three times.[24]

Analysis by Grant Williams led to the same conclusion of debt's diminishing economic impact. Williams calculated that the increase in real US GDP for each dollar of incremental debt amounted to US$4.61 between 1947 and 1952, falling to US$0.63 between 1953 and 1984. That period ended with the takeoff of debt-driven activity. Between 1985 and 2000 the extra output per dollar had fallen further to US$0.24, which then declined another two-thirds to US$0.08 between 2001 and 2012.[25]

Using a different measure, Christopher Rupe and Nathan Martin have similarly calculated this diminishing impact of debt, reproduced here as Figure 12.1. As more debt enters the system, its 'productivity' in terms of output gained for each unit diminishes.

Destabilisation

The prolonged use of coping mechanisms also creates dilemmas that introduce new potential instabilities. Again, financialisation demonstrates this third limitation of muddling through. The financialised measures taken in furtherance of preserving stability fuel financial and, sometimes, economic instability. Expanding debt and fictitious capital alongside the deteriorating course of real capital is an incendiary combination. The divergence between the fictitious and the real eventually implodes.

Figure 12.1 Diminishing marginal productivity of debt in the US

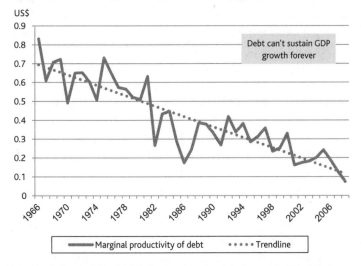

Note: Marginal productivity of debt is the annual nominal dollar increase in GDP relative to a $1 increase in debt.

Source: latest published data based on Christopher Rupe and Nathan Martin, published in the Economic Edge blog, 'The most important chart of the century' by Nathan Martin on 20 March 2010. http://economicedge.blogspot.co.uk/2010/03/most-important-chart-of-century.html. The data sources are the Federal Reserve Z.1 Report for the total credit market debt figure (All Sectors; Debt Securities and Loans), and the Bureau of Economic Analysis for the annual nominal GDP numbers (NIPA table 1.1.5)

The underlying problem remains the barriers to expanding production, rather than the expansion of debt and financial capital. If credit were used for productive investment then new values would be created from which to repay the debt. There would be no problem.

But when investment languishes the expanded money supply runs ahead of value production and boosts financial prices. At some point reality intervenes and brings those prices down. Financialisation has therefore helped to moderate and dampen the business cycle at the cost of generating a series of financial cycles. These contain the possibility of disruptive crises of their own making.[26]

Economies kept afloat on debt induce three sources of instability. First, the costs of servicing debt may rise, forcing defaults. We saw this when US mortgage rates rose from 2005, kicking off the chain of events leading to Lehman Brothers' collapse three years later. Second, the refinancing of existing debt becomes arduous, or impossible, when financial capital flows slacken or evaporate. Again this can precipitate defaults. Indebted developing countries have seen this many times over the last four decades when inward capital swiftly dries up.

Third, asset price bubbles fuelled by leveraged buying burst, causing distress to asset holders. Fictitious values contract. Their owners, including financial institutions, can fail. This often sparks wider financial and, sometimes, economic turmoil. Occasionally, as in 2008, the *debt* bubble itself bursts, with greater disorderly consequence when banking relations seize up.

The more the fictitious volumes expand relative to genuine value creation, the greater is the potential for instability. The level of debt, as a measure of the amount of outstanding fictitious capital, suggests the financial system's state of fragility. There are no absolute limits to debt. However, the credibility and therefore the soundness of debt are based on it being serviceable in the present, as well as the prospect of it being repaid. The servicing of existing debt can come from new debt, which postpones the day of reckoning. But somewhere value needs to be produced to fund repayments. Without this, instability beckons.

Stabilisation backfires

When instability becomes realised some call this a 'Minsky Moment', named after the American economist Hyman Minsky. Minsky is best known for his 'financial instability hypothesis', which argues that stability breeds instability. It describes how periods of stability encourage lots more financial asset buying, producing price bubbles that eventually burst – the 'Minsky Moment'. The structures that are established during a period of stability eventually become shaky, leading to a collapse.[27]

While providing a reasonable description of what tends to happen in a financialised economy, Minsky didn't get to grips with what's specific about such an economy, and why one occasionally develops. The key aspect is that a financialised economy is intrinsically more prone to volatility than an economy where the productive core is working well. When value production is depressed, financial prices tend to fluctuate more.

Lacking a direct connection to real values, financialised prices can deviate further from the underlying fundamentals than the prices of produced services or goods deviate from their real values. For example, the share price of a company can diverge widely from the underlying value of the business, whether based on its balance sheet value, or on its projected cash flows from profits.

As a general rule, high indebtedness relative to production means that the elastic relationship between prices and underlying values stretches, creating the potential for financial implosions. Claudio Borio appropriately calls this property of the financialised economy 'excess elasticity'. 'The analogy is with an elastic band, which one can stretch further and further until at some point it snaps.'[28]

The timing and the specific catalyst for bubbles bursting are unpredictable. The pinprick is clear only in hindsight. In the late 2000s it was US subprime mortgages, but it could have been some other mispriced, overvalued financial asset that cracked first. It is like the game of Jenga where removing one wooden block leads to the tower of blocks collapsing. It is rarely obvious which particular block's removal will precipitate collapse. Removing another one might have been just as destabilising.

Sometimes in the game the whole tower, not just parts of it, topples. Similarly financial crises can sometimes be contained, but, alternatively, once underway they can develop a momentum that is difficult to control. That's what happened at the end of the 2000s.

In 2006 US home prices started a rapid decline consequent on the increasing cost of mortgages. This proved too much for borrowers, especially the most income-strapped subprime ones. Homes went into foreclosure and a relative excess supply of homes put further downward pressure on prices. With increasing defaults on subprime loans, more than 25 subprime lending firms declared bankruptcy in February and March 2007, while the US's largest subprime lender, New Century, went under in April.

By July 2007 Bear Stearns announced major losses in two of its hedge funds as the asset-backed securities that were based on the subprime loans also started to fail. The following March, the US government prodded JP Morgan Chase to purchase Bear

Stearns at a knockdown price since it was on the brink of collapse from this exposure. The rest, as they say, is financial history.[29]

Central banks aggravate instability

The state's financial policies hoping to stabilise capitalism usually recreate the conditions for the next bout of debt-driven financial instability. Even though previous rounds of liquidity contributed to the development of earlier bubbles, the common response when they burst has been another slug of central bank-backed liquidity. In a state-financialised economy debt habitually goes in one direction – upwards.

The post-crash retrenchments in borrowing barely interrupted its overall expansion, as was discussed in Chapter Five with regard to corporate debt. Rolling back debt is easier pledged than done. This is a structural dilemma, not an absence of will. Debt reduction can come from only two sources. Borrowings can be repaid with real values: difficult today, given that value creation is what the economy lacks. Or it can come from 'debt restructuring' – a euphemism for debt being written off.

But writeoffs are another source of instability, as they can spread quickly. One bad debt written off here can have a knock-on effect elsewhere, potentially undermining the credibility of the whole credit system: in Latin, 'credit' means trust. This discourages debt restructuring for fear of destabilising the entire fictitious structure.

After 2008, debt writeoffs were concentrated in household debt, and were especially marked among US mortgages. While causing misery for the broke families who were forced to find new places to live, the overall amount of fictitious value destroyed was relatively modest. From the end of 2009 to mid-2015 total credit to households in the UK and the US fell respectively by just over 13% and 16% of GDP. However, in absolute terms these represented significant money *increases* in household indebtedness of US$108 billion and US$226 billion respectively.[30]

Across the advanced economies collectively, nonfinancial debt grew by the equivalent of one-third of annual output from the end of 2007 to reach 260% of GDP in mid-2014. Private debt fell by 2% of GDP, which was more than offset by the 35% of

GDP rise in public debt.[31] By country, from 2007 to mid-2015 total nonfinancial debt increased by nearly 20% of GDP in the US, by 71% in Japan, by 7% in Germany and by nearly 33% in the UK. Not much deleveraging there.

Debt growth has been reinforced by the exceptional central bank measures taken to boost liquidity since the crash. This contributes to greater financial price disparities and the potential for new bubbles. In 2014 Richard Fisher, president of the Federal Reserve Bank of Dallas, openly warned of the US central bank's liquidity policies: 'I believe we are experiencing financial excess that is of our own making. When money is dirt cheap and ubiquitous, it is in the nature of financial operators to reach for yield.'[32]

In these circumstances financial prices rise through three main channels. First, the extra money held by the commercial banks or other financial institutions arising from QE is spent on financial assets directly, boosting demand and pushing up prices. Second, these financial institutions might lend some of this extra liquidity to other individuals or businesses that use it not for productive investment or even for consumption, but for financial asset purchases.

Either way central bank-backed liquidity drives up asset prices. When this upward price movement occurs, there is a third, follow-on momentum effect. Other buyers drive prices even higher on the assumption that this extra liquidity is going to be around for some time. Central bank signalling of the continuation of easy money policies leads to even greater financial asset price appreciation.

The overpricing of financial assets has become persistent under state financialisation. This is known in financial circles as the 'mispricing of risk', because the other side of overpriced assets is lower financial returns. Financial investors do not get the appropriate returns for the risk they run in possibly not getting their money back.

The resulting lower incomes from mainstream financial assets, such as government bonds and top-quality corporate debt, spur financial investors into more volatile assets. Helped by state-supported liquidity, they look elsewhere for better returns. A 'search for yield' drives financial investors into riskier pieces of paper and more outlandish forms of financial activity. As John Plender wrote, this 'search for yield' is simply a euphemism for buying a higher income while ignoring higher financial risk.[33]

Some give up on finding decent income flows. Instead money goes into the search for capital appreciation. 'Exotic' financial investments and 'alternative' assets, from property to commodities, to fine wines or works of art, are bought speculatively. Equity, property and alternative investment prices soar, drawing more money into climbing markets that make the price rises self-perpetuating. Until a bubble bursts again.

Recall from earlier that manipulating financial prices in this way is one of the goals of easy money state policies. Boosting financial asset prices is hoped to induce a wealth effect that encourages more spending. Andrew Haldane from the Bank of England accepted that monetary policy had clearly 'aided and abetted risk-taking' by investors. He reminded people that this had been their intention, using higher asset prices as a means to stimulate the wider economy. 'That is how [monetary policy] is meant to work, that's why we did it.' Higher asset prices were for him a 'good news story'.[34] Central banks as the previous gamekeeper of price stability have turned poacher.

In conclusion

Despite its threefold limitations, muddling through retains great staying power. Its paradox as a state methodology is that it is both powerless and powerful. Muddling-through mechanisms – not least state financialisation – can only be palliatives to the dominant tendencies of decay. Like all palliatives they are partial and limited. They will never be able to fix the underlying problems.

But by giving relief from the worst manifestations of decay they also alleviate pressures to act more decisively on the root causes. They work well enough to maintain an air of prosperity. They generally avoid calamitous economic collapses. However, the underlying problems of weakness in productive dynamism, of ageing and deteriorating infrastructure, plant and equipment, and of narrow and sluggish innovation all continue to inflict damage.

An unhelpful spiral unfolds. By staving off economic restructuring decay festers, and the prospect of radical intervention seems even more daunting. In contrast, the practice of muddling through remains appealing. Until this complacency is shaken up and appropriate actions taken, this spiral foretells the West's continued slide to economic irrelevance.

'Irrelevance' does not necessarily herald a slow, boring demise, though that would be grim enough. A combination of the limits of coping and of the tendencies to decay mean that the West's drift to the economic margins of the world will be interspersed with bouts of great instability and tumult. The necessity to restructure the economy to fix production can be delayed. It can't be avoided forever.

Part IV
The way out

The something that we should do is to stop. (Angus Deaton, 2013, p 15[1])

THIRTEEN

Escaping the Long Depression

Escaping from the grip of the Long Depression will not be easy, but it is necessary and it is possible. Western economies need rebuilding, not saving. This involves stopping doing some things and starting to do others. There are many barriers to economic health and prosperity, yet none is insuperable. The biggest challenges are not objective, economic, constraints. They lie in the realms of ideas and imagination, culture and politics.

The alternative to economic malaise is industrial renewal. This does not mean trying to reverse the decline of coal mining and steel production, shipbuilding plants or car factories. It is not a quest to revive heavy industry and manufacturing of old. It is about the creation of new sectors for generating wealth across multiple services and goods. Economic renewal must embrace transport and energy, construction and communications, agriculture and healthcare, clothing and household goods, leisure and food.

A revival of productive wealth creation would bring higher-paid jobs, and reduce the human and social waste from unemployment and underemployment. It would increase tax revenues and fund public spending on scientific discovery and invention. The appropriate focus for progress now is to unlock the existing potential for higher productivity and social improvement through ending the Long Depression.

There are still some on the radical left who argue for the revolutionary overthrow of capitalism.[2] This had meaning when the working class existed as a political force. But the working class's demise as described in Chapter Nine brought that era of possibilities to an end. The question remains of how the existing system of production can be organised, or transformed, or transcended in such a way as to advance the best interests of humanity. Once we have escaped the Long Depression, the resulting phase of economic expansion would not be forever. Economic growth would at some time hit limits, just as the post-war boom did. Working out how to overcome the limitations of a profit-driven economy is not today's priority.

The economic challenge

For economic renewal there is no alternative to creative destruction. The burden of sustaining unproductive enterprises has been sapping the vitality of Western economies for decades. We need to act collectively and purposefully to dispense with the old and develop the new. Culling outdated capital stock would eliminate stagnating sectors and free resources for innovative investment in more productive businesses and in new sectors of production. The first step is to call a halt to the state's pragmatic muddling-through policies. We need to cast off the blanket of regulations and subsidies that sustains economic decay.

The key to future prosperity lies in the scope of developments in science and technology to generate a 'fourth industrial revolution'. The digital technologies that have emerged over the Long Depression have the potential to transform production. But, so far, their promise has extended little beyond the spheres of entertainment, communications, finance and commerce.

There has not been an absolute shortage of scientific advances since the depression began (though not as many as in earlier decades). Bioscience and nanoscience remain promising areas for research and development. Yet the development of potentially revolutionary technologies, for example in genomic medicine, stem cell therapies and robotics, has been frustratingly slow.[3] Boxes 13.1 (autonomous transport), 13.2 (quantum technology) and 13.3 (virtual reality) indicate other technologies that have been developing too slowly or narrowly. Newer areas, including wider medical and agrarian technologies, have been starved of the funds they need to develop rapidly.

And there is no shortage of problems to solve. People around the world need better ways of producing goods and services.

They need improvements in the delivery of health services, accommodation and information management. We need concerted responses to the challenges of energy production and storage, and to problems of climate change and environmental destruction.

Box 13.1

AUTONOMOUS TRANSPORT

What is it?

Companies are split on which path to take: fully autonomous or semi-autonomous driverless cars. Ford is working on launching a car that can manage whole journeys without human intervention. ICT companies like Alphabet – Google's parent – also mostly favour this 'big-bang' approach.

In contrast, General Motors is taking a more gradual route that starts by automating the most routine driving tasks, such as motorway driving. Volvo, Daimler and the electric car manufacturer Tesla endorse this step-by-step approach.

There are benefits and drawbacks to both methods. Going straight to full self-driving doesn't take away the role of humans because autonomous cars are going to be sharing roads with non-autonomous vehicles for a long time. Also working out how to hand back control at short notice to the occupant immersed in something else is tough.

What could it do?

Eliminate the time and effort people put into driving from A to B, giving people scope to do other things instead.

Cut journey times and fuel usage. Programmed vehicles could move faster and brake less frequently; it is the use of throttle to speed up after braking that most wastes fuel.

Reduce accidents. Most car accidents occur not because of speeding or alcohol, but because people lose concentration. Machines do not get tired or lose focus not because of their programmed 'smartness' but because they lack the human characteristic of imagination. Imagination needs occasional recharging – sleep – and also allows minds to wander: both bad for driving. Automation will not stop accidents immediately.

Remember how often PCs used to 'crash'? This was more frequent in their early days, before the bugs were discovered and – mostly – repaired.

Where are we today?

Fully automated driverless tractors on farmland, and driverless industrial trucks in warehouses and on private factory land are being trialled by several manufacturers. They are close to commercial rollout. These can iron out some of the technical challenges with driverless cars.

The incremental approach to automated driving is also already available. Jaguar launched 'adaptive cruise control' in 1996, which speeds the car up or slows it down to maintain a preset distance to the vehicle in front. Mercedes-Benz launched 'active lane keeping assist' in 2013, which takes control of the brakes to rectify matters when the car wrongly crosses road lane markings.

However, there remain many technical challenges to be resolved as automation takes on more aspects of driving. For example, during tests driverless cars have been baffled by tumbleweed. On cold days they can interpret other vehicles' exhaust gases as solid objects.[4]

More important is the question of social acceptance, which appears as ethical, legal or regulatory issues. There needs to be clarity on responsibility when things go wrong, when accidents happen: the car manufacturer, the software supplier, the telecommunications network provider in the case of an outage, the owner/occupant? The question of responsibility is more problematic during the transition to full automation. How to allocate responsibility when a driven and a fully, or partly, automated vehicle collide?

What about decisions over programming vehicles to avoid collisions? This could mean a choice between hitting a coach full of people, or striking a pedestrian with a pram, or killing the occupant by veering into a wall instead.[5]

One solution to some of these challenges would be to segregate driverless vehicles from all pedestrians, non-car road transport and driven vehicles. Dedicated, distinct transport routes would maximise the benefits from automation and minimise technical compromises, but at considerable infrastructure expense.

Box 13.2
QUANTUM TECHNOLOGY
What is it?
Quantum technology can be regarded as a third stage on from first stage analogue and second stage digital technologies, taking society to a phase surpassing existing digitisation. It is derived from science that goes beyond the classical physics of Newton's law of motion, thermodynamics, and Maxwell's equations for electromagnetism.

What could it do?
Some of the properties of quantum mechanics are taken into practical applications such as quantum computing, quantum sensing, quantum cryptography, quantum simulation, quantum metrology and quantum imaging.

Applications being worked on range from precision clocks, to communications, sensing and computing. For example, quantum technology would bring much more powerful quantum computers which can store and process quantum data, as opposed to binary data. Among other possibilities, this will enhance machine-learning capabilities. New encryption techniques will also follow.

Quantum systems can take existing laser light technologies into new areas. One project already underway aims to measure gravity and the mass of objects. This would allow people to measure a wall and 'see' through it. Users could 'look' into a floor and see what cables are where, which could also help in locating oil, gas and minerals in the ground.

Quantum systems would enable much more accurate modelling of biological systems. Another use relates to chemical sensing, with potential applications ranging from authenticating products to safety controls in petrochemical plants.

It is anticipated that the first quantum devices deployed commercially will be in the semiconductor manufacturing industry. Chips that currently have about 300 million transistors on them could have 1.2 billion.[6]

Where are we today?

We already have quantum 1.0 devices, which are reliant on the effects of quantum physics. These include lasers, microprocessors, transistors and semiconductor devices, magnetic resonance imaging (MRI) scanners, and nuclear power. Quantum *technologies* represent the second quantum revolution or quantum 2.0, which will bring devices that actively create, manipulate and read out quantum states of matter.

Quantum technology research – much of it at the theoretical stage – is underway in several countries including the US, UK, China, Germany, Russia and Japan. While the full potential of quantum technologies remains unknown, with sustained investment and effort even the areas outlined above are likely to yield immense economic benefit (as well as security and defence capabilities).[7] In 2013 the British government announced a five-year investment of £270 million. This is a helpful initial injection of funding, though much more needs to be invested in Britain and all around the world.

Box 13.3
VIRTUAL REALITY
What is it?

Virtual reality has become the generic term for both straight virtual reality (VR) and also for augmented reality (AR), sometimes called mixed reality (MR). In practice there is a major difference between them. Virtual reality technology refers to a full immersive experience in a virtual world, while augmented/mixed reality refers to a modified view of the real world.

Their potential applications vary widely. VR isolates people from their physical surroundings so they can interact with fictitious worlds. AR provides computer-generated context and information about the world around people, allowing them to interact with their surroundings. VR headsets replace the real world with a simulated world, while AR devices overlay extra information onto a real-world view. This additional information could be about the history of what is being looked at;

directions about how to move in relation to it; services that are available, such as a menu for a restaurant, price comparisons and user reviews.

What could it do?

Dubbed the 'internet of experiences', VR/AR could transform much more than the world of entertainment. Obvious applications include education, travel, retailing, property sales, architecture, videoconferencing and social networking.

Consider how the technology could transform medical training. On 14 April 2016 in a London hospital cancer surgeon Dr Shafi Ahmed operated to remove the tumour from a man with colon cancer. About 20 medical students in a nearby lecture theatre watched a live streaming through VR/AR goggles, while another medic took part from Tanzania.

Dr Ahmed is also founder of a company developing VR-based training and believes that VR/AR could revolutionise surgical education and training, particularly for developing countries that don't have the resources and facilities of Western hospitals.[8] With more development it should be possible to go beyond students simply observing to have a more interactive experience with trainees simulating the surgery.

Where are we today?

So far most development has been concentrated on gaming and other kinds of entertainment and leisure, such as the Pokémon Go AR game. The running in this is being made by the familiar technology companies, Facebook – through the US$19 billion purchase of Oculus – Google, Microsoft, Apple, HTC and Samsung.

Goldman Sachs projects that the VR applications software market could reach US$35 billion by 2025.[9] On current trends the lion's share of that – US$19 billion – will still be entertainment-related, with another US$4 billion for retail and property sales. That would leave only a relatively small share for path-breaking productive applications in engineering, health care, training and education. A much broader perspective is needed.

In combination, letting go of the old and pushing ahead with the new can help to realise what is required through bringing about an upward shift in the rate of profit. The value expressed in capital stock, in capital assets, would fall relative to the rise in new surplus created. Economic restructuring would boost profitability across the economy. The social benefit would be the return to a dynamic of innovative investment and productivity growth. This would result in more freedom from want, as well as offering individuals the possibility of more time free from the burden of work.

There are no pain-free routes out of the Long Depression. The processes of creative destruction will mean economic ruin, adding to areas already severely affected by deindustrialisation. Hence it is imperative that any plan for economic restructuring provides support for individuals and families faced with transitional periods of unemployment. People will need support, in terms of skills training, as well as housing and welfare benefit. This will be essential to enable people to move from jobs in declining sectors to more dynamic enterprises.

Putting off action is the worst option of all. As Niccolò Machiavelli, the Italian Renaissance humanist, observed, 'Prudence consists in knowing how to recognise the nature of disadvantages, and how to choose the least sorry one as good.'[10] Perpetuating the way things are means condemning people to poorly paid jobs with no future. It means preserving a zombie economy, which staggers on without any prospect of rejuvenation, punctuated by spikes of more intense crisis.

State-led restructuring

One thing is clear from the decades of the Long Depression: the private sector is incapable of achieving economic renewal on its own.[11] Too much is at stake in currently existing businesses, however moribund, for them to initiate their own destruction. Though today's corporate leaders often proclaim wider social objectives, in practice their companies exist primarily to make profits. This focus limits their capacity to act in the wider or long-term interests of society.

The criterion of profitability deters private firms from independent engagement in long-term, open-ended research. Since most research 'fails', a successful innovation-based economy depends on sources of funding that are 'decoupled from economic return'.[12] Being closely 'coupled' to economic return, the private sector is unsuited to expensive and unpredictable research activities.[13]

Private business structures are also not conducive to the collaboration that is invaluable for scientific advance. Protecting the self-interest of each firm inhibits the dissemination of knowledge that makes faster progress possible. Property rights over newly discovered ideas allow firms to restrict access to other scientists, thereby limiting their scope to take new discoveries further.

Tim Berners-Lee, the inventor of the World Wide Web, is the exception proving the rule that individual entrepreneurs play a less significant role than collectivities in pioneering technological advance. As a matter of principle, Berners-Lee refused to commercialise his creation, preferring instead to develop it as a channel for free expression and collaboration.[14] But, in general, collective public institutions have taken the leading role in developing new technologies and in promoting their implementation as practical innovations.

The leading role for the state in innovation has been evident over the past century.[15] The Manhattan Project that produced the atom bomb and the Apollo Program that saw man walk on the moon both illustrate how the state can push science forward.[16] During the post-war boom, a handful of companies did remarkable scientific research. These include AT&T (the parent of Bell Labs), IBM, Xerox (the parent of the Palo Alto Research Center), Hewlett Packard, Motorola and General Electric. The achievements of these firms were not, however, testimony to the potential of private enterprise. They were all primarily the result of collaboration with the state.[17] The 'military–industrial complex' came to symbolise the close collaboration of the state and business in post-war America.[18]

The apparatus of state has not been restricted to supporting the creative aspects of economic advance. It was also central to the reorganisation that laid the basis for post-war innovation. In the 1930s and 1940s state institutions in several of the world's leading nations oversaw a huge destruction of antiquated capital values.

The state and the Second World War

The Second World War was the culmination of long-running conflicts among the major developed capitalist nations. It also marked the resolution, through concerted state intervention, of the Great Depression that had ravaged Western economies in the 1930s. The primary focus of state activity was on military conflict rather than economic renewal. In practice, however, the demands of war took precedence over the constraints of private profitability and of limited public resources. The result was the 'economic miracle' that rescued the Western world from the slump.[19]

The war effort accelerated the destruction of capital values that had already started during the depression. Even in the US, the country least affected by the physical devastation of war, estimates suggest that between 1931 and 1945 the ratio of capital stock to national output fell by more than a third. As a result of this enormous devaluation of capital relative to the size of the economy, profitability approximated doubled, thereby establishing the basis for economic recovery.[20] It is doubtful the post-war boom could have taken off without this state-organised restructuring.

In their preparation and conduct of the war, state institutions became closely involved in the creative aspects of reorganising production. Whereas in 1930 the US federal government's share of R&D spending was 16%, it increased dramatically as war approached. It continued to account for between half and two-thirds throughout the post-war boom.[21] State sponsorship of R&D brought about dramatic advances. Not just nuclear energy coming out of the Manhattan Project, but also electronic computers, jet engines and radar.[22] Concerns about returns on capital were irrelevant to those engaged in splitting the atom, cracking enemy codes and winning supremacy in battles in the air.

Wartime technologies long outlasted military objectives: they underpinned the peacetime industrial resurgence. The 'necessity of war became the mother of invention of improved production techniques'; these innovations were not subsequently 'forgotten'.[23] During the conflict the US government invested in the productive sectors most critical to the war effort. These included synthetic rubber, aluminium, airframes and engines, and aviation fuel refining, all having non-military applications.

During the war the government purchased industrial plant that amounted to about 50% of the stock of privately owned equipment that existed in 1941. The number of machine tools in the US doubled between 1940 and 1945. After the war, many government-owned, privately operated plants were sold off in 'sweetheart deals' at low prices to the private sector.[24] The state thus encouraged the developments and innovations of which the private sector later took advantage.

The Second World War gave a tremendous boost to productivity as well as to profitability. As Joseph Stiglitz observed: although Americans tend to be 'allergic' to terms like 'industrial policy', it is the appropriate term for the systematic government intervention in this period. It was a policy that 'permanently changed the nature of the economy' for the post-war decades.[25]

The impetus for state promotion of innovation continued through the Cold War years. In her elaboration of the concept of the 'entrepreneurial state', Mariana Mazzucato notes how many subsequent technological advances emerged from the immediate post-war surge of state activity. These included developments in biotechnology and pharmaceuticals as well as computers and communications. It was the state, not the private sector, that 'kick-started and developed the engine of growth' in the years leading up to the Long Depression.[26]

The development of the internet provides a vivid illustration of the importance of state intervention in innovation. The internet evolved out of ARPANET, the US state-run data communications network which connected research sites across the country in the 1960s. Its sponsor, the US government's Defense Advanced Research Projects Agency (DARPA) was set up in 1958, a year after the American establishment was shaken by the Soviet Union's successful launch of the Sputnik space satellite. DARPA's goal was to ensure that the US military had more sophisticated technology that any of its potential enemies. Yet it had extensive economic influence through funding the establishment of university computer science departments and startup firms. These firms in turn pioneered advances in semiconductors and other ICT early stage technologies.[27] The state was thus at the heart of the ICT revolution.[28] David King expressed the 'simple fact' was that 'there would have been no Silicon Valley in the United States without DARPA funding'.[29]

The restoration of economic growth in the 1950s was achieved through state intervention, but at a terrible cost in terms of human life and social devastation in the Second World War. Yet it cannot be beyond the bounds of human imagination to implement a programme of reconstruction that does not involve a lapse into barbarism.

The great evasion: political obstacle to change

The practical measures required to stimulate an economic renaissance can be readily summarised. We need to stop propping up moribund enterprises. We should promote investment in innovation. We must support people through the transition to new employment.

Perhaps in the future new collective institutions will be created, but the state is the only existing one that is comprehensive enough to orchestrate the transformation of the economy on the scale required. The particular interests of any company or sector will need to be subordinated to the general development of production. The solutions needed go far beyond simply devising a radical economic strategy. Indeed, they go beyond the sphere of economics. In the past, the state has only undertaken a radical programme of change under extreme duress. This may have arisen in the form of the external threat of war or from the internal pressure of working class militancy. Today the challenge arises from 40 years of economic decay.

The key problem apparent in all advanced economies is that the state shows a marked reluctance to meet this challenge of tackling the legacy of the Long Depression. Governments have had many opportunities to deal with the problems of decay but have consistently failed to rise to the occasion. In economic affairs they have either ignored or denied the gravity of the situation. Successful muddling through has provided false comfort. It has allowed them to hide from their failures to revive productive activity and to promote decent employment. This is the *great evasion* that was introduced in the previous chapter. Throughout the Long Depression political leaders have displayed failures of understanding, failures of leadership and failures of accountability. The great evasion both reflects and reinforces the political elite's distance from the demos – from the populace as a political entity.

Many commentators have drawn attention to the propensity of politicians to evade economic reality. Richard Duncan has been highly critical of government failures to target the economy's structural flaws.[30] Andre Geim has expressed frustration that the government seems oblivious to the fact that progress has stalled.[31] George Magnus has argued that we are in a political crisis, resulting from the fact that no government in any major advanced economy has done anything substantive to promote growth and jobs.[32]

For Fareed Zakaria, industrial societies have spent the last few decades 'managing or ignoring their problems rather than tackling them head-on'.[33] Nouriel Roubini and Stephen Mihm have noted the reluctance of politicians to act 'decisively'. They highlighted that kicking the can down the road runs the risk of also letting banks slowly sink into a financial coma, becoming 'zombies dependent on public credit'.[34] Edmund Phelps has described the 'dogged denial' of the era of slowdown by politicians who 'did not dare to speak the truth'.[35] An influential columnist insisted that necessary policies 'of destructive creativity can come only from strong and innovative political leaders'. But, 'Sadly, there are none of those in sight.'[36]

Recognising the political form of the economic challenge is vital, but how to deal with it? Geim has ventured one solution, which came to him in the form of a 'dream', prompted by his frustration that political leaders do not recognise the urgency of reversing the slowdown in the rate of scientific discovery and innovation. His fantasy is that astrophysicists find a huge cosmic rock on course to hit planet Earth in about 50 years' time. This 'scary' spectre galvanises human efforts to escape the stasis. The world deflects the existential threat by developing new technologies, which in turn serve to revive economic progress. In this scenario, an asteroid re-enacts the role of the Second World War in the prehistory of the post-war boom.[37]

But the problems of contemporary politics cannot be sidestepped. Today's elites are bound to the status quo. They seem incapable of abandoning their commitment to conserving a stagnant economy and taking the risks required to forge a new one. Their actions have perpetuated the Long Depression, and they are reluctant to break with their legacy. Rather than passively anticipating an intergalactic collision, we require a new approach to political leadership. We need leaders who are prepared to reject the traditions of the zombie economy and launch a programme for the revival of production.

Challenging the great evasion demands a renewal of democratic politics. The politicians who have dominated the parliaments of the Western world during the Long Depression have pursued a cautious and risk-averse approach in economic affairs. They have also presided over measures that have diminished civil liberties and democratic freedoms. The quest for economic transformation requires opening up democratic debate and holding politicians and governments to account. That is why democracy-imbued occasions like Britain's referendum decision to leave the EU offer opportunities for forging new economic, as well as new political, thinking.

'Political restructuring' is the precondition for economic restructuring. In a period when faith in humanity and the future have reached a low ebb, the values of the Enlightenment – the power of reason, the pursuit of liberty, individual autonomy and progress – have come into question. Yet these values, which can be most fully expressed through democratic forms, offer the best prospect of both political and economic advance.

Creating the political climate for restructuring

We need to create a political climate that is conducive to productive creativity. The essential precondition for this political transformation is a battle with the ideas that sustain the current situation. The staying power of the great evasion rests particularly on the contemporary notion that human-led change generally makes thing worse. This reinforces the fatalist acquiescence to modest levels of economic growth in the two decades before the crash, and to the torpor since. Meanwhile, the relative success of coping with the implications of moribund production has helped disguise this hollowing out of purpose.

Fundamentally, we need to rescue belief in human agency and in the creative potential of humanity to solve the problems of society. Reconstituting a sense of agency is a prerequisite for people re-engaging with political life. For people to embrace a programme of economic renewal requires a revolution in imagination. It means restoring the conviction that transformative change is desirable, necessary and possible. As Michael Ignatieff emphasised: change should be what politics is about. The purpose of political ideas is to bring us together and enable us to believe that we can control our collective destinies. Without a political vision of where we should be headed we are instead merely 'spectators of our own drift'.[38]

Viktor Frankl explained that for the individual a lost sense of meaning could start to be restored by 'becoming aware of *what can be done* about a particular situation'.[39] It is similar for society as a collective of individuals. Understanding what is possible in shaking up the economy provides a basis for purpose in bringing it about.

Promoting an intellectual alternative begins with bringing economic affairs back into the sphere of politics. It means challenging the prevailing scepticism about the possibility, and even the desirability, of economic growth. And it means exposing the high costs – individual and social – of the zombie economy.

Transcending the separation between economics and politics

As we saw in Chapter Eleven, the retreat of political elites from economic responsibility has been a pervasive feature of the Long Depression. For too long this has been ignored in mainstream discussion. The return of economic affairs to political controversy is essential to reinvigorate public debate. This is particularly difficult because the division between the private realm of exploitation and accumulation and the public world of political life is a constitutive feature of capitalist society.[40]

The separation of economic and political spheres has proved to be an enduring strength of the capitalist system. Unlike earlier forms of production such as feudalism and slavery, capitalism has not generally needed to exercise coercion to ensure that production continues. As a result, production tends to be regarded as a technical 'economic' process, with natural rather than social properties. Hence the depoliticisation of state economic intervention since the 1980s did not provoke much opposition. Given the apparent autonomy of economics from politics, it seems natural that questions such as how to promote growth are removed from political controversy. The outsourcing of responsibility for economic affairs to unaccountable agencies of state appears to be merely a technical adjustment.

Any programme of economic revival will require the reversal of the trend to outsource economic policy to experts, regulators and nongovernmental organisations. This is not a question of financial expediency. Nor is it a matter of suspicion about the motives of private businesses in seeking to provide public services. It is a matter, above all, of democratic accountability.

Overcoming scepticism about growth, and about making growth

We need to engage with the argument for the social, as well as the material, benefits of economic development. This means re-establishing the merits of risk-taking and reversing the sorts of state regulation that deter innovation. For too long the mantra of 'sustainability' has had the ascendancy. This outlook has led to the imposition of restraints on innovation and economic development, from stem cell research in the US to genetically modified foods in Europe.

We need to challenge the sustainable development consensus that puts the 'natural' environment above economic growth. Economic development actually gives us the means to control environmental damage, whether this results from natural events or human activities. The revered 'state of nature' is a reactionary place because it implies a return to struggling for survival and being exposed to premature death from disease and natural disasters.

The modern environmentalist ideas that inform sustainability are a problem not only because they lead to restrictions on development. They have also become the acceptable way of criticising humanism and of discrediting human-led change. From this perspective people are ascribed a minor and unremarkable role in the bigger historical picture. The forces of nature limit what people may seek to do to take control of their lives, while people's attempts to control nature are construed as the acts of an arrogant and harmful species. Human history and civilisation are recast as a tale of environmental destruction, thereby denigrating the powers of reason, knowledge and science.

Challenging today's environmentalist and sustainability notions is vital for restoring belief in the capacity of people to reason and to influence events positively. The mistakes people have made with the environment, and with much more besides, are not justifications for giving up on change. Rather they provide lessons that can guide us in moving forward. But the prospects of *moving forward* are undermined while the ideas of environmental determinism and sustainable development retain the sway they do currently.

Making conscious the barriers posed by a zombie economy

The state's muddle-through activities that preserve what exists have to stop. The corporate dependency on the state has become every bit as noxious as personal welfare dependency. The spreading intrusion of the welfare state into people's lives has gone way beyond a safety net for people. It encourages a corrosive dependence on third party intervention, undermining individual self-reliance and community solidarity.

For the economy, corporate dependency on state handouts also has caustic effects in sustaining the current moribund situation. Surviving on corporate welfare both puts off the disruptive technological transformation of businesses, and also makes it harder for new firms to replace them. Pulling away the state props to zombie capitalism will help clear out the old and less productive, making a start on economic rejuvenation.

Democratic disruption

Moving towards a programme of economic renewal will require fundamental changes in perspective. We need to promote public debate over the core assumptions that underlie both conventional and critical narratives. If existing political elites are unable to lead economic transformation, how will change happen? Can we challenge them effectively, and hold them to account? What can be done to foster both intellectual and practical alternatives to the status quo? How can we persuade people that a disruptive phase seems unavoidable before we can emerge from the Long Depression?

The extent to which successive governments have been complicit in sustaining the zombie economy needs to be recognised. This precludes the possibility of any straightforward shift in state economic policy. Forging a new political leadership is going to prove more demanding than simply reorienting government priorities.

Capitalism will not collapse – or transform itself

The economics editor Paul Mason fudges the scale of the political challenge when he suggests in his *Postcapitalism* that we should 'think positively' about the role of the state in promoting the transition to the new society of his title.[41] Mason argues that over the past 25 years capitalism has been successfully driving technology forwards. He believes that the resulting innovations are not compatible with basic capitalist institutions, such as the market, prices, private ownership and wages. From this perspective, capitalism has reached its limits and is metamorphosing into 'postcapitalism'. He argues that postcapitalism is possible because alternative forms of economic activity have already been appearing 'spontaneously' through the use of the new information technologies.[42]

In Mason's view, the state nurtures non-market economic forms by enabling new technologies and business models. In a similar way it could also reshape 'markets to favour sustainable, collaborative and socially just outcomes'.[43] Yet he ignores the proliferation of anti-democratic and illiberal state practices in recent years. His conception of the benign 'spontaneous' emergence of 'postcapitalism' avoids the challenge of forging the alternative political leadership required to secure any such transition.

What can be done to foster an alternative force for political and economic transformation? Denying the necessity for an appropriate agency for change is another form of evasion. Some critics of capitalism seem to think this doesn't matter because the system is so moribund that it will simply destroy itself. The appeal of this perspective is that it avoids the political tasks of effecting transformation. We simply need to await capitalism's collapse and then embark on the tasks of economic renewal.

The economic sociologist Wolfgang Streeck, for example, argues that capitalism will die from 'an overdose of itself'.[44] He believes that the collapse of labour movements in Western Europe over the past 30 years has deprived capitalism of the opposition it needs to provide stability. As a result, capitalism has become less restrained and more unstable. Now that its erstwhile challengers have been vanquished, the threat to the system comes from within.

In his view, 'unfettered' capitalism, characterised by stagnation, corruption and growing inequality – echoing the focus of Piketty and Stiglitz[45] – tends towards implosion. It is true, as discussed in Chapter Twelve, that the interaction between the forces of decay and those of resilience is likely to lead to greater instability. But this does not herald the collapse of the system. Streeck's thesis reveals a profound pessimism about the possibility of political transformation. He contends that, as a result of the destruction of collective agency 'we cannot even dream' of any degree of control over our common fate.[46]

Streeck offers a sophisticated variant of the old left dogma that capitalism is destined to inevitable collapse. In the past, this determinist perspective led to the evasion of the political challenges of building an anti-capitalist movement. Today, we cannot afford to ignore the problem of the absence of any agency capable of leading the economic transformation we need.

The fact that there is at present no determinate answer to this problem is no excuse for fantasising about capitalist collapse. There will be no final crisis of capitalism. History should have taught us not to underestimate the resilience of this system and its capacity to survive even the grimmest times. Bringing the Long Depression to a successful end will require a political force capable of providing conscious leadership towards the process of economic transformation.

Some critics of capitalism avoid the problem of the apparent absence of an agency for change by imagining that a force for capitalist transformation already exists. Paul Mason identifies this agency in the networks of educated individuals fostered by smartphone technology, new social media and 'info-capitalism'.[47] He celebrates collaborative networks, such as Wikipedia, that provide free access to information, and the business subculture of the 'sharing economy'.[48]

Mason argues that through the power of information technology, capitalism is subverting itself. But the fact that street protestors around the world now use social media to communicate does not imply that their grievances go 'to the heart of what is broken in modern capitalism'.[49] A mobile phone is simply a device for communication. It does not signify an anti-capitalist consciousness.

Wikipedia has been a boon for students and journalists, and a catastrophe for purveyors of encyclopaedias and dictionaries. But even the thousands of volunteers who maintain it have yet to discover through its millions of pages any way of eating, clothing, sheltering and entertaining themselves free of charge. They need income from somewhere else. Contributing to Wikipedia is the sort of activity that used to be called a hobby, or a voluntary service to the community. People may have all sorts of motivations for supplying Wikipedia, but interpreting this activity as a commitment to a postcapitalist mode of production is a leap too far.

Meanwhile the 'sharing economy' can certainly cut prices for services. But participation in such activities does not signify a conscious challenge to the market. Organisations like Airbnb and Uber have succeeded through adopting an asset-lite, employee-lite form of capitalist production. The individuals who directly provide the shared services are using their own assets and their own time. They often lack the pay, benefits and modest levels of job security enjoyed by their colleagues in conventional hotels and taxi firms.

Such 'sharing' activities used to be called the informal sector – the black economy – or, at best, self-employment. For some, these sorts of work provide an attractive supplement to the income derived from a regular job. For those lacking regular employment, these jobs are a poor substitute.

Mason suggests that having the 'whole of human intelligence one thumb-swipe away'[50] has the effect of turning a collection of disparate individuals into a force for postcapitalist transformation. But transforming capitalism will need more than thumb-swipes. It will require a widespread intellectual recognition of the level of productive decay and an awareness of what can be done to overcome it.

The harsh realities of transformation

There can be no economic transformation without the destruction of unproductive firms and sectors as well as the creation of new centres of production. Too many advocates of state industrial policy focus one-sidedly on the feel-good *creative* aspects. They minimise the associated processes of destruction and the resulting disruption of the lives of individuals, families and communities. This underestimates the political challenge involved in winning public support for economic restructuring, and in particular for ending the current state activities that sustain the stable zombie economy. In fact, many proponents of a more active industrial policy blur the contrast between earlier state actions that promoted growth with those in more recent decades that have become a barrier to economic development.

For example, Mazzucato, in documenting the role of the state in leading innovation in the late 20th century, fails to recognise the political transformation required before it could assume such a role again in the 21st century.[51] Her appreciation of the contribution of the 'entrepreneurial state' in the US during the post-war boom is popular in Britain, particularly among leftists. But she underplays the extent to which the state has not only retreated from this role, but also now props up zombie capitalism. She neglects the gulf between the cautious, stabilising contemporary state and the bold, risk-taking agency required to meet the challenges of the Long Depression.

The wider rehabilitation of industrial policy since the 1990s, and especially since the crash-time bailouts,[52] has confused matters further, creating the impression within radical commentators that state policies of recent decades are enlightened, and that we could do with more of them. In fact, the term 'industrial policy' has now become synonymous with any state economic intervention.[53] This has muddied the distinction between regressive and progressive economic interventions.

Justin Lin and Celestin Monga, for example, defined industrial policy as 'broadly' referring to any government decision or action that encourages 'ongoing activity' or investment in an industry.[54] Such a broad definition obscures the distinctions between propping up and restructuring, between saving old industries and firms and investing in new ones. Yet such different interventions have opposite economic and social consequences.

An industrial policy that extends corporate dependence is the opposite of what is needed. Economic revival necessitates closing down low-productivity, low-profit businesses. The political challenge is to popularise the recognition that saving the old economy is not only futile but is a barrier to prosperity.

It is misleading for commentators like Mazzucato, who know better about creative destruction, to offer a vision of a new innovation economy without also spelling out the disruption that is the inevitable accompaniment of this process.[55] People will not spontaneously embrace a programme of economic restructuring that may require them to change jobs, retrain and move home. Without a compelling and convincing vision of a better future, the prospect of personal and family hardship will inevitably loom large. Avoiding the hard political arguments about the disruptiveness of transition will inevitably backfire. It will undermine any possibility of rallying popular support for thoroughgoing economic transformation.

The case for disruptive change has to be argued openly. After more than four decades of depression, resisting change is worse than settling for the status quo, because it means resignation to continuing decline. As Hathaway and Litan argued, 'Policy makers, citizens, owners, employers and entrepreneurs' must not be afraid of dynamism or change even though it can be unsettling for a time.[56] Winning this acceptance of change is at the core of the necessary battle of ideas.

Ending the Long Depression means persuading people that conserving decadence is mistaken and that rebuilding is necessary. Worthwhile economic change can't happen unless people make it happen. A programme of economic restructuring and renewal can only work with active popular engagement. It is not a top-down initiative that can occur somewhere remote in the 'economy', divorced from everyday life.

There is no painless and easy route out of the current economic malaise. Tough decisions will have to be made. Decisions about research, capital investment, innovation and new industries are made by human beings, not by machines. The selection of new industries and techniques, along with their operation, are always deeply human affairs. Freedom of economic, scientific and technological opinion, together with democratic discussion and accountability, are the best guarantees that people make the appropriate decisions.

Short-term goals will need to be balanced with the wider priorities of the economy and society. We could do with some new democratic vehicles to help resolve these choices, but one principle should be paramount. Let the people decide.

Notes

Introduction

[1] The common term for the turbulent events of 2007–09 is the Global Financial Crisis. The use of 'global' is misleading: the crisis was made in the West. It had worldwide ramifications but obscuring its source as being within the productive decay of the advanced industrial countries is detrimental to learning how it happened.

[2] UN, 2016, p 9.

[3] Summers, 2016.

[4] Olivier Blanchard, 'Slow growth is a fact of life in the post-crisis world', *Financial Times,* 14 April 2016.

[5] McKinsey Global Institute, 2016.

[6] A term coined by Christine Lagarde, Managing Director of the International Monetary Fund. Lagarde, 2014.

[7] Aaronson et al, 2014, p 199.

[8] Koo, 2011.

[9] Reinhart and Rogoff, 2009.

[10] Reinhart, Reinhart and Rogoff, 2012.

[11] Dobbs et al, 2015.

[12] UN, 2016, p 23.

[13] Hilary Osborne, 'Rise in consumer borrowing is fastest since pre-crisis, says Bank of England', *The Guardian*, 4 January 2016; US Federal Reserve, Consumer Credit Release, February 2016. www.federalreserve.gov/releases/g19/current/

[14] UN, 2016, p 23.

[15] Olivier Blanchard, 'Slow growth is a fact of life in the post-crisis world', *Financial Times*, 14 April 2016.

[16] 'Too much of a good thing', *The Economist*, 26 March 2016.

[17] Cowen, 2011.

[18] Gordon, 2016, p 522.

[19] Timothy Aeppel, 'Silicon Valley doesn't believe U.S. productivity is down', *Wall Street Journal*, 16 July 2015.

[20] Brynjolfsson, 1993.

[21] Martin Feldstein, 'The U.S. underestimates growth', *Wall Street Journal,* 18 May 2015; Bean, 2016.

[22] Bureau of Labor Statistics (BLS), 2015, p 15; Gordon, 2016, pp 527–8.

23 The four Western economies focused on in this book: US, UK, Germany and Japan, plus France, Italy and Canada.

24 A term promoted since 2009 by Pimco (the Pacific Investment Management Company), which was then running the world's biggest bond fund. See Mohamed El-Erian, 'Mohamed A. El-Erian discusses PIMCO's secular outlook and investment strategy', *PIMCO Economic Outlook*, May 2009. http://europe.pimco.com/EN/Insights/Pages/Secular%20Outlook%20 Q%20and%20A%20May%202009%20El-Erian.aspx. The consultants McKinsey also used the term the same year: Davis, 2009.

25 Wolf, 2014, p xxii.

26 Krippner, 2012, pp 2-3.

27 Wolf, 2014, p 5.

28 Antolin-Diaz, Drechsel and Petrella, 2014.

29 Coyle, 2014, p 4.

30 Sarah O'Connor, 'Drugs and prostitution add £10bn to UK economy', *Financial Times,* 30 May 2014.

31 Burgess, 2011, pp 234, 245.

32 David Pilling, 'Has GDP outgrown its use?', *Financial Times*, 5 July 2014.

Chapter One

1 Ed Conway, 'Deep-freeze Britain faces its own lost decade', *The Times*, 12 January 2016.

2 Despite the geography Japan is regarded as a member of the 'Western' club of industrial economies.

3 Caballero and Hammour, 1994.

4 Foster, Grim and Haltiwanger, 2013, pp 24, 31.

5 Krippner, 2012.

6 Lapavitsas, 2013, pp 312-13.

7 'Group of 7, Meet the Group of 33', *The New York Times*, 26 December 1987.

8 Sirkin, Zinser and Hohner, 2011.

9 Dominic O'Connell, 'I see no evil', *The Sunday Times,* 27 January 2013.

10 IMF, 2014b, pp 28-9, 32.

Chapter Two

1 This value measure distorts the indicative *volume* productivity measure since the direct effect of rising productivity is to *reduce* the value of each unit produced.

2 Adalet McGowan et al, 2015.

3 This illustration ignores the effects of other changes in the purchasing power of a currency. It is primarily because post-war generations have become used to inflation and generally rising prices that this cheapening of things from increasing productivity is not more evident.

4 Frankl, 2004, p 76.

[5]   Teulings and Baldwin, 2014; BIS, 2014, pp 58-60, and 2015, pp 50-51; IMF, 2015, pp 69-110.

[6]   BIS, 2014, p 58.

[7]   Dabla-Norris et al, 2015.

[8]   Brenke, 2009, pp 193-4; Plunkett, 2011, pp 17-18.

[9]   See the annual *Global Wage Reports* from the International Labour Organization (ILO), and the press release 'Global wage growth stagnates, lags behind pre-crisis rates' launching the *Global Wage Report 2014/15*, 5 December 2014. www.ilo.org/global/about-the-ilo/newsroom/news/WCMS_324645/lang--en/index.htm

[10] BLS, Weekly and hourly earnings data from the Current Population Survey, Series LEU0252881600 (all); LEU0252881900 (men).

[11] Gordon, 2016, p 569.

[12] Adalet McGowan et al, 2015, p 12.

[13] Solow, 1956, 1957.

[14] As Stephen Oliner, Daniel Sichel and Kevin Stiroh, users of the model admitted, this represents an inherent weakness in it. Oliner, Sichel and Stiroh, 2007, p 1.

[15] Abramovitz, 1956, p 11.

[16] Bernanke and Gurkaynak, 2002, p 12.

[17] See also Bond, Leblebicioğlu and Schiantarelli, 2010.

[18] Former British Labour Prime Minister Gordon Brown famously popularised this theory in a speech in 1994, drafted by his advisor Ed Balls.

[19] Romer, 1986, 1990.

[20] Marshall, 1920, p 84.

[21] Peter Coy, 'The rise of the intangible economy: U.S. GDP counts R&D, artistic creation', *Bloomberg Businessweek*, 18 July 2013.

[22] Gordon, 2016, p 569.

[23] Phelps, 2013, p 220.

[24] Gordon, 2016, p 635.

[25] Gordon, 2012, p 1. Gordon's thesis is expanded in his book: Gordon, 2016.

[26] Robert Solow, 'We'd better watch out', *New York Times Book Review*, 12 July 1987, p 36.

[27] Oliner and Sichel, 2000, 2002; Jorgenson and Stiroh, 2000.

[28] OECD data: ICT investment. https://data.oecd.org/ict/ict-investment.htm#indicator-chart

[29] Baily, 2003, p 283.

[30] McKinsey Global Institute, 2001; Baily, 2003, p 283.

[31] Gordon, 2004, p 1.

[32] Gordon, 2004, p 5.

[33] Gordon, 2010a, pp 10-11.

[34] Roxburgh et al, 2010, p 23. World Bank data reports that household consumption as a share of GDP between 1996 and 2000 averaged 55% in France, 57% in Germany, 60% in Italy, while it was 65% in the US and 64% in Britain. http://data.worldbank.org/indicator/NE.CON.PETC.ZS?page=3

[35] Van Ark, Inklaar and McGuckin, 2003, pp 56-99.

[36] Elliott and Atkinson, 2008, p 232.

[37] Nordhaus, 2002; Triplett and Bosworth, 2002.

[38] O'Mahony and van Ark, 2003.

[39] Janeway, 2012, p 165.

[40] US Department of the Treasury, 2008, p 14.

[41] Cowen, 2011, pp 24-5.

[42] Gordon, 2004, p 8; Gordon, 2010a, p 23.

[43] Edmund Phelps quoted in 'Comments and discussion' in Gordon, 2003, p 294.

[44] Gordon, 2012, p 2.

[45] Field, 2003, pp 24-5.

[46] Mokyr, 2013.

[47] ONS, 2015b, p 8.

[48] ONS, 2015a, p 3.

[49] Butcher and Bursnall, 2013, p F8.

[50] Bryson and Forth, 2015, p 9.

[51] OECD data: gross domestic spending on R&D. https://data.oecd.org/rd/gross-domestic-spending-on-r-d.htm

[52] ONS, 2015b, pp 1, 3.

[53] Chris Giles, 'New order threatens economic growth', *Financial Times,* 11 May 2011.

[54] Corry, Valero and Van Reenen, 2011, p 14.

[55] Patterson, 2012, p 12.

[56] Haldane, Brennan and Madouros, 2010, pp 95-100.

[57] McCafferty, 2014.

[58] Goodridge, Haskel and Wallis, 2015, pp 3, 5.

[59] Martin Arnold and Patrick Jenkins, 'Barclays: Captain credible', *Financial Times,* 17 October 2015.

[60] Chris Giles, 'Pace of UK growth under threat', *Financial Times,* 11 May 2011.

[61] Roxburgh et al, 2010, p 23.

[62] Martin, 2010, p 40.

[63] LSE Growth Commission, 2013, p 9.

[64] Corry, Valero and Van Reenen, 2011, pp 14-15.

[65] Srinivasan, 2012, p 2.

[66] The Conference Board *Total Economy Database*, May 2016. www.conference-board.org/data/economydatabase/

[67] See Crafts, 2011b; Corry, Valero and Van Reenen, 2011.

Chapter Three

[1] BLS, Data series 0500000008 from Current Employment Statistics. The 2014 values for 1973 wages and phone costs were calculated at: www.measuringworth.com/uscompare/relativevalue.php

[2] Paul Ledak, 'How much more computing power does an iPhone 6 have than Apollo 11?', *Quora*, 29 December 2014. www.quora.com/How-much-

more-computing-power-does-an-iPhone-6-have-than-Apollo-11-What-
is-another-modern-object-I-can-relate-the-same-computing-power-to

3 Drew Desilver, 'For most workers, real wages have barely budged for
decades', Pew Research Center Fact Tank, 9 October 2014. www.
pewresearch.org/fact-tank/2014/10/09/for-most-workers-real-wages-
have-barely-budged-for-decades/

4 Martin Baily quoted by Sam Fleming, 'US productivity slowdown adds to
concerns among policy makers', *Financial Times,* 7 May 2015.

5 Kurzweil, 2001.

6 Erik Brynjolfsson, 'Advice for the second machine age', *Financial Times,*
31 March 2015.

7 Garry Kasparov and Peter Thiel, 'Our dangerous illusion of technological
progress', *Financial Times,* 9 November 2012.

8 James Bessen also believes that the multibillion-dollar valuations in Silicon
Valley have obscured the underlying problems in the way the US develops
and adopts technology. Bessen, 2015.

9 Andre Geim, 'Be afraid, very afraid, of the world's tech crisis', *Financial
Times,* 6 February 2013.

10 Hooker and Achur, 2014, p 6.

11 NESTA, 2008.

12 Designer Michael Bierut told an innovation conference that one of his rules
for being innovative is to 'shut up and listen' to customers. Ravi Mattu,
'Innovation is all about the customer', *Financial Times,* 15 November 2011.

13 Collins and Hansen, 2011.

14 Gordon, 2016, p 567.

15 Alan Blinder observed of Facebook and the Apple Watch: though
inventiveness may not have waned, its productivity-enhancing impacts
have. Alan Blinder, 'The mystery of declining productivity growth', *The
Wall Street Journal,* 14 May 2015.

16 Royal Society, 2011, pp 17, 24-5.

17 Allas, 2014.

18 Aghion, 2006, p 3.

19 Barnett, Batten et al, 2014, p 122.

20 Manyika et al, 2012, p 34.

21 Mazzucato, 2013, p 25.

22 Arora, Belenzon and Patacconi, 2015.

23 Mazzucato, 2013, pp 24-5.

24 John Carroll, 'Pfizer on track to chop R&D budget back to $6.5B-$7B
range', *FierceBiotech,* 29 January 2013.

25 Chesbrough, 2003.

26 Woudhuysen and Kaplinsky, 2009, pp 438-41.

27 Mazzucato, 2013, pp 50-51.

28 Mazzoleni and Nelson, 1998, p 273; Nelson, 2000, pp 12, 15; National
Research Council, 2007, p 168.

29 Smart, 2005.

30 Bessen and Meurer, 2007; Bessen, 2015.

[31] Mazzucato, 2013, p 50.

[32] The website singularity.com that accompanies Kurzweil's book *The Singularity is Near* is a common source for this claim.

[33] Alexander Fleming identified penicillin in 1928; Gerhard Domagk discovered the first systemically active antibacterial drug, prontosil, in 1933.

[34] Gordon, 2016, p 398.

[35] Syverson, 2016.

[36] Christensen is the author of the *Innovator's Dilemma,* an influential book on innovation from 1997.

[37] Jorgenson, Ho and Samuels, 2010, p 2.

[38] Conference Board, 'Global productivity slowdown moderated in 2013', *2014 Productivity Brief Press Release*, PRNewswire, 14 January 2014. www.prnewswire.com/news-releases/global-productivity-slowdown-moderated-in-2013-240097261.html

[39] Stiglitz, Lin and Monga, 2013, p 7.

[40] Harvard Business Review, 2002.

[41] Quoted in the *BusinessWeek* Report: The CEO guide to technology, 'Tech's "dearth of innovation"', *BusinessWeek,* 26 July 2005.

[42] Jeffrey Immelt, 'The CEO of General Electric on sparking an American manufacturing renewal', *Harvard Business Review,* March 2012.

[43] George Yip and Bruce McKern, 'China's many types of innovation', *Forbes Asia*, 19 September 2014.

[44] Edward Luce, 'America reassembles industrial policy', *Financial Times,* 9 April 2012.

[45] Professor James Wilsdon thinks that on most measures of research and innovation, China already exceeds many people's expectations: Clive Cookson, 'Government in danger of stifling bright ideas', *Financial Times*, 17 October 2013.

[46] Andre Geim, 'Be afraid, very afraid, of the world's tech crisis', *Financial Times,* 6 February 2013.

[47] National Research Council, 2007.

[48] Arora, Belenzon and Patacconi, 2015.

[49] Andre Geim, 'Be afraid, very afraid, of the world's tech crisis', *Financial Times,* 6 February 2013.

[50] Janeway, 2012, pp 10, 274.

Chapter Four

[1] Connors and Franklin, 2015, p 7.

[2] Knight, 1921, Part 3, chapter 12, paragraph 41.

[3] Jorgenson, Ho and Samuels, 2010, p 15.

[4] Phelps, 2013, p 225.

[5] Poynter, 2000, pp 47-8.

[6] Chart 2A, HM Treasury, 2014.

[7] IMF, 2014b, pp 79-81.

[8]   European Commission AMECO database. http://ec.europa.eu/economy_finance/db_indicators/index_en.htm

[9]   BIS, 2014, p 56.

[10] Bureau of Economic Analysis (BEA), National Income and Product Account (NIPA) table 5.1, line 51. www.bea.gov/iTable/index_nipa.cfm

[11] BEA, Fixed assets: Table 1.9 Current-cost average age at year-end of fixed assets and consumer durable goods. www.bea.gov/iTable/iTable.cfm?ReqID=10&step=1#reqid=10&step=3&isuri=1&1003=125

[12] The shift to shorter-lived ICT assets is an international phenomenon. Jorgenson, 2011, pp 282, 288-9; OECD, 2015a. Because these assets have to be replaced more frequently, gross investment figures will also be flattered as the ICT share of investment rises.

[13] ONS, 2015c.

[14] ONS, 2015c, p 21.

[15] IMF, 2015, chapter 4, 'Private Investment: What's the holdup?', pp 114-18.

[16] Gros, 2014.

[17] US gross investment to GDP ratio averaged 15.8% between 1890 and 1913, and 13.2% between 1950 and 1973. Maddison, 1991.

[18] Dobbs et al, 2010, p 14.

[19] US manufacturing's share of GDP halved from 24% in 1970 to 12% in 2008. In Britain the fall was even steeper from 32% also to 12%. In Japan and Germany the shares fell from 34% to 20% and from 36% to 23% respectively. OECD.Stat. www.oecd-ilibrary.org/economics/data/oecd-stat_data-00285-en

[20] The capital-output ratio of telecommunications is about 345% and of education about 290%, while for manufacturing it is only about 150%. Dobbs et al, 2010, p 14.

[21] Tom Heyden, 'The cows that queue up to milk themselves', *BBC News*, 7 May 2005.

[22] Frey claims that most industries formed since 2000 – electronic auctions, Internet news publishers, social-networking sites, and video and audio streaming services, all of which appeared in official industry classifications for the first time in 2010 – employ far fewer people than earlier computer-based industries and require little capital to get going. Frey, 2015.

[23] UN, 2016, p 23.

[24] Scott, 1989, p 69.

[25] Corrado, Hulten and Sichel, 2009, p 683.

[26] Corrado et al, 2012, pp 35-7.

[27] Goodridge, Haskel and Wallis, 2014, p 10.

[28] Corrado et al, 2012, pp 4, 32-4.

[29] Goodridge, Haskel and Wallis, 2014, pp 9, 11-22.

[30] Corrado, Hulten and Sichel, 2009, p 662.

[31] Peter Coy, 'The rise of the intangible economy: U.S. GDP counts R&D, artistic creation', *Bloomberg Businessweek*, 18 July 2013.

[32] Agreed for the 2008 version of the UN's *System of National Accounts*.

[33] This approach has now been adopted in most countries, including by the US in 2013 and by Britain in 2014.

[34] James Woudhuysen, 'R&D: why failure is necessary', *spiked*, 1 October 2013.

[35] Goodridge, Haskel and Wallis, 2014.

[36] This is a random selection of suggested academic research topics taken from the web: http://libguides.umflint.edu/topics

[37] US studies of intangibles include the same three main areas of spending that are not yet treated in the official accounts as investment. Slightly different terms are used in the US compared to Britain but the coverage is similar: brand-building, worker training, and the development of organisational practices and processes. Corrado, Hulten and Sichel, 2009.

[38] Goodridge, Haskel and Wallis, 2014, p 9.

[39] Lauren Henderson, 'For what it's worth', *FT Creative Business*, 3 February 2004, p 6.

[40] Becker, 1994.

[41] O'Mahony and de Boer, 2002, pp 9–12.

[42] Aston and Bekhradnia, 2003, pp 34–45.

[43] Knight, 1921, Part 3, chapter 11, paragraph 36.

Chapter Five

[1] Activist Insight, 2014, p 4.

[2] Rana Foroohar, 'Shareholder "activists" - are they good or bad?', *Time*, 26 March 2014.

[3] Jackson, 2011.

[4] A typical example is an OECD business and public sector discussion in 2011. Wehinger, 2011.

[5] Rajan, 2010, p 48.

[6] According to surveys conducted by Bank of America Merrill Lynch the majority of fund managers – people who look after large portfolios of financial investments for their clients – want companies to invest in growth instead of using corporate cash for buybacks, dividends or balance sheet repair. http://newsroom.bankofamerica.com/press-releases/economic-and-industry-outlooks/bofa-merrill-lynch-fund-manager-survey-finds-investo-3

[7] IMF, 2014b, chapter 3, 'Is it time for an infrastructure push? The macroeconomic effects of public investment'.

[8] Standard & Poor's Ratings Services, 2014, pp 4–5.

[9] 'Corporate spending: two steps forward, one step back', *Global Equity Strategy*, Credit Suisse, 12 October 2012.

[10] Koller, Lovallo and Williams, 2011.

[11] Macmillan, Prakash and Shoult, 2014. 'Cash reserves' refers to cash and near-cash items and short-term financial assets that are easily turned into cash.

[12] Bates, Kahle and Stulz, 2009, p 1985.

Notes

13 Cash reserves are derived from savings: gross corporate savings are the retained earnings (with an adjustment for depreciation) after dividends have been paid to shareholders. Dobbs et al, 2010, p 20.

14 Corporate savings have also been used for other financial activities including acquiring other businesses and paying down debt: it is what is left over that accumulates in cash holdings.

15 IMF, 2006, p 136.

16 Loeys et al, 2005.

17 In 2005 a discussion took off about a 'global savings glut', a term popularised by Bernanke. Bernanke, 2005. Many, including Bernanke, blamed China for the excess in savings, fuelling a bout of China-bashing for the troubles facing Western, and especially the US, economies.

18 Macmillan, Prakash and Shoult, 2014.

19 Alison Smith, 'Cash mountains have become a feature of the corporate landscape', *Financial Times*, 19 March 2015.

20 Mike Cherney, 'Apple dives again into bond market', *The Wall Street Journal*, 6 May 2015.

21 Foroohar, 2016.

22 BIS Statistics Explorer: Credit to the nonfinancial sector, updated to 1 December 2015. http://stats.bis.org/statx/toc/CRE.html

23 Dobbs et al, 2015, p 21.

24 IMF, 2014a, p 1.

25 For example, the British Federation of Small Businesses, in Bank of England, 2014, p 10.

26 Bank of England, 2014, p 14.

27 Bank of England, 2014, p 10.

28 Roxburgh et al, 2012, p 21.

29 Broadbent, 2012b, p 12.

30 Charles Goodhart, 'Failure to reform housing finance is a missed opportunity', *Financial Times,* 30 September 2014.

31 Bates, Kahle and Stulz, 2009, p 2018. The authors added that this factor had been reinforced by a heightened perception of risk, encouraging firms to maintain a bigger cushion of cash.

32 Bernanke, 2005.

33 Dobbs et al, 2010, pp 10, 17.

34 While central banks can for a time push some interest rates to their zero extreme (and below it), this capability depends on the level and direction of *market* interest rates. State interventions adjust official rates but these can't escape or reverse market trends for long.

35 Kothari, Lewellen and Warner, 2014, p 15.

36 Kothari, Lewellen and Warner, 2014, pp 27-30.

37 Kothari, Lewellen and Warner, 2014, p 5.

38 Banerjee, Kearns and Lombardi, 2015, p 76.

39 Coyle, 2014, p 44.

40 At a party rally in Bedford.

41 Allman, 1983, pp 24-5.

[42]   Financial services are an unproductive area of economic activity. The profits this sector reports are not the result of new value created but derive from its ability to benefit through charges and interest rate spreads from appropriating some of the value and profits produced elsewhere. Allman also drew attention to the 'serious problems associated with the measurement of profit rates in the financial sector'. Allman, 1983, p 25 footnote.

[43]   Blanchard, Rhee and Summers, 1990, p 15.

[44]   One can use current nominal prices, or inflation adjusted ones; the historical cost of the capital assets, or their replacement cost; profits before or after taxation; and many other variants besides.

[45]   Kliman, 2012, chapter 5.

[46]   Maito, 2014, pp 9-10.

[47]   Marx, 1973, p 748.

[48]   The *net* profit figures that are often used in profitability ratios are the profits left over after the deduction of all other expenses *including* interest and taxes. Net profits tend to move in the same direction as operating profits.

[49]   Marx, 1974, p 213.

[50]   Kothari, Lewellen and Warner, 2014, pp 18-19.

[51]   Many later followers of Marx ignored this qualification when they crudely equated a falling rate of profit with economic crisis.

[52]   Marx, 1974, p 239.

[53]   For an excellent exposition of the relationship between the rate and mass of profit and the confusions this has sometimes caused see Grossmann, 1992, especially pp 101-3.

[54]   Mattick, 1974, p 68.

[55]   Jorgenson, Ho and Samuels, 2010, p 15.

[56]   For example, Nordhaus et al, 1972.

Chapter Six

[1]   Phelps, 2013, p 219.

[2]   Phelps, 2013, p 175.

[3]   Marx, 1974, p 239.

[4]   Mattick, 1974, p 68.

[5]   Standard & Poor's Ratings Services, 2013, pp 27-8, 33.

[6]   Andrew Bounds, 'Graphene's leading lights unveil mass market bulb', *Financial Times,* 28 March 2015.

[7]   Lazonick and O'Sullivan, 2000, p 15.

[8]   Smithers, 2013, pp 15-16.

[9]   Economic 'records' need to be seen in perspective. Even in a slow growing economy with low or zero inflation, many economic measures are regularly hitting *nominal* record levels: consumption, disposable income, exports, even business investment and profits. Records *relative* to some contemporaneous measure like GDP might be more meaningful.

[10] Kliman, 2012, pp 5-10, and throughout. The intense disputes within parts of the left over whether corporate profitability rose a little in the 1980s is an intellectual distraction.

[11] Alliance for Competitive Taxation, 2014.

[12] Kevin Farnsworth, 'Britain's corporate welfare is out of control – increasing it makes no sense', *The Guardian,* 10 July 2015.

[13] BEA, federal government tax as a share of corporate profits, data retrieved from FRED, Federal Reserve Bank of St. Louis. https://fred.stlouisfed. org/graph/?g=aWA

[14] Calculated from BEA, NIPA tables 1.1.5, 6.17 and 6.19. www.bea.gov/ iTable/index_nipa.cfm

[15] Plunkett, 2011, p 22.

[16] OECD.Stat, GDP (income approach), SNA93 table. http://stats.oecd.org/ Index.aspx?DatasetCode=SNA_TABLE1

[17] Whittaker and Savage, 2011, p 23.

[18] BEA, NIPA table 6.17. www.bea.gov/iTable/index_nipa.cfm

[19] Kothari, Lewellen and Warner, 2014, p 7.

[20] Keynes, 1936.

[21] Fisher, 1933.

[22] Hansen, 1938.

[23] Hayek, 1931.

[24] Stiglitz, 2012b; Krugman, 2013; Summers, 2014; Wolf, 2014.

[25] Hayek, 1991; Friedman, 2002.

Chapter Seven

[1] Blum, Cameron and Barnes, 1970, p 885.

[2] Granados, 2010, p 110.

[3] IMF World Economic Outlook Database, October 2015. https://www. imf.org/external/pubs/ft/weo/2015/02/weodata/index.aspx

[4] Stock and Watson, 2003. A more recent update of their approach contrasted a standard deviation in growth rates of 2.7% between 1960 and 1983 to almost half that level, 1.5%, from 1984 to 2006. Fosler, 2011.

[5] Bernanke, 2004.

[6] Clark, 2009, p 16.

[7] Clark, 2009, p 25; Craig Hakkio, 'The Great Moderation', US Federal Reserve History website. www.federalreservehistory.org/Events/ DetailView/65

[8] Caballero and Hammour, 2000, p 8.

[9] Schumpeter, 1975.

[10] Marx, 1973, pp 749-50.

[11] Marx, 1975, p 496.

[12] The *Grundrisse* (written in 1857-58) was only published in 1939 and 1941.

[13] Schumpeter, 1975, pp 82-5.

[14] Mazzucato, 2011, p 49.

[15] Steinbeck, 1962, p 181.

16 Field, 2003, p 7.
17 Gordon, 2016, p 528.
18 Haltiwanger, 2012.
19 Hathaway and Litan, 2014a, p 1.
20 Caballero and Hammour, 2000, p 19.
21 Disney, Haskel and Heden, 2003; Haltiwanger, Jarmin and Miranda, 2008, p 2; Barnett, Chiu et al, 2014, p 7.
22 An 'establishment', or 'plant', is a single physical location where economic activity takes place, so a 'firm' can comprise one or more establishments or plants.
23 Foster, Haltiwanger and Krizan, 2001.
24 Barnett, Chiu et al, 2014, p 22.
25 Disney, Haskel and Heden, 2003; Bank of England, 2013, p 27.
26 Haltiwanger, 2012.
27 Fujita, 2008, p 14.
28 Haltiwanger, 2012, pp 25-7.
29 Adalet McGowan et al, 2015, pp 12, 32, 45.
30 Adalet McGowan et al, 2015, p 12.
31 Hathaway and Litan, 2014a, pp 1-2.
32 Hathaway and Litan, 2014b, p 9.
33 Criscuolo, Gal and Menon, 2014, p 30.
34 Barnett, Chiu et al, 2014, pp 19-20, based on ONS Business Demography data.
35 Broadbent, 2012b, pp 11-12.
36 For example, Michael Hayman, 'Britain can produce world-beaters – if business speaks up for capitalism', *City A.M.*, 29 April 2015. Such claims about strong entrepreneurialism tend to rely on conflating the rise in self-employment with the expansion of businesses that employ people.
37 Barnett, Chiu et al, 2014, p 22.
38 Barnett, Batten et al, 2014, p 123.
39 Davis and Haltiwanger, 2014, p 14.
40 Haltiwanger, 2012, p 29.
41 Foster, Grim and Haltiwanger, 2013, pp 30-31.
42 BLS Business Employment Dynamics (BED) database. http://www.bls.gov/bdm/home.htm
43 Haltiwanger, Hathaway and Miranda, 2014, pp 4-5.
44 Davis and Haltiwanger, 2014, p 14.
45 Manyika et al, 2011, p 12.
46 BLS. http://www.bls.gov/data/#employment
47 Manyika et al, 2011, p 19.
48 Haltiwanger, Jarmin and Miranda, 2008, p 18.
49 Haltiwanger, Jarmin and Miranda, 2011, p 3.
50 Davis and Haltiwanger, 2014, pp 3-4. This complements the BED data with the Job Openings and Labor Turnover (JOLT) series, also from the Bureau of Labor Statistics, that measures turnover at the level of the individual worker.

[51] Davis and Haltiwanger, 2014, p 11.

[52] Butcher and Bursnall, 2013, p F9.

[53] Hijzen, Upward and Wright, 2010, p 628.

[54] Butcher and Bursnall, 2013, p F8.

[55] ILOSTAT database. www.ilo.org/ilostat/faces/oracle/webcenter/ portalapp/pagehierarchy/Page137.jspx?_afrLoop=109873536189758&cl ean=true&_adf.ctrl-state=rmohmu4tp_9

[56] ILO, 2013, p 4.

Chapter Eight

[1]   Broadbent, 2012b, p 9.

[2]   Restuccia and Rogerson, 2012.

[3]   BIS, 2014, p 49.

[4]   Ferdinando Giugliano, 'What not to do in a crisis', *Financial Times*, 10–11 January 2015, quoting from Eichengreen, 2014.

[5]   Crafts, 2011a, p 24.

[6]   Nordhaus and Tobin, 1972, pp 3–4.

[7]   Furedi, 1997.

[8]   Deborah Summers, 'No return to boom and bust: what Brown said when he was chancellor', *The Guardian*, 11 September 2008.

[9]   Queen's Speech, UK Cabinet Office and Her Majesty The Queen, 15 November 1995. www.publications.parliament.uk/pa/ld199596/ldhansrd/ vo951115/text/51115-01.htm

[10] Queen's Speech, UK Cabinet Office and Her Majesty The Queen, 17 May 2005. www.publications.parliament.uk/pa/ld200506/ldhansrd/vo050517/ text/50517-01.htm

[11] Queen's Speech, UK Cabinet Office and Her Majesty The Queen, 27 May 2015. www.gov.uk/government/speeches/queens-speech-2015

[12] Lapavitsas, 2013 pp 172, 198.

[13] Cabarello, Hoshi and Kashyap, 2008, pp 1943–4, 1947.

[14] OECD, 2015b, p 4.

[15] Adalet McGowan et al, 2015, pp 59–60.

[16] OECD, 2015b, p 4.

[17] Adalet McGowan et al, 2015, p 54.

[18] Farnsworth, 2015.

[19] 'Reality dawns for artificial world created by Fed activism', *Financial Times*, 19 December 2013.

[20] Broadbent, 2012b, p 13.

[21] The Insolvency Service, Insolvency statistics. https://www.gov.uk/ government/collections/insolvency-service-official-statistics

[22] Barnett, Batten et al, 2014, pp 124–5.

[23] Kate Burgess, 'Insolvencies practitioners feel the squeeze', *Financial Times*, 7 June 2016.

[24] Arrowsmith et al, 2013, p 297.

[25] Pessoa and Van Reenan, 2013, p 12.

[26] Arrowsmith et al, 2013, p 300.
[27] Arrowsmith et al, 2013, pp 301-2.
[28] Broadbent, 2012a, p 11.
[29] King, 2013, pp 82-3.
[30] Caballero, Hoshi and Kashyap, 2008, pp 1946, 1965.
[31] Caballero, Hoshi and Kashyap, 2008, pp 1944-5.
[32] Haldane, 2015, p 1.
[33] Caballero, Hoshi and Kashyap, 2008, p 1970.
[34] ILO, 2012; Quak and van de Vijsel, 2014.

Chapter Nine

[1] Advice attributed, maybe apocryphally, to the banker Nathan Mayer Rothschild, who made a fortune during the uncertainties of the Napoleonic Wars.
[2] Bates, Kahle and Stulz, 2009.
[3] Roxburgh et al, 2012, p 19.
[4] Marcel Fratzscher, 'The German locomotive has become Europe's liability', *Financial Times*, 28 August 2014.
[5] Standard & Poor's Ratings Services, 2013, pp 27, 34.
[6] White, 2012, p 13.
[7] Kay, 2012, p 36.
[8] Philip Stephens, 'Why the business of risk is booming', *Financial Times*, 13 March 2015.
[9] Toksöz, 2014.
[10] 'Political uncertainty holding back transformational progress on infrastructure', CBI/URS, 3 November 2014. www.cbi.org.uk/media-centre/press-releases/2014/11/political-uncertainty-holding-back-transformational-progress-on-infrastructure-cbi-urs/
[11] Lawrence Mishel, 'Regulatory uncertainty: a phony explanation for our jobs problem', *Economic Policy Institute*, 27 September 2011.
[12] Keynes, 1936.
[13] For example, Angeletos, Collard and Dellas, 2015.
[14] For example, Baum, Caglayan and Talavera, 2008.
[15] Kothari, Lewellen and Warner, 2014, p 15.
[16] Simms, 2014, pp 211-21.
[17] Field, 2003, 2006.
[18] Mazzucato, 2011, footnote 97, p 128.
[19] Boyle and Guthrie, 2003, pp 2143, 2160; Baum, Caglayan and Talavera, 2008, p 18.
[20] Knight, 1921, Part 3, chapter 9, paragraph 7.
[21] http://quoteinvestigator.com/2012/09/27/invent-the-future
[22] Knight, 1921, Part 1, chapter 2, paragraph 27.
[23] Knight, 1921, Part 3, chapter 10, paragraph 36.
[24] Knight, 1921, Part 2, chapter 5, paragraph 39.

[25] Knight, 1921, Part 3, chapter 11, paragraph 5; Part 3, chapter 12, paragraph 39.

[26] Knight, 1921, Part 3, chapter 11, paragraph 43.

[27] For example, Janan Ganesh, 'The fatal flaw at the heart of the campaign for Brexit', *Financial Times*, 15 December 2015.

[28] Janan Ganesh, 'Lynton Crosby is right about the "politics of fear"', *Financial Times*, 29 December 2015.

[29] Fukuyama, 1992, p 4.

[30] Furedi, 2014, p 14.

[31] Furedi, 2014, p 56.

[32] Schumpeter, 1975, p 63.

[33] Schumpeter, 1975, p 61.

[34] Schumpeter, 1975, p 142.

[35] A sentiment that many on the left were arguing again after the British people voted in 2016 to leave the EU.

[36] Adorno and Horkheimer, 1979, p xvi.

[37] Ignatieff, 1999.

[38] William Safire, 'The Cold War's hot kitchen', *The New York Times*, 23 July 2009.

[39] Crafts, 2000, p 14.

[40] In America the elite had extra ordeals to contend with from military defeat in Vietnam, the Watergate scandal and the forced resignation of President Richard Nixon under threat of impeachment in 1974.

[41] Thatcher's standing benefited too from taking on and defeating Argentina over the occupation of the Falkland Islands in 1982.

[42] Mizruchi, 2007, p 8.

[43] Frank Furedi, '25 years after the Berlin Wall fell, a culture wall has replaced it', *Spiked*, 10 November 2014.

[44] Frank Furedi, 'We need to inject some humanism into British politics', *Spiked*, 6 May 2015.

[45] Lasch, 1991, p 224.

[46] Measured in '1990 International Geary-Khamis' dollars.

[47] Maddison, 2003. Britain was a slight exception: material living standards there had been drifting upwards a little bit faster than the world average in the first two-thirds of the second millennium.

[48] Bailey, 2012.

[49] Mokyr, 2010, p 33.

[50] Magnus, 2011, pp 45-6.

[51] For example, the British government's Productivity Plan. HM Treasury, 2015.

[52] Paul Ormerod, 'There's nothing inevitable about slower growth – but we must embrace change', *City A.M.*, 4 March 2015.

Chapter Ten

[1] Ben Casselman, 'Risk-averse culture infects U.S. workers, entrepreneurs', *The Wall Street Journal*, 3 June 2013.

[2] Koller, Lovallo and Williams, 2011.

[3] Mikes, 2014; Caroline Binham, 'Risk officers rise in UK executive ranks', *Financial Times*, 6 April 2015.

[4] Poterba and Summers, 1995.

[5] Roxburgh et al, 2012, p 47.

[6] Broadbent, 2012a, p 2.

[7] Broadbent, 2012a, pp 3, 10-11.

[8] Haldane 2015, pp 3-11.

[9] Taleb, 2007, pp 225-6.

[10] Le Merle, 2011.

[11] Mazzucato, 2011, p 50.

[12] Mazzucato, 2011, pp 71, 111.

[13] Clive Cookson, 'Twelve ways the world could end', *Financial Times*, 14 February 2015.

[14] Schwab's warning came in the run up to the 2016 event: John Thornhill's review of Klaus Schwab, *The Fourth Industrial Revolution* (2016), *Financial Times*, 18 January 2016.

[15] Lanier, 2014.

[16] Rory Cellan-Jones, 'Stephen Hawking warns artificial intelligence could end mankind', *BBC News*, 2 December 2014; Sally Davies, 'Hawking warns earth could go to Hal as intelligent computers take over', *Financial Times*, 3 December 2014.

[17] Samuel Gibbs, 'Elon Musk: artificial intelligence is our biggest existential threat', *The Guardian*, 27 October 2014.

[18] Eric Mack, 'Bill Gates says you should worry about artificial intelligence', *Forbes*, 28 January 2015.

[19] Frey, 2015; Karabell, 2016.

[20] Ford, 2015.

[21] Lynda Gratton, 'Advice for the second machine age', *Financial Times*, 31 March 2015.

[22] Binfield, 2004.

[23] Plunkett, 2011, p 33.

[24] Brynjolfsson and McAfee, 2011.

[25] Frey and Osborne, 2013; George Bowden, 'Robots taking 35% of UK jobs: 8 roles artificial intelligence may replace', *The Huffington Post UK*, 14 September 2015.

[26] See, for instance, Jackson, 2011.

[27] Mishan, 1967, p 208.

[28] Coyle, 2014, p 60.

[29] Bell, 1996, p 80.

[30] King and Schneider, 1993, p 70.

[31] King and Schneider, 1993, p 115.

[32] Ben-Ami, 2010, pp 31-57.

33 The first big *endorsement* of the principle had been in 1982 when the World Charter for Nature was adopted by the UN General Assembly.

34 Nordhaus and Tobin, 1972.

35 Nordhaus and Tobin, 1972, p 17.

36 Bernstein, 2010.

Chapter Eleven

1   Public Administration Select Committee, 2012, pp 19, 20, 7.

2   Timothy Garton Ash, 'Fading memories of the brutal history that created Europe', *Financial Times*, 19-20 December 2015.

3   Gordon Crovitz, 'Steve Jobs's advice for Obama', *The Wall Street Journal*, 31 October 2011.

4   Corey Robin, 'Endgame: Conservatives after the Cold War', *Boston Review*, February/March 2004.

5   Graebner, D. (2015) *The Utopia of Rules: On Technology, Stupidity and the Secret Joys of Bureaucracy*, Melville House, quoted in Gillian Tett, 'Time to tear up the paperwork', *Financial Times*, 21 February 2015.

6   *The New York Times*, 7 January 1971.

7   Labour Party, 1976, p 188.

8   Bruce Bartlett, 'Keynes and Keynesianism', *The New York Times*, 14 May 2013.

9   The lion's share of British steel production subsequently merged with a Dutch steel producer and was renamed as Corus before being taken over by the Indian operator Tata Steel in 2007.

10 Foreign firms from Japan, the US, Germany and India (another part of Tata took over Jaguar Land-Rover from Ford in 2008) have dominated UK car production since.

11 Burgin, 2012.

12 Clinton's 1996 State of the Union Address. https://clinton4.nara.gov/WH/New/other/sotu.html

13 Quoted by Germaine Greer, 'The making of Maggie', *The Guardian*, 11 April 2009.

14 Fukuyama, 1989.

15 Anne-Sylvaine Chassany, 'Emmanuel Macron bets on French political realignment', *Financial Times*, 18 April 2016.

16 'UK politics: "Stability is a sexy thing"', *BBC News*, 16 November 1998. http://news.bbc.co.uk/1/hi/uk_politics/215777.stm

17 Emma Dunkley and Martin Arnold, 'Sale of RBS stake marks start of the UK's biggest privatisation', *Financial Times*, 4 August 2015.

18 James Politi, 'Pope Francis calls Europe an "elderly and haggard" grandmother', *Financial Times*, 25 November 2014.

19 Philpott, 2004. Philpott was then chief economist at the UK's Chartered Institute of Personnel and Development, the UK's professional association for human resources staff.

20 Gordon, 2010a, pp 4-5.

21 Gordon, 2010a, p 9, quoting Jon E. Hilsenrath, 'While economy lifts, severe profit crunch haunts companies; nervous CEOs could slow recovery by continuing layoffs, plant closings', *The Wall Street Journal,* 1 April 2002, A1.

22 Gordon, 2010b, pp 4–5.

23 Oliner, Sichel and Stiroh, 2007, p 4.

24 Manyika et al, 2011, pp 13–14.

25 Magnus, 2011, p 64.

26 Borio, 2012, pp 7–8.

27 Irwin Stelzer, 'America remains the best engine for global growth', *The Sunday Times,* 17 January 2016.

28 Jill Treanor and Nicholas Watt, 'Mark Carney fears Brexit would leave UK relying on "kindness of strangers"', *The Guardian,* 26 January 2016.

29 It took Britain's referendum vote to leave the EU in June 2016 to trigger a fall in the value of sterling to something closer to fair value, after years of being overvalued resulting from high capital inflows.

30 US Department of the Treasury, 2014, p 5.

31 UK Debt Management Office database. http://www.dmo.gov.uk/ rpt_parameters.aspx?rptCode=D5N&page=Gilts/Overseas_Holdings

32 Andritzy, 2012, p 26.

33 Greenspan, 2005.

34 IMF, 2014a, p 13.

35 Mendoza and Quadrini, 2009, pp 4, 29.

36 See, for example, Wolf, 2014.

Chapter Twelve

1   Szu Ping Chan and Ben Wright, 'Can anything stop this global cycle of doom?', *The Telegraph,* 16 April 2016.

2   Julian Baggini, 'Should we cultivate resilience?', *FT Weekend Magazine,* 4–5 October 2014.

3   Jonathan O'Connell, 'The FBI's headquarters is falling apart. Why is it so hard for America to build a new one?', *The Washington Post,* 16 October 2015.

4   'I-10 in California closed after bridge collapses', *USA Today,* 20 July 2015.

5   Stefan Wagstyl, 'Germany: in a spin', *Financial Times,* 1 September 2014.

6   Zakaria, 2013.

7   Turner, 2014b, pp 2, 18.

8   The title of Mohamed El-Erian's 2016 book.

9   Lapavitsas, 2013, p 107.

10 The base rate was cut further following the EU referendum vote.

11 http://news.sky.com/story/1263732/carney-house-prices-biggest-risk-to economy, 18 May 2014.

12 Orphanides, 2013, pp 7, 18.

13 Nellis, 2013.

14 Robin Harding, 'Bernanke joke underscores questions on QE's efficacy', *Financial Times,* 14 October 2014.

15 Joyce, Tong and Woods, 2011, pp 201-2.
16 Jonathan Davis, 'Nightmare of debt deflation stalks Europe', *Financial Times*, 25 August 2014.
17 Elaine Moore and Thomas Hale, 'Negative bond yield universe hits US$5.5tn after Japan eases', *Financial Times*, 30 January 2016.
18 Jorda, Schularick and Taylor, 2012, pp 4, 10.
19 Turner, 2014b, p 16.
20 Roxburgh et al, 2010, p 10.
21 Turner, 2014a, p 5.
22 Mauldin and Tepper, 2011, pp 148-9.
23 Dobbs et al, 2010, p 17.
24 J. Kyle Bass, Hayman Advisors client letter, 'The cognitive dissonance of it all', reprinted in John Mauldin's *Outside the Box*, 6 March 2010.
25 Grant Williams, 'The consequences of the economic peace', *Things that make you go hmmm...*, Mauldin Economics, 6 October 2014.
26 Drehmann, Borio and Tsatsaronis, 2012.
27 Minsky, 1992, pp 7-8.
28 Borio, 2012, p 7.
29 Gillian Tett's *Fool's Gold* (2009) is a well written guide to what happened.
30 BIS Statistics: Credit to the nonfinancial sector, updated to 6 December 2015. www.bis.org/statistics/totcredit.htm?m=6%7C326
31 Dobbs et al, 2015, p 20.
32 Fisher, 2014, p 1.
33 John Plender, 'Yield chasers cross the beta desert at their peril', *Financial Times*, 1 September 2014.
34 Chris Giles and Sarah O'Connor, 'Haldane backs central banks' actions in a "nutty" world', *Financial Times*, 3 July 2014.

Chapter Thirteen

1 Deaton was referring to overseas aid, but his exortation to 'stop' is pertinent to all state actions getting in the way of growth.
2 For example, Kliman, 2012.
3 Gordon, 2016, pp 478-80.
4 Robert Wright, 'Self-driving car makers take different routes', *Financial Times*, 15 April 2016.
5 'Why self-driving cars must be programmed to kill', *MIT Technology Review*, 22 October 2015.
6 Harriet Green, 'Quantum leap: interview with Graeme Malcolm, CEO of M Squared Lasers', *City A.M.*, 18 April 2016.
7 Dr. Jonathan Pritchard and Dr. Stephen Till, 'UK quantum technology landscape 2014', UK Defence Science and Technology Laboratory, Porton Down.
8 Andrew Ward, 'Cutting edge virtual reality streams live operation to trainees', *Financial Times*, 15 April 2016.

9   Heather Bellini et al, 'Virtual & Augmented Reality: Understanding the Race for the Next Computing Platform', Goldman Sachs, January 2016.

10 Machiavelli, 2008, p 78.

11 Stiglitz, Lin and Monga, 2013, p 10.

12 Janeway, 2012, p 1.

13 Gary Pisano, a Harvard Business School professor, used the example of the biotechnology industry to show that research and development is not best managed as a private business. Pisano, 2006.

14 John Llewellyn, 'Give the geniuses a reason to make earth a better place', *Financial Times*, 30 June 2014.

15 The state's role goes back much further. James Bessen described how since the early 19th century US government procurement activities had played an important role in spurring technological innovation. Bessen, 2015.

16 Peter Thiel quoted the reasonable claim made in the *New York Times* the day after the bombing of Hiroshima of the superiority of collaborative working and centralised direction in matters scientific: 'End result: an invention [the nuclear bomb] was given to the world in three years which it would have taken perhaps half a century to develop if we had to rely on prima donna research scientists who work alone.' Thiel, 2011.

17 Pisano, 2006.

18 Lazonick and O'Sullivan, 2000, pp 30-31.

19 Gordon, 2016, pp 536-7.

20 Kliman calculated that American GDP increased by 164% while the amount of capital stock advanced by US companies grew by only 3% in nominal terms: Kliman, 2012, p 77.

21 Lin and Monga, 2010, p 10.

22 Bessen highlights that it was during the 1940s that the Pentagon funded the making of the first general-purpose computer. Bessen, 2015.

23 Gordon, 2016, p 564.

24 Field, 2003, p 16.

25 Stiglitz, 2012a.

26 Mazzucato, 2013, p 13.

27 Mazzucato, 2013, p 76.

28 Mazzucato, 2013, p 63.

29 Public Administration Select Committee, 2012, evidence p 48.

30 Duncan, 2009.

31 Andre Geim, 'Be afraid, be very afraid, of the world's tech crisis', *Financial Times*, 6 February 2013.

32 Alan Beattie, 'Politics and the markets: week of the living dread', *Financial Times*, 6 August 2011.

33 Zakaria, 2013.

34 Roubini and Mihm, 2011, p 176.

35 Phelps, 2013, p 236.

36 Lex column, 'Minding its own BISness', *Financial Times*, 28 June 2011.

37 Andre Geim, 'Be afraid, be very afraid, of the world's tech crisis', *Financial Times*, 6 February 2013.

[38] Michael Ignatieff, 'Free polarised politics from its intellectual vacuum', *Financial Times*, 10 January 2014.

[39] Frankl, 2004, p 145.

[40] Meiksins Wood, 1995.

[41] Mason, 2015, p 243.

[42] Mason, 2015, pp xiii–xiv.

[43] Mason, 2015, pp 273–5.

[44] Streeck, 2014, p 55.

[45] Stiglitz, 2012b; Piketty, 2014.

[46] Streeck, 2014, p 46.

[47] Mason, 2015, pp 212–13.

[48] Mason, 2015, pp xv–xvi.

[49] Mason, 2015, p xvii.

[50] Mason, 2015, p xvii.

[51] Mazzucato, 2013, especially chapters 1 and 10. She argues that what is necessary to expand our vision of what the state can do is 'to change the ways we talk about the State' (p 9) 'and the images and ideas we use to describe' it (p 198).

[52] 'The global revival of industrial policy: picking winners, saving losers', *The Economist*, 5 August 2010; Stiglitz, Lin and Monga, 2013.

[53] Nester, 1997. William Nester argued that every nation has an industrial policy, whether it admits or not, drawing on the fact that all major industries are now deeply involved with and dependent on government.

[54] Lin and Monga, 2013, p 23.

[55] Mariana Mazzucato, 'A new wealth-creating agenda for the Labour Party', *The Guardian*, 15 June 2015.

[56] Hathaway and Litan, 2014a, p 6.

References

Aaronson, S., Cajner, T., Fallick, B., Gaibis-Reig, F., Smith, C. and Wascher, W. (2014) 'Labor force participation: recent developments and future prospects', *Brookings Papers on Economic Activity*, Fall.

Abramovitz, M. (1956) 'Resource and output trends in the U.S. since 1870', *American Economic Review*, 46(2), May.

Activist Insight (2014) *Activist Investing Review 2014*, Activist Insight and Schulte Roth & Zabel LLP.

Adalet McGowan, M., Andrews, D., Criscuolo, C. and Nicoletti, G. (2015) *The Future of Productivity*, OECD.

Adorno, T. and Horkheimer, M. (1979) *Dialectic of Enlightenment* (first published in 1944), Verso.

Aghion, P. (2006) 'A primer on innovation and growth', Bruegel Policy Brief 2006/06, October.

Allas, T. (2014) 'Insights from international benchmarking of the UK science and innovation system', Department for Business, Innovation and Skills Analysis Paper 3, January.

Alliance for Competitive Taxation (2014) *ACT Tax Facts: By Standing Still on Taxes, the U.S. Has Fallen Behind the Rest of the World*, Alliance for Competitive Taxation, 25 September.

Allman, D. (1983) 'The decline in business profitability: a disaggregated analysis', *Federal Reserve Bank of Kansas City Economic Review*, January.

Andritzky, J. (2012) 'Government bonds and their investors; what are the facts and do they matter?', International Monetary Fund Working Paper 12/158.

Angeletos, G., Collard, F. and Dellas, H. (2015) 'Confidence, aggregate demand, and the business cycle: a new framework', Vox policy portal, Centre for Economic Policy Research, 16 March. www.voxeu.org/article/confidence-aggregate-demand-and-business-cycle-new-framework

Antolin-Diaz, J., Drechsel, T. and Petrella, I. (2014) 'Is economic growth permanently lower?', *Fulcrum Research Notes*, Fulcrum, October.

Arora, A., Belenzon, S. and Patacconi, A. (2015) 'Killing the golden goose? The decline of science in corporate R&D', National Bureau of Economic Research Working Paper 20902, January.

Arrowsmith, M., Griffiths, M., Franklin, J., Wohlmann, E., Young, G. and Gregory, D. (2013) 'SME forbearance and its implications for monetary and financial stability', *Bank of England Quarterly Bulletin*, 53(4).

Aston, L. and Bekhradnia, B. (2003) *Demand for Graduates: A Review of the Economic Evidence*, The Higher Education Policy Institute, September.

Bailey, R. (2012) 'Is U.S. economic growth over? Forget the stagnationists. Here are reasons to be cheerful', *Reason*, 16 October.

Baily, M. (2003) 'Comments and discussion', in Gordon, R. (2003) 'Exploding productivity growth: context, causes and implications', *Brookings Papers on Economic Activity*, 2003(2).

Banerjee, R., Kearns, J. and Lombardi, M. (2015) '(Why) is investment weak?', *Bank for International Settlements Quarterly Review*, March.

Bank for International Settlements (2014) *84th Annual Report*.

Bank for International Settlements (2015) *85th Annual Report*.

Bank of England (2013) *Inflation Report*, August.

Bank of England (2014) *Trends in Lending*, October.

Barnett, A., Chiu, A., Franklin, J. and Sebastiá-Barriel, M. (2014) 'The productivity puzzle: a firm-level investigation into employment behaviour and resource allocation over the crisis', Bank of England Working Paper 495, April.

Barnett, A., Batten, S., Chiu, A., Franklin, J. and Sebastiá-Barriel, M. (2014) 'The UK productivity puzzle', *Bank of England Quarterly Bulletin*, Q2.

Bates, T., Kahle, K. and Stulz, R. (2009) 'Why do U.S. firms hold so much more cash than they used to?', *The Journal of Finance*, 64(5), October.

Baum, C., Caglayan, M. and Talavera, O. (2008) 'On the sensitivity of firms' investment to cash flow and uncertainty', Boston College Department of Economics Working Paper 638, August.

Bean, C. (2016) *Independent Review of UK Economic Statistics*, HM Treasury and Cabinet Office, March.

Becker, G. (1994) *Human Capital: A Theoretical and Empirical Analysis, with Special Reference to Education*, University of Chicago.

Bell, D. (1996) *The Cultural Contradictions of Capitalism*, Basic Books.

Ben-Ami, D. (2010) *Ferraris for All: In Defence of Economic Progress*, Policy Press.

Bernanke, B. (2004) 'The Great Moderation', speech given at the Eastern Economic Association, Washington, DC, 20 February.

Bernanke, B. (2005) 'The global saving glut and the U.S. current account deficit', speech given to the Virginia Association of Economists, Richmond, VA, 10 March.

Bernanke, B. and Gurkaynak, R. (2002) 'Is growth exogenous? Taking Mankiw, Romer and Weil seriously', *NBER Macroeconomics Annual 2001*, Massachusetts Institute of Technology Press, 16.

Bernstein, A. (2010), *The Case for Business in Developing Economies*, Penguin.

Bessen, J. (2015) 'The anti-innovators: how special interests undermine entrepreneurship', *Foreign Affairs*, January/February.

Bessen, J. and Meurer, M. (2007) 'What's wrong with the patent system? Fuzzy boundaries and the patent tax', *First Monday*, 12(6), June.

Binfield, K. (ed) (2004) *Writings of the Luddites*, Johns Hopkins University Press.

Blanchard, O., Rhee, C. and Summers, L. (1990) 'The stock market, profit and investment', National Bureau of Economic Research Working Paper 3370, May.

Blum, J., Cameron, R. and Barnes, T. (1970) *The European World: A History*, Little, Brown Book Group.

Bond, S., Leblebicioğlu, A. and Schiantarelli, F. (2010) 'Capital accumulation and growth: a new look at the empirical evidence', *Journal of Applied Econometrics*, 25(7), November/ December.

Borio, C. (2012) 'On time, stocks and flows: understanding the global macroeconomic challenges', a lecture co-organised by the University of Munich, the Ifo Institute for Economic Research and the Sueddeutsche Zeitung, Munich, 15 October.

Boyle, G. and Guthrie, G. (2003) 'Investment, uncertainty, and liquidity', *The Journal of Finance*, 58(5), October.

Brenke, K. (2009) 'Real wages in Germany: numerous years of decline', *Weekly Report*, 5(28), German Institute for Economic Research (DIW).

Broadbent, B. (2012a) 'Costly capital and the risk of rare disasters', speech given at Bloomberg, London, Bank of England, 28 May.

Broadbent, B. (2012b) 'Productivity and the allocation of resources', speech given at Durham Business School, Bank of England, 12 September.

Brundtland Commission (1987) *Our Common Future*, Report of the World Commission on Environment and Development, United Nations.

Brynjolfsson, E. (1993) 'The productivity paradox of information technology: review and assessment', *Communications of the ACM*, December.

Brynjolfsson, E. and McAfee, A. (2011) *Race Against the Machine: How the Digital Revolution is Accelerating Innovation, Driving Productivity, and Irreversibly Transforming Employment and the Economy*, Digital Frontier Press.

Brynjolfsson, E. and McAfee, A. (2014) *The Second Machine Age: Work, Progress, and Prosperity in a Time of Brilliant Technologies*, W.W. Norton.

Bryson, A. and Forth, J. (2015) 'The UK's productivity puzzle', National Institute of Economic and Social Research Discussion Paper 448.

Bureau of Labor Statistics (2015) 'Producer prices' (chapter 14), *BLS Handbook of Methods*.

Burgess, S. (2011) 'Measuring financial sector output and its contribution to UK GDP', *Bank of England Quarterly Bulletin*, Q3.

Burgin, A. (2012) *The Great Persuasion: Reinventing Free Markets Since the Depression*, Harvard University Press.

Butcher, B. and Bursnall, M. (2013) 'How dynamic is the private sector? Job creation and insights from workplace-level data', *National Institute Economic Review*, 225, August.

Caballero, R. and Hammour, M. (1994) 'The cleansing effect of recessions', *American Economic Review*, 84(5).

Caballero, R. and Hammour, M. (2000) 'Institutions, restructuring, and macroeconomic performance', paper based on a lecture given in Buenos Aires on 25 August 1999 at the XII World Congress of the International Economic Association, Massachusetts Institute of Technology.

Caballero, R., Hoshi, T. and Kashyap A. (2008) 'Zombie lending and depressed restructuring in Japan', *American Economic Review*, 98(5).

Carson, R (1962) *Silent Spring,* Houghton Mifflin.

Chesbrough, H. (2003) *Open Innovation: The New Imperative for Creating and Profiting from Technology*, Harvard Business School Press.

Christensen, C. (1997) *Innovator's Dilemma: When New Technologies Cause Great Firms to Fail*, Harvard Business School Press.

Clark, T. (2009) 'Is the Great Moderation over? An empirical analysis', *Federal Reserve Bank of Kansas City Economic Review*, Q4.

Collins, J. and Hansen, M. (2011) *Great by Choice: Uncertainty, Chaos and Luck – Why Some Thrive Despite Them All*, Random House Business.

Conference Board (2014) *2014 Productivity Brief – Key Findings: Global Productivity Slowdown Moderated in 2013; 2014 May See Better Performance*, The Conference Board.

Connors, E. and Franklin, M. (2015) *Multi-factor Productivity (Experimental), Estimates to 2013*, Office for National Statistics, 23 January.

Corrado, C., Haskel, J., Jona-Lasinio, C. and Iommi, M. (2012) 'Intangible capital and growth in advanced economies: measurement methods and comparative results', The Institute for the Study of Labor (IZA) Discussion Paper 6733, July.

Corrado, C., Hulten, C. and Sichel, D. (2009) 'Intangible capital and U.S. economic growth', *Review of Income and Wealth*, 55(3), September.

Corry, D., Valero, A. and Van Reenen, J. (2011) *UK Economic Performance Since 1997: Growth, Productivity and Jobs*, London School of Economics Centre for Economic Performance, November.

Cowen, T. (2011) *The Great Stagnation: How America Ate All the Low-Hanging Fruit of Modern History, Got Sick, and Will (Eventually) Feel Better*, Dutton.

Coyle, D. (2014) *GDP: A Brief but Affectionate History*, Princeton University Press.

Crafts, N. (2000) 'Globalization and growth in the twentieth century', International Monetary Fund Working Paper WP/00/44, March.

Crafts, N. (2011a) *Delivering Growth while Reducing Deficits: Lessons from the 1930s*, Centre Forum.

Crafts, N. (2011b) *British Relative Economic Decline Revisited*, University of Warwick.

Criscuolo, C., Gal, P.N. and Menon, C. (2014) 'The dynamics of employment growth: new evidence from 18 countries', OECD Science, Technology and Industry Policy Paper 14.

Dabla-Norris, E., Guo, S., Haksar, V., Kim, M., Kochhar, K., Wiseman, K. and Zdzienicka, A. (2015) 'The new normal: a sector-level perspective on growth and productivity trends in advanced economies', International Monetary Fund Staff Discussion Note SDN/15/03, March.

Davis, I. (2009) 'The new normal', *McKinsey Quarterly*, March.

Davis, S. and Haltiwanger, J. (2014) 'Labor market fluidity and economic performance', revised paper presented at the Federal Reserve Bank of Kansas City's economic policy symposium in August 2014, November.

Deaton, A. (2013) *The Great Escape: Health, Wealth and the Origins of Inequality*, Princeton University Press.

Disney, R., Haskel, J. and Heden, Y. (2003) 'Restructuring and productivity growth in UK manufacturing', *The Economic Journal*, 113(489).

Dobbs, R., Manyika, J., Roxburgh C. and Lund, S. (2010) *Farewell to Cheap Capital? The Implications of Long-term Shifts in Global Investment and Saving*, McKinsey Global Institute, December.

Dobbs, R., Lund, S., Woetzel, J. and Mutafchieva, M. (2015) *Debt and (Not Much) Deleveraging*, McKinsey Global Institute, February.

Drehmann, M., Borio, C. and Tsatsaronis, K. (2012) 'Characterising the financial cycle: don't lose sight of the medium term!', Bank for International Settlements Working Paper 380, June.

Duncan, R. (2009) *The Corruption of Capitalism: A Strategy to Rebalance the Global Economy and Restore Sustainable Growth*, CLSA Books.

Eichengreen, B. (2014) *Hall of Mirrors: The Great Depression, the Great Recession and the Uses – and Misuses – of History*, Oxford University Press.

El-Erian, M. (2016) *The Only Game in Town*, Random House.

Elliott, L. and Atkinson, D. (2008) *The Gods that Failed: How Blind Faith in Markets has Cost Us Our Future*, Bodley Head.

Farnsworth, K. (2015) 'The British corporate welfare state: public provision for private businesses', Sheffield Political Economy Research Institute Paper 24, July.

Field, A. (2003) 'The most technologically progressive decade of the century', *American Economic Review*, September.

Field, A. (2006) 'Technological change and U.S. productivity growth during the interwar years', *Journal of Economic History*, 66(1), March.

Fisher, I. (1933) 'The debt–deflation theory of great depressions', *Econometrica*.

Fisher, R. (2014) 'Monetary policy and the Maginot Line (with reference to Jonathan Swift, Neil Irwin, Shakespeare's Portia, Duck Hunting, the Virtues of Nuisance and Paul Volcker)', speech delivered at the University of Southern California, Los Angeles, 16 July.

Ford, M. (2015) *The Rise of the Robots – Technology and the Threat of Mass Unemployment*, Oneworld Publications.

Foroohar, R. (2016) *Makers and Takers: The Rise of Finance and the Fall of American Business*, Crown Business.

Fosler, G. (2011) 'The return of the "old normal"', *Economic Assessments*, GailFosler Group LLP, 14 June.

Foster, L., Haltiwanger, J. and Krizan, C.J. (2001) 'Aggregate productivity growth: lessons from microeconomic evidence', in E. Dean, M. Harper and C. Hulten (eds) *New Developments in Productivity Analysis*, University of Chicago Press.

Foster, L., Grim, C. and Haltiwanger, J. (2013) 'Reallocation in the Great Recession: cleansing or not?', Center for Economic Studies Discussion Paper CES-WP-13-42, August.

Frankl, V. (2004) *Man's Search for Meaning*, Rider.

Frey, C.B. (2015) 'The end of economic growth? How the digital economy could lead to secular stagnation', *Scientific American*, 312(1), January.

Frey, C.B. and Osborne, M. (2013) 'The future of employment: how susceptible are jobs to computerisation?', Oxford Martin Programme on the Impacts of Future Technology Working Paper, 17 September.

Friedman, M. (2002) *Capitalism and Freedom: Fortieth Anniversary Edition*, University of Chicago Press.

Fujita, S. (2008) 'Creative destruction and aggregate productivity growth', *Federal Reserve Bank of Philadelphia Business Review*, Q3.

Fukuyama, F. (1989) 'The end of history', *The National Interest*, Summer.

Fukuyama, F. (1992) *The End of History and the Last Man*, Free Press.

Furedi, F. (1997) *Culture of Fear: Risk-taking and the Morality of Low Expectation*, Cassell.

Furedi, F. (2014) *First World War – Still No End in Sight*, Bloomsbury.

Goodridge, P., Haskel, J. and Wallis, G. (2014) *Estimating UK Investment in Intangible Assets and Intellectual Property Rights*, Intellectual Property Office.

Goodridge, P., Haskel, J. and Wallis, G. (2015) 'Accounting for the UK productivity puzzle: a decomposition and predictions', Imperial College London Business School Discussion Paper 2015/02.

Gordon, R. (2003) 'Exploding productivity growth: context, causes and implications', *Brookings Papers on Economic Activity*, 2003(2).

Gordon, R. (2004) 'Why was Europe left at the station when America's productivity locomotive departed?', CEPR Discussion Paper 4416, Centre for Economic Policy Research, 31 March.

Gordon, R. (2010a) 'Revisiting U.S. productivity growth over the past century with a view of the future', National Bureau of Economic Research Working Paper 15834, March.

Gordon, R. (2010b) 'Okun's Law, productivity innovations, and conundrums in business cycle dating', *American Economic Review: Papers & Proceedings*, 100(2), May.

Gordon, R. (2012) 'Is US economic growth over? Faltering innovation confronts the six headwinds', *Policy Insight 63*, Centre for Economic Policy Research, September.

Gordon, R. (2016) *The Rise and Fall of American Growth: The U.S. Standard of Living since the Civil War*, Princeton University Press.

Graebner, D. (2015) *The Utopia of Rules: On Technology, Stupidity and the Secret Joys of Bureaucracy*, Melville House.

Granados, J.T. (2010) 'Economists, recessions and profits', *Capitalism Nature Socialism*, 21(1), March.

Greenspan, A. (2005) 'The Federal Reserve Board's semi-annual Monetary Policy Report to the Congress', Federal Reserve, 16 February.

Gros, D. (2014) 'Investment as the key to recovery in the euro area?', CEPS Policy Briefs 326, Centre for European Policy Studies, 18 November.

Grossmann, H. (1992) *The Law of Accumulation and Breakdown of the Capitalist System*, Pluto Press.

Haldane, A. (2015) 'Stuck', speech at the Open University, Milton Keynes, Bank of England, 30 June.

Haldane, A., Brennan, S. and Madouros, V. (2010) 'What is the contribution of the financial sector: miracle or mirage?', in Adair Turner et al, *The Future of Finance: The LSE Report*, London School of Economics and Political Science.

Haltiwanger, J. (2012) 'Job creation and firm dynamics in the U.S.', *Innovation Policy and the Economy*, 12, National Bureau of Economic Research.

Haltiwanger, J., Jarmin, R. and Miranda, J. (2008) 'Business formation and dynamics by business age: results from the new business dynamics statistics', Preliminary Draft, Center for Economic Studies, US Census Bureau, May.

Haltiwanger, J., Jarmin, R. and Miranda, J. (2011) 'Historically large decline in job creation from startup and existing firms in the 2008–2009 recession', Business Dynamics Statistics Briefing, Ewing Marion Kauffman Foundation, March.

Haltiwanger, J., Hathaway, I. and Miranda, J. (2014) *Declining Business Dynamism in the U.S. High-Technology Sector*, Ewing Marion Kauffman Foundation, February.

Hansen A. (1938) *Full Recovery or Stagnation?*, W.W. Norton.

Harvard Business Review (2002) 'Inspiring innovation', *Harvard Business Review*, August.

Hathaway, I. and Litan, R. (2014a) 'Declining business dynamism in the United States: a look at states and metros', *Economic Studies at Brookings*, The Brookings Institution, May.

Hathaway, I. and Litan, R. (2014b) 'The other aging of America: the increasing dominance of older firms', *Economic Studies at Brookings*, The Brookings Institution, July.

Hayek, F.A. (1931) *Prices and Production*, Augustus M. Kelly.

Hayek, F.A. (1991) *The Fatal Conceit: The Errors of Socialism*, University of Chicago Press.

Hijzen, A., Upward, R. and Wright, P. (2010) 'Job creation, job destruction and the role of small firms: firm-level evidence form the UK', *Oxford Bulletin of Economics and Statistics*, 72.

HM Treasury (2014) *Review of the Oil and Gas Fiscal Regime: Call for Evidence*, HM Treasury.

HM Treasury (2015) *Fixing the Foundations: Creating a More Prosperous Nation*, Cm 9098, HM Treasury, July.

Hooker, H. and Achur, J. (2014) *First Findings from the UK Innovation Survey 2013*, Department for Business, Innovation and Skills, October.

Ignatieff, M. (1999) 'Ascent of man', *Prospect Magazine*, October.

International Labour Organization Bureau for Workers' Activities (2012) *From Precarious Work to Decent Work*, Symposium Outcome Document, ILO.

International Labour Organization (2013) *Global Employment Trends for Youth 2013 – A Generation at Risk*, ILO.

International Monetary Fund (2006) 'Awash with cash: why are corporate savings so high?', *World Economic Outlook*, April.

International Monetary Fund (2014a) 'Perspectives on global real interest rates', *World Economic Outlook: Recovery Strengthens, Remains Uneven*, April.

International Monetary Fund (2014b) *World Economic Outlook: Legacies, Clouds, Uncertainties*, October.

International Monetary Fund (2015) *World Economic Outlook: Uneven Growth: Short- and Long-Term Factors*, April.

Jackson, T. (2011) *Prosperity without Growth: Economics for a Finite Planet*, Routledge.

Janeway, W. (2012) *Doing Capitalism in the Innovation Economy: Markets, Speculation and the State*, Cambridge University Press.

Jorda, O., Schularick, M. and Taylor, A. (2012) 'When credit bites back: leverage, business cycles, and crises', Federal Reserve Bank of San Francisco Working Paper 2011-27, October.

Jorgenson, D. (2011) 'Innovation and productivity growth', *American Journal of Agricultural Economics*, 93(2).

Jorgenson, D., Ho, M. and Samuels, J. (2010) 'Information technology and US productivity growth: evidence from a prototype industry production account'. http://scholar.harvard.edu/files/jorgenson/files/02_jorgenson_ho_samuels19nov20101_2.pdf. Prepared for M. Mas and R. Stehrer (eds) (2012) *Industrial Productivity in Europe: Growth and Crisis*, Edward Elgar.

Jorgenson, D. and Stiroh, K. (2000) 'Raising the speed limit: U.S. growth in the information age', *Brookings Papers on Economic Activity*, 1.

Joyce, M., Tong, M. and Woods, R. (2011) 'The United Kingdom's quantitative easing policy: design, operation and impact', *Bank of England Quarterly Bulletin*, Q3.

Karabell, Z. (2016) 'Learning to love stagnation', *Foreign Affairs*, March/April.

Kay, J. (2012) *The Kay Review of UK Equity Markets and Long-Term Decision Making*, Department for Business, Innovation and Skills.

Keynes, J.M. (1936) *General Theory of Employment Interest and Money*, Macmillan.

King, A. and Schneider, B. (1993) *The First Global Revolution*, The Club of Rome.

King, S. (2013) *When the Money Runs Out: The End of Western Affluence*, Yale University Press.

Kliman, A. (2012) *The Failure of Capitalist Production: Underlying Causes of the Great Recession*, Pluto Press.

Knight, F. (1921) *Risk, Uncertainty, and Profit*, Hart, Schaffner & Marx, Houghton Mifflin Co. Available at the Library of Economics and Liberty Online: www.econlib.org/library/Knight/knRUP4.html

Koller, T., Lovallo, D. and Williams, Z. (2011) 'A bias against investment?', *McKinsey Quarterly*, September.

Koo, R. (2011) 'The world in balance sheet recession: causes, cure, and politics', *Real-World Economics Review*, 58.

Kothari, S.P., Lewellen, J. and Warner, J. (2014) 'The behavior of aggregate corporate investment', The Bradley Policy Research Center Financial Research and Policy Working Paper FR 14-18, William E. Simon Graduate School of Business Administration, 12 September.

Krippner, G. (2012) *Capitalizing on Crisis: The Political Origins of the Rise of Finance*, Harvard University Press.

Krugman, P. (2013) *End This Depression Now!*, W.W. Norton.

Kurzweil, R. (2001) *The Law of Accelerating Returns*, Kurzweil Accelerating Intelligence website. www.kurzweilai.net/the-law-of-accelerating-returns

Kurzweil, R. (2006) *The Singularity is Near*, Gerald Duckworth & Co.

Labour Party (1976) *Annual Conference Report*, Labour Party.

Lagarde, C. (2014) 'The challenge facing the global economy: new momentum to overcome a new mediocre', speech given at the School of Foreign Service, Georgetown University, Washington, DC, 2 October.

Lanier, J. (2014) *Who Owns the Future?*, Penguin.

Lapavitsas, C. (2013) *Profiting Without Producing: How Finance Exploits Us All*, Verso.

Lasch, C. (1991) *The Culture of Narcissism: American Life in An Age of Diminishing Expectations*, W.W. Norton.

Lazonick, W. and O'Sullivan, M. (2000) 'Maximizing shareholder value: a new ideology for corporate governance', *Economy and Society*, 29(1).

Le Merle, M. (2011) 'How to prepare for a black swan', *Strategy+Business*, 64, Autumn.

Lin, J.Y. and Monga, C. (2010) 'Growth identification and facilitations: the role of the state in the dynamics of structural change', World Bank Policy Research Working Paper 5313, May.

Lin, J.Y. and Monga, C. (2013) 'Comparative advantage: the silver bullet of industrial policy', in J. Stiglitz and J. Y. Lin (eds) *The Industrial Policy Revolution I: The Role of Government Beyond Ideology*, Palgrave Macmillan for the International Economic Association.

Loeys, L., Mackie, D., Meggyesi, P. and Panigirtzoglou, N. (2005) *Corporates are driving the global savings glut*, JP Morgan Research, 24 June.

LSE Growth Commission (2013) *Investing for Prosperity: Skills, Infrastructure and Innovation*, London School of Economics and Political Science, February.

McCafferty, I. (2014) 'The UK productivity puzzle – a sectoral perspective', speech given at the Bank of England, London, 19 June.

Machiavelli, N. (2008) *The Prince*, Oxford University Press.

McKinsey Global Institute (2001) *US Productivity Growth, 1995–2000*, McKinsey Global Institute, October.

McKinsey Global Institute (2016) *Diminishing Returns: Why Investors may Need to Lower their Expectations*, McKinsey Global Institute, May.

Macmillan, I., Prakash, S. and Shoult, R. (2014) 'The cash paradox: how record cash reserves are influencing corporate behavior', *Deloitte Review*, 15, 28 July.

Maddison, A. (1991) *Dynamic Forces in Capitalist Development*, Oxford University Press.

Maddison, A. (2003) *The World Economy: Historical Statistics*, OECD.

Magnus, G. (2011) *Uprising: Will Emerging Markets Shape or Shake the World Economy*, Wiley.

Maito, E.E. (2014) 'The historical transience of capital: the downward trend in the rate of profit since XIX century', Munich Personal RePEc Archive (MPRA) Paper 55894, University of Munich.

Manyika, J., Lund, S., Auguste, B., Meddonca, L., Welsh, T. and Ramaswamy, S. (2011) *An Economy that Works: Job Creation and America's Future*, McKinsey Global Institute, June.

Manyika, J., Sinclair, J., Dobbs, R., Strube, G., Rassey, L., Mischke, J., Remes, J., Roxburgh, C., George, K., O'Halloran, D. and Ramaswamy, S. (2012) *Manufacturing the Future: The Next Era of Global Growth and Innovation*, McKinsey Global Institute, November.

Marshall, A. (1920) *Principles of Economics* (8th edn), Macmillan and Co. Available at the Online Library of Liberty: http://oll.libertyfund.org

Martin, B. (2010) *Rebalancing the British Economy: A Strategic Assessment*, Centre for Business Research, University of Cambridge, July.

Marx, K. (1973) *Grundrisse: Foundations of the Critique of Political Economy*, translated by Martin Nicolaus, Penguin.

Marx, K. (1974) *Capital: A Critique of Political Economy, Volume 3*, Lawrence and Wishart.

Marx, K. (1975) *Theories of Surplus Value, Part 2*, Lawrence and Wishart.

Mason, P. (2015) *Postcapitalism*, Allen Lane.

Mattick, P. (1974) *Marx and Keynes: The Limits of the Mixed Economy*, Merlin Press.

Mauldin, J. and Tepper, J. (2011) *End Game: The End of the Debt Supercycle and How it Changes Everything*, John Wiley.

Mazzoleni, R. and Nelson, R. (1998) 'The benefits and costs of strong patent protection: a contribution to the current debate', *Research Policy*, 27.

Mazzucato, M. (2011) *The Entrepreneurial State*, Demos.

Mazzucato, M. (2013) *The Entrepreneurial State: Debunking Public vs. Private Sector Myths*, Anthem Press.

Meadows, D.H., Meadows, D.L., Randers, J. and Behrens III, W.W. (1972) *The Limits to Growth: A Report for the Club of Rome*, Universe Books.

Meiksins Wood, E. (1995) *Democracy against Capitalism: Renewing Historical Materialism*, Cambridge University Press.

Mendoza, E. and Quadrini, V. (2009) 'Financial globalization, financial crises and contagion', National Bureau of Economic Research Working Paper 15432, October.

Mikes, A. (2014) 'The triumph of the humble chief risk officer', Harvard Business School Working Paper 14-114, May.

Minsky, H. (1992) 'The financial instability hypothesis', The Levy Economics Institute of Bard College Working Paper 74, May.

Mishan, E. (1967) *The Costs of Economic Growth*, Staples Press.

Mizruchi, M. (2007) 'Power without efficacy: the decline of the American corporate elite', seminar paper, University of Michigan.

Mokyr, J. (2010) *The Enlightened Economy: An Economic History of Britain 1700–1850*, Yale University Press.

Mokyr, J. (2013) 'Is technological progress a thing of the past?', Vox policy portal, Centre for Economic Policy Research, 8 September. www.voxeu.org/article/technological-progress-thing-past

National Research Council (2007) *Condensed-Matter and Materials Physics: The Science of the World Around Us*, The National Academies Press.

Nellis, D. (2013) 'Measuring the change in effectiveness of quantitative easing', *Issues in Political Economy*, 22.

Nelson, R. (2000) 'Observations on the post Bayh–Dole rise of patenting at American universities', paper for the Swedish International Symposium on Economics, Law and Intellectual Property, Gothenburg, June.

NESTA (2008) *Social Innovation: New Approaches to Transforming Public Services*, Policy Briefing SI/18, NESTA, January.

Nester, W. (1997) *American Industrial Policy: Free or Managed Markets?*, Palgrave Macmillan.

Nordhaus, W. (2002) 'Productivity growth and the new economy', *Brookings Papers on Economic Activity*, 2002(2).

Nordhaus, W., Bosworth, B., Solow, R. and Vaccara, B.N. (1972) 'The recent productivity slowdown', *Brookings Papers on Economic Activity*, 1972(3).

Nordhaus, W. and Tobin, J. (1972) 'Is growth obsolete?', in W. Nordhaus and J. Tobin, *Economic Research: Retrospect and Prospect: Economic Growth*, National Bureau of Economic Research.

Office for National Statistics (2015a) *Labour Productivity, Quarter 4 2014*, Office for National Statistics, 1 April.

Office for National Statistics (2015b) *International Comparisons of Productivity – First Estimates, 2014*, Office for National Statistics, 18 September.

Office for National Statistics (2015c) *Capital Stocks, Consumption of Fixed Capital, 2015*, Office for National Statistics, 1 December.

Oliner, S. and Sichel, D. (2000) 'The resurgence of growth in the late 1990s: is information technology the story?', *Journal of Economic Perspectives*, 14(4), Fall.

Oliner, S. and Sichel, D. (2002) 'Information technology and productivity: where are we now and where are we going?', *Federal Reserve Bank of Atlanta Economic Review*, 87(3).

Oliner, S., Sichel, D. and Stiroh, K. (2007) *Explaining a Productive Decade*, Federal Reserve.

O'Mahony, M. and de Boer, W. (2002) *Britain's Relative Productivity Performance: Updates to 1999*, National Institute of Economic and Social Research.

O'Mahony, M. and van Ark, B. (2003) *EU Productivity and Competitiveness: An Industry Perspective: Can Europe Resume the Catching-up Process?*, European Commission DG Enterprise.

Organisation for Economic Co-operation and Development (2015a) *Business and Finance Outlook 2015*, OECD.

Organisation for Economic Co-operation and Development (2015b) *The Future of Productivity*, Joint Economics Department and the Directorate for Science, Technology and Innovation Policy Note, OECD.

Orphanides, A. (2013) 'Is monetary policy over burdened?', paper presented at the BIS 12th Annual Conference Navigating the Great Recession: What Role for Monetary Policy?, Bank for International Settlements Working Paper 435, December.

Patterson, P. (2012) *The Productivity Conundrum, Explanations and Preliminary Analysis*, Office for National Statistics, 16 October.

Pessoa, J. and Van Reenen, J. (2013) 'The UK productivity and jobs puzzle: does the answer lie in labour market flexibility?', London School of Economics Centre for Economic Performance Special Paper 31.

Phelps, E. (2013) *Mass Flourishing: How Grassroots Innovations Created Jobs, Challenge, and Change*, Princeton University Press.

Philpott, J. (2004) *Quarterly HR Trends and Indicators Survey*, Chartered Institute of Personnel and Development, April.

Piketty, T. (2014) *Capital in the Twenty-First Century*, Harvard University Press.

Pisano, G. (2006) 'Can science be a business? Lessons from biotech', *Harvard Business Review*, October.

Plunkett, J. (2011) *Growth without Gain? The Faltering Living Standards of People on Low-to-Middle Incomes*, Resolution Foundation Commission on Living Standards, May.

Poterba, J. and Summers, L. (1995) 'A CEO survey of U.S. companies' time horizons and hurdle rates', *MIT Sloan Management Review*, 15 October.

Poynter, G. (2000) *Restructuring in the Service Industries: Management Reform and Workplace Relations in the UK Service Sector*, Mansell Publishing.

Public Administration Select Committee (2012) *Strategic Thinking in Government: without National Strategy, can Viable Government Strategy Emerge?*, HC 1625, UK Stationery Office, 24 April.

Quak, E. and van de Vijsel, A. (2014) 'Low wages and job insecurity as a destructive global standard', *The Broker*, 26 November.

Rajan, R. (2010) *Fault Lines: How Hidden Fractures Still Threaten the World Economy*, Princeton University Press.

Reinhart, C., Reinhart, V. and Rogoff, K. (2012) 'Debt overhangs: past and present', National Bureau of Economic Research Working Paper 18015, April.

Reinhart, C. and Rogoff, K. (2009) *This Time is Different: Eight Hundred Centuries of Financial Folly*, Princeton University Press.

Restuccia, D. and Rogerson, R. (2012) 'Misallocation and productivity', University of Toronto Department of Economics Working Paper 468, 23 November.

Romer, P. (1986) 'Increasing returns and long-run growth', *Journal of Political Economy*, 94(5).

Romer, P. (1990) 'Endogenous technological change', *Journal of Political Economy*, 98(5).

Roubini, N. and Mihm, S. (2011) *Crisis Economics: A Crash Course in the Future of Finance*, Penguin.

Roxburgh, C., Labaye, E., Thompson, F., Tacke, T. and Kauffman, D. (2012) *Investing in Growth: Europe's Next Challenge*, McKinsey Global Institute, December.

Roxburgh, C., Lund, S., Wimmer, T., Amar, E., Atkins, C., Kwek, J., Dobbs, R. and Manyika, J. (2010) *Debt and Deleveraging: The Global Credit Bubble and its Economic Consequences*, McKinsey Global Institute, January.

Royal Society, (2011) *Knowledge, Networks and Nations: Global Scientific Collaboration in the 21st Century*, The Royal Society.

Sachs, J.D. (2015) *The Age of Sustainable Development*, Columbia University Press.

Schumacher, E.F. (1988) *Small Is Beautiful: A Study of Economics As If People Mattered*, Abacus.

Schumpeter, J. (1975) *Capitalism, Socialism and Democracy*, Harper & Brothers.

Scott, M.F. (1989) *A New View of Economic Growth*, Oxford University Press.

Simms, B. (2014) *Europe: The Struggle for Supremacy 1453 to the Present*, Penguin.

Sirkin, H., Zinser, M. and Hohner, D. (2011) *Made in America, Again: Why Manufacturing Will Return to the US*, Boston Consulting Group, August.

Smart, J. (2005) 'Measuring innovation in an accelerating world: review of "A possible declining trend for worldwide innovation," Jonathan Huebner', *Technological Forecasting and Social Change*, 72(8).

Smithers, A. (2013) *The Road to Recovery: How and Why Economic Policy Must Change*, Wiley.

Solow, R. (1956) 'A contribution to the theory of economic growth', *Quarterly Journal of Economics*, 70(1), February.

Solow, R. (1957) 'Technical change and the aggregate production function', *Review of Economics and Statistics*, 39(3), August.

Spengler O. (1991) *The Decline of the West*, Oxford University Press.

Srinivasan, S. (2012) 'A new measure of consumer credit', *Bank of England Monetary & Financial Statistics*, July.

Standard & Poor's Ratings Services (2013) *Global Corporate Capital Expenditure Survey 2013*, Standard & Poor's Ratings Direct, July.

Standard & Poor's Ratings Services (2014) *Global Corporate Capital Expenditure Survey 2014*, McGraw Hill Financial, June.

Steinbeck, J. (1962) *Travels with Charley: In Search of America*, Viking.

Stiglitz, J. (2012a) 'The book of Jobs', *Vanity Fair*, January.

Stiglitz, J. (2012b) *The Price of Inequality*, Allen Lane.

Stiglitz, J., Lin, J.Y., and Monga, C. (2013) 'The rejuvenation of industrial policy', World Bank Policy Research Working Paper 6628.

Stock, J. and Watson, M. (2003) 'Has the business cycle changed and why?', *NBER Macroeconomics Annual 2002*, Massachusetts Institute of Technology Press, 17.

Streeck, W. (2014) 'How will capitalism end?', *New Left Review*, 87, May–June.

Summers, L. (2014) 'U.S. economic prospects: secular stagnation, hysteresis, and the zero lower bound', *Business Economics*, 49(2).

Summers, L. (2016) 'The age of secular stagnation: what it is and what to do about it', *Foreign Affairs*, March/April.

Syverson, C. (2016) 'Challenges to mismeasurement explanations for the U.S. productivity slowdown', National Bureau of Economic Research Working Paper 21974, February.

Taleb, N.N. (2007) *The Black Swan: The Impact of the Highly Improbable*, Penguin.

Tett, G. (2009) *Fool's Gold*, Little, Brown.

Teulings, C. and Baldwin, R. (eds) (2014) *Secular Stagnation: Facts, Causes, and Cures*, Vox e-book, Centre for Economic Policy Research, 16 March. www.voxeu.org/article/secular-stagnation-facts-causes-and-cures-new-vox-ebook

Thiel, P. (2011) 'The end of the future', *National Review*, 3 October.

Toksöz, M. (2014) *Guide to Country Risk: How to Identify, Manage and Mitigate the Risks of Doing Business across Borders*, The Economist in association with Profile Books.

Triplett, J. and Bosworth, B. (2002) '"Baumol's disease" has been cured: IT and multifactor productivity in U.S. services industries', paper presented at a conference on 'The New Economy: How New? How Resilient?', Texas, 19 April.

Turner, A. (2014a) 'Escaping the debt addiction: monetary and macroprudential policy in the post crisis world', lecture at the Centre for Financial Studies, Frankfurt, 19 February.

Turner, A. (2014b) 'Wealth, debt, inequality and low interest rates: four big trends and some implications', speech at Cass Business School, London, 26 March.

United Nations (2016) *World Economic Situation and Prospects 2016*, United Nations.

US Department of the Treasury (2008) *Report to Congress on International Economic and Exchange Rate Policies*, US Department of the Treasury, May.

US Department of the Treasury, the Federal Reserve Bank of New York, and the Board of Governors of the Federal Reserve System (2014) *Foreign Portfolio Holdings of U.S. Securities as of June 30, 2013*, US Department of the Treasury, April.

Van Ark, B., Inklaar, R. and McGuckin, R. (2003) 'Changing gear: productivity, ICT and service industries in Europe and the United States', in J. Christensen and P. Maskell (eds) *The Industrial Dynamics of the New Digital Economy*, Edward Elgar.

Wehinger, G. (2011) 'Fostering long-term investment and economic growth', a summary of discussions at the OECD High-Level Financial Roundtable on 7 April 2011, *OECD Journal: Financial Market Trends*, 1.

White, W. (2012) 'Ultra easy monetary policy and the law of unintended consequences', Federal Reserve Bank of Dallas Globalization and Monetary Policy Institute Working Paper 126, September.

Whittaker, M. and Savage, L. (2011) *Missing Out: Why Ordinary Workers are Experiencing Growth without Gain*, Resolution Foundation Commission on Living Standards, July.

Wolf, M. (2014) *The Shifts and the Shocks: What We've Learned – and Have Still to Learn – from the Financial Crisis*, Allen Lane.

Woudhuysen, J. and Kaplinsky, J. (2009) *Energise: A Future for Energy Innovation*, Beautiful Books.

Zakaria, F. (2013) 'Can America be fixed? The new crisis of democracy', *Foreign Affairs*, January/February.

Index